My Life, My Travels

Kev Richardson

A Wings ePress, Inc.
Travel Memoir

Wings ePress, Inc.

Edited by: Jeanne Smith
Copy Edited by: Joan C. Powell
Executive Editor: Jeanne Smith
Cover Artist: Trisha FitzGerald-Jung

All rights reserved

Names, characters and incidents depicted in this book are products of the author's imagination or are used fictitiously. Any resemblance to actual events, locales, organizations, or persons, living or dead, is entirely coincidental and beyond the intent of the author or the publisher.

No part of this book may be reproduced or transmitted in any form or by any means, electronic or mechanical, including photocopying, recording, or by any information storage and retrieval system, without permission in writing from the publisher.

Wings ePress Books
www.wingsepress.com

Copyright © 2020 by: Kev Richardson
ISBN 978-1-61309-569-0
ISBN-10: 1-61309-569-4

Published In the United States Of America

Wings ePress Inc.
3000 N. Rock Road
Newton, KS 67114

What They Are Saying About

My Life, My Travels

I catch my breath as Ric Richardson describes his world-wide travels, his single piece of luggage seemly weighing him down as he sprints train to plane, ferry to taxi to keep his departure times on schedule. Once home, he writes his articles in solitude for his explorer, sending them off like leaves in the wind.

I was absolutely enchanted by the story of his life as a traveling-man, meeting new people at every turn, finding new places to explore. I wanted to grab my bag and keep pace with him. I'm sure you will too.

—JoEllen Conger – *Conger Book reviews USA.*

Kev Richardson cannot stop telling wonderful tales in wonderful ways.

Now he's wallowing in memories of places he travelled in and writing articles for airline magazines on what? On thirty-nine countries!

He keeps asking, "And where to next?" And off he goes to some of them, taking you with him!

At least leaving you wishing he is taking you with him.

Go get'em, Ric! You are a wonder!

—Libby Abbott – *Aussie eBook Reviews*

The travel books of Kev Richardson are not merely the telling of his lifelong adventures. Kev embodies his travels – he lives the places he visits and is totally absorbed by the customs and traditions of the people he meets. It is his passion for the people and places he has been, and the delightful telling of his journeys, that so embraces his readers. And intimately connects the people who read his books to the life of this remarkable person.

—Robert Jameson - *Living Body Earth*

"They must be interesting people in every essence." quote by Mr. Richardson

A stunning travel log of nearly the entire world. As you read, tidbits of his earlier life sprout then bloom, which reveal the essence of who this author is. In his 60s and retired from the day job, this is a splendid way to meet and greet a great novelist who has embraced life with extraordinary acumen. I enjoyed every minute of his travels, of learning more of the complexities of Mr. Richardson, and highly recommend all his memoirs.

—Katherine Pym, historian and novelist.

It was a real pleasure to read Kev Richardson's account of his travels around the world during a life that so far stretches to ninety years...actually several lives, as Ric tells it. Travelling on business, he grasps every chance to squeeze some recreational travel into every trip. From watching morris dancers in rural England to driving the longest car he's ever seen in Milwaukee, he doesn't miss an opportunity. On an assignment to New Zealand, he finds time to drive both the east and west coasts. Later, travel becomes his business, beginning with a commission to write of the Easter festival in Cuzco, Peru...he turns it into a three-month tour of South America.

Along the way, we are transported to an era of travellers' cheques and bomb-damaged European cities, much of which are long gone. Positioned somewhere between a memoir and a travel guide, the book has a brisk, honest and refreshing style so readers experience his enjoyment in the sights, sounds and smells of the places he visits. Ric loves good food and interesting company and makes friends everywhere he goes. Whether trapped in Turkey and can't get out, or being mugged in Bogotá, he seems irrepressible. His writing is full of humour and gives the reader a no-holds-barred view of the cultures he encounters. Trying to change local currency in a Lima teetering on the edge of civil war, he wishes someone would invent mobile phones.

—Peter Dixon, Author of *Setting the Med Ablaze*

5 Big Stars! Reading Ric's life story. I was transported back to an era when travelling was full of surprises and most of all, interaction with other people. He had to cope without Tripadvisor or online booking and instead met a lot of interesting people in those fascinating places, exchanging information and making life-long friends. Let yourself be carried back to the good old times of travelling!

—Eveline Willi, Avid Swiss

Preface

How many lifetimes can a guy pack into a childhood, let alone life?

On turning ninety I decided on a future of 'Let's see what each day still has to offer'!

By my tenth birthday, I and my family of four had already lived in four houses in four suburbs of two cities a thousand road miles apart.

Yes, in those days, road travel between Sydney and Brisbane, because of several wide rivers interrupting the straight line, emptying into the Pacific Ocean and which yet had no bridges, one had to drive a long way west over the Great Dividing Range before being able to turn north on then 'country roads, 'country' in this sense meaning dirt and stony because there was damn little bitumen once leaving large towns.

Anyway, in those days, only the rich had motorcars.

Or there was the train, but the line also had to cross those mountains each way. And there were no sleepers in those days. It was sit-up for fourteen hours of travel.

I'm talking about the years I was a kid and once World War II started in 1939, all fit men were shipped off to Europe to help save England. Those were the days when the only air travel to England was via big-float planes that took 10 days and were for only the multi-rich.

And yes, I interrupt my own story here to say that in this work, I'll be repeatedly talking about numbers—numbers of people, number of years, numbers of age etcetera, so shall use numbers rather than spell them out on every occasion as literacy demands... Once into this world of retirement, ain't I my own boss and I can do what I like with everything? So please excuse my 3s and 4s.

The entire object of this work is to talk about the travels I've experienced, only realised of late that travel began early in life for me and I was never able to steer life around it. And travel is ever a NOW thing, so once into the tale I shall be writing in the first person. Life for me in dotage is just that...everything plotted around NOW, for there is likely little that is left of it. Measuring life these days is no longer counting in years; it has somewhere boiled down into days.

So for the nonce, let's get back to my 'past-tense-preface'...

Travel was certainly an early time for me...while still at primary school age I can recall today is certainly not what it was before 9/11, certainly not the adventurous pleasures I recall of 'the good old days!'

My first 'travel' title was granted when, at age 8, I had the opportunity of being driven by car to Sydney. By the score of times we had to stop to move rocks off the road, it was a four-day journey. But on return (by train), being the first kid at Brisbane's biggest state school (Windsor by name, first school I'd ever come across with its own swimming pool) I was lauded for having been the only kid in school that had ever travelled as far as Sydney by motor car. So, I was learning to get the 'travel bug' early in life.

Already at age 5, I was the only kid in my class who'd ever travelled by ocean liner...our family moved from Sydney to Brisbane, two nights and three days!

I got lost aboard so many times, taking our young Labrador, Gypsy for walks on her leash. I got lost so many times that I had a paper sign with cabin number and name pinned on to my shirt. Dad had already taken off by train to begin his new role in Brisbane as Queensland Manager of his printing paper company, and just Mum, sister Val some three years older than me, and Gypsy were travelling the comfortable way...by sea. But Mum always got seasick and Val sat with her while I had the run of the ship. On the first morning at sea, even wangled breakfast sitting at the captain's table and got very well looked after.

Then just a couple of years later I was travelling again...had to stand up in class on return, telling my adventures of being the only kid in Brisbane's big Windsor State school, who ever travelled so far as Sydney by motor-car...we made it in four days! I must admit having to pull over to move rocks on the dirt roads certainly took many hours.

'Travel' first meant to me, 'where we lived' and by the time Mum brought Valerie and me back to Sydney after dad died of cancer when I was but 11 years old, 4 years in Sydney and 7 in Brisbane, I'd lived in 5 homes! With Mum staying in Brisbane to sell the house etc, one of dad's brothers and a sister had come for the funeral, and to bring Val, me and Gypsy back to Sydney by train. Val and I spent a couple of years with Aunt Moogs (nickname of course), at Chatswood and me with Gypsy with Uncle Eric at Northbridge until Mum was able to get a flat (a damned hard job during the war!) for us in Crows Nest on Sydney's north shore where all the Richardson tribes (Dad was the youngest of 11 children!) had their homes in the Willoughby and Mosman areas.

Ever looked at your own life and arranged it into stages? Mine had already been in six...

Life 1: 1929-1939: A kid. Where? 5 different homes all told, in Sydney and Brisbane.

Life 2: 1940-1947: Student. Objective? Learn all I can - in Brisbane and then Sydney (3 different homes, the most recent the house I had built in West Chatswood's Millwood Avenue).

Life 3: 1951-1964: Kit and Kids. Objective? To be as good a father as mine - Sydney then Brisbane then Sydney again. In total three different homes in these 13 years.

Life 4: 1963-1971: Widowed in Sydney. Objective? Make my working career a success. (3 different homes during these 8 years.

Life 5: 1971-1989: Marry Maggie. Objective? Success achieved, discover world travel - Melbourne. (During these 18 years, Maggie and I had 5 homes, buying in need of restoration and selling at peaks in the Toorak, Malvern district...during full-time jobs all that time).

Life 6: 1989 until now: Alone again but writing and travelling – Qld Gold Coast and Chiang Mai, Thailand.

My working life with one little hiccup, indeed proved a happy one for me.

~ * ~

I finished high-school in the year WW2 finished and began work in Sydney with a substantial print-packaging company, so large that our three major clients were Colgate-Palmolive, Wrigley's and Nestlé. The hiccup happened after some ten years when it was my choice to leave the company, selling the house we'd built and moving to Brisbane. We built at Kenmore. After only 8 months in the house and two years after quitting my Sydney job, that boss came to Brisbane and over lunch sold me on all the advantages that would be mine if I were to return to that job with considerable management power. I did and 'never looked back.'

So travel again and yet a different home. This Dickinson Robinson Group (DRG of Bristol UK) employed 24,000 people in 12 countries around the world. I was given management of my own company in Melbourne, so it was sell-up again and travel to a new home there. Over the next several years, most Melbourne operations were assembled in one massive plant in South Melbourne and progressively I became general manager of the entire operation.

When it came time for me to retire, as you will read between the lines later, that 'travel' urge childhood bred into my younger life, began preparing me for retirement. After two marriages and having become a great-grandfather, I have only body strength and determination in achieving more. Apart from the lives of convict ancestors, I read up on Aboriginal life before, during and after 'Whiteman' stole their country. There is little to find for they had no written language.

Business taught me to never go off half-cocked, so at 62 years of age, before trying to write a book I signed a two-year correspondence course on English Literacy. I qualified. I joined the Gold Coast Writers Club to get the feel of published authors, to quickly become its president. In my 6th life in this world, I began plotting serious study of both parents' family lives. I would write books on each.

Having written one's memoirs only to find there is nowt to do but sit around waiting to die, my life became utterly boring! What can a man busy all his life, do?

Retiring from Australian business at the age of 62 was the time of the new thing called computer... "It will do away with paper!" it was claimed.

What's happened since is that the world's use of paper has increased 53%.

I attained a stage when writing a book on my mother's family history. My studies oozed with startling information on convict life. In 1986 Australia opened library and museum doors on history that had been hidden by law from all the world...that 'White Australia' had begun in January 1788 as an English prison for 'minor' criminals, e.g. robbery or perjury. Internet had yet too little information on what I needed to find...I wanted the hidden history of those eight convicts, which meant I had to go where written history was available...it had to be on the bloody site. There was no 'internet!'

Most of those families had left no background records, for most were illiterate. My only way of learning was to visit those seven counties in England and one in Ireland, sit in their libraries recording weddings, births and deaths, then fly home to transcribe to paper.

Having lost America's War of Independence, England had to find somewhere else to despatch minor criminals, also to defeat France in founding a Pacific Ocean colony. In 1770 Captain Cook charted the east coast of Australia reporting water enough to feed to his ship and that black natives lived along the south to north coastline...

"If it feeds blacks it can feed convicts," was the decision to relieve bulging gaols. Eleven ships with some 650 male and 50 female convicts, 200 redcoats, some with wives, and an administration team of a few score, total on the thousand mark (records vary in numbers), set sail for the world's biggest island.

After a year's study of libraries, I was shocked at what I found. I wrote my first book *Gurrewa* (local native name for the country's white cockatoo). In 1989 my 5th life, near its twenty-year mark, Maggie and I agree on a mutual separation (all covered in detail in *A Home for Old Ladies*). She remains in Melbourne and I move into the Gold Coast beach-house I'd purchased as an investment.

There, the then president of its Writers Club, editor of the local newspaper, introduces me to a friend in London who buys travel articles to sell to airline magazines. This too proves a successful move, so I begin with places already visited. He likes what I write, so living alone I begin travelling with a dual purpose. When in Europe it is easy to then spend time in English counties to study my family history, and wherever that takes me I can write about. This soon becomes my purposeful way of fulfilling a now selfish life. If I travel for three months and write for three months, I've a half a year to beach-bum.

Having written *Gurrewa*, I need a publisher and the internet convinces me agents are best skilled in influencing publishers. Business taught me to always shoot for the top on any project, so internet convinces me Australia's best agent in historical genre is Sydney's Selwa Anthony. I phone her.

"I'm snowed under. I cannot take on more clients."

"Please just read it?"

"Sorry m'dear. I'm overloaded with work."

Another thing business taught me is to never accept a 'No' answer. I must go crawling like a persistent cat! All this is before e-mails, so I write a pleading note that I am a patient man and can wait until she finds a spare few minutes to read even its first chapter. I post the entire 75,000 words.

Three nail-biting months later, she phones… "Apart from your first page, you start this story wrong. Make page 'two' where you have Chapter 3 and feed what precedes it as afterthoughts throughout the next few chapters. And…"

I never argue. I get straight on to it and send it back.

Several days later, she phones… "I have a few publishers who could be interested. I like it, it has real guts."

I have plenty else to take up my time so begin plotting my first three-month trip.

Selwa phones, explaining that there are no more large Australian publishers. "All the big ones have been taken over by foreign publishers and locally print only proved successes. I've failed with my regulars. Are you happy if I try an English publisher?"

I have to say yes. All it costs me is time.

She sells it and two months later I receive by airmail, my first copy of *Gurrewa*.

A wonderful objective achieved! I put a tick on my wall.

A month later she phones. "It's won an award! We need to talk here in Sydney!"

"I leave next week for Europe."

"Then depart from Sydney. When a first attempt wins an award, we must quickly get two sequels. There are many important things about writing sequels I need to talk about with you. Come an hour early. When you have your ticket, give me the date."

I do that quickly with all my gear for Britain and fly to Sydney.

"I love your book. It has as brilliant an ending, as its stunning beginning. I need two sequels in two years."

"I cannot write two books in two years. *Gurrewa* took two years and I'm president of the Gold Coast Writers Club, secretary of the Sunlovers Club—"

She slams the table with the flat of one hand and shakes a finger with the other...

"If you are really dedicated, Kev Richardson, you'll put all that on a shelf, take two years leave of absence from those clubs, go somewhere nobody knows you, crawl into a corner and write!"

She holds out her hand. "Have a happy trip. You've hours ahead of you right now, so use them carefully." She marches out the door without looking back.

I begin thinking about how I might write both beginning and end of the first sequel.

That becomes, for every book I am to write, a habit. But now... London, here I come.

BOOK ONE

5th & 6th Lives

1952 - 1992

First Flight
Business travels
(England, Germany, Canada, USA)
Greece
Amsterdam
England
South Pacific Islands
Hawaii
Yosemite
Turtle Island
New Zealand

One

Here with a loaf of Bread beneath the Bough,
A Flask of Wine, a Book of verse – and Thou
Beside me in the wilderness –
And Wilderness is Paradise enow.
—*Rubáiyát of Omar Khayyam #XI*

    Everyone's first airflight is exciting and a simple little expression in mine has stuck in my memory ever since my first. Today it seems hilarious.
    In 1951, neither Kit nor I had flown, so decide to begin our honeymoon by air. The secluded little beach...just 220 road miles away that we've chosen is so close that the flight must be short... fly Sydney to Newcastle and bus from there.
    It is a thrilling experience to start what we hope will be a thrilling new life.
    Australia's largest airliner in 1951 is the DC 3 and as we taxi into the take-off queue our excitement begins. Here is the line I've ever remembered...

Our hostess announces...
"Everybody up the front please, until we are off the ground."

In the 1950s, international travel is only for the rich and business chiefs. It isn't until 1974 that working my way up in one of Australia's largest printing companies now owned by DRG (Dickinson-Robinson-Group) of Bristol in England, that my first one occurs. DRG employs 24,000 people in 12 countries. I am to visit an industrial exhibition in Germany, then go to England to see and learn from our company's leaders, returning via Toronto, Milwaukee and San Francisco. The home flight is via Honolulu, Fiji and New Zealand.

What does my first exciting travel experience chance on? All accommodation and flights are First Class and by chance, my first international aircraft is the Boeing 707 jumbo jet, newest aircraft in the world!

A two-storied aircraft? Sheesh? What will the world offer next?

~ * ~

In 1974 the Qantas upstairs is a First-Class lounge. We come down only to eat, sleep, take-offs and landings. The upstairs lounge on the Melbourne to London run via Sydney, Perth and Bombay has a baby-grand piano with pianist, tables for chess, monopoly, bridge etc., also a library of hundreds of books and magazines.

My mind flies back to being asked up-front until air-bound on a DC3!

When the 19-hour flight lands in the dead of night in Bombay, we are sent ashore for an hour while the plane is cleaned and refuelled. But oh, what a stench tortures every nostril in the waiting room. It's the stench of garbage and the room has no air-conditioning. A bus trip into the city is offered First Class passengers, yet all refuse.

I still have that nasty memory of India.

Saturday morning, Maggie's parents meet me at Heathrow, drive me to Luton for Saturday and Sunday touring the district and meeting family. Early Monday, my mother-in-law drives me to the station for an early train to London, where I change trains for

Paddington then head west. It is a wonderful journey. Many times, I feel like jumping out to take pictures, especially in Bath.

At Bristol, a DRG uniformed man seeks me out, relieves me of my huge leather bag, huge because I require for a month many different forms of clothing and need spare space for souvenirs. Luggage on wheels has not yet been invented and it is heavy to have to carry. He leads me to a huge vintage Daimler. I learn the company has seven such, as well as a small aircraft. It is also Bristol's major employer.

He drives me to Hotel Dragonara (later to become Bristol Hilton). I don't see much of the city and in those days Bristol had but one 'skyscraper,' the 14 story DRG House.

So much had to be crammed into my week and my Friday train has me at London's 'Inn on the Park', not only on Park Lane but it shares Hyde Park Corner with Buckingham Palace. My shock is a bad one on arriving. They have no record of my booking and are booked out. I fortunately always insist on hotel booking copies for I travelled around Australia often. So now I can show them my Qantas confirmation of having booked me into this hotel from Friday dinner through Monday breakfast.

I quietly tell them to please find my room; I shall wait in the bar.

It takes them ten minutes and they proffer a whole load of apologies.

In 2020 of course, one has computers to assure this. Without a copy, however, you can find yourself stranded in the gutter.

Saturday free I walk so many of London's crowded streets, each with too narrow a pavement. Strolling Regent Street is indeed a glorifying experience and with a slight detour, Savile Row where Gerard Rawes, one of my great-grandfathers had his tailor-shop (see *Gerard Rawes* published November 2010). Sunday is another strolling day taking in Trafalgar Square where Gerard married at St. Martin's in the Field, Nelson's column and so many places of renown. I taxi back for a delightful Inn on the Park dinner and very tired, have an early night.

The morning sees me early to breakfast and after a quick look around Hyde Park Corner on which the hotel is situated, and Belgrave Square, I head for the airport.

~ * ~

Germany...

I fly to Düsseldorf and taxi to Duisburg where DRG staff from the 13 countries are booked. I have an extremely busy four days and the DRG two-storied 'stand' is huge. I have a long Must-Do-List, looking at new things available in our industry. Come morning, on checking out of my hotel, as I signed my name to DRG's account, the clerk nods as a parting gesture. I answer with a rehearsed *"Danke Meneer"*.

The cheeky bastard congratulates me on having so quickly learned to speak German, but then has a giggle at his own sense of humour.

From Germany, my week-end freedoms must be paid for from my out-of-pocket expenses which are generous. I may decide from where I append my week-end so long as I fly out on my Diners Club Card to Toronto. I love train travel and would love to see something of Holland, so buy myself a first-class train ticket for a weekend in Amsterdam.

~ * ~

Holland...

I love trains and Europe's are of excellent standard. One stop short of my goal is Utrecht, where the station is so dramatically smothered in floral displays that I reckon there must be something remarkable going on. I grasp my bag and jump off the train, and book the bag into the station's luggage bay so my hands are free for photographing. I expect to find excitement everywhere I look. As I stroll, I get only repeated reminders that I have never seen such beautiful floral displays. All I find is this wonderful surprise repeated on every side of me. This is simply the way Holland cities 'dress' every summer.

I return to the station where I had seen a cash-exchange window and exchange *deutschmarks* for Dutch *guilders*, take several shots of the 'smothered in flowers' station then resume my strolling until dusk. Not wanting to seek accommodation in the dark of night in Amsterdam, I tear myself way from the beautifully adorned Utrecht.

Amsterdam is like Utrecht, smothered in flowers. I quickly learn that one can save tiring legs by taking a *kanaalboot,* a ferry on one of Amsterdam's scores of canals. Many streets deny motor vehicles, so walking in crowds is also comfortable. In many streets, buildings are being reinforced to save further crumbling. At every building, house or shop or business house, flowers bloom on every window sill. Few buildings are taller than three or four stories and few have lifts. I have to quickly buy more snapshot film.

At every time of day, however, one needs care when gazing into Amsterdam shop windows. Even along canals, a sparsely dressed damsel beckons a man in so she can please your sexual desires. I respond only by returning her broad smiles.

Two Dutch places on my 'must see' list call for a short train ride to Den Hague. On its city edge is their biggest surf beach, Scheveningen. I am keen to see how Dutch people use it. I quickly leave again, for everyone on the beach is tucked within a tent to avoid an absolute gale, blowing sand so thick in the air it almost hides the North Sea.

The other 'attraction' nearby is clever, amazing and amusing, a miniature city named Maduradam. Tiny but mobile people 10cm tall stroll about their tiny gardens; others go shopping. Miniature cars move about streets and rail traffic seems and sounds real. Even aeroplanes take off as cows graze on the lawns between its runways as I will apparently see on the morrow. The display even includes its own tiny flower park. Amazing!

Next day I am not ashamed to find myself aboard my KLM airliner in tears. Here am I, a grown man, crying. The worried stewardess brings me brandy. Holland had given me so much pleasure I feel cheated at being torn from it so quickly.

I swear to one day return and see more. I am to do so, many times.

Canada...

My Canadian visit is even briefer but a working visit. Despite insisting Australia's biggest biscuit manufacturers are satisfied that cellulose packaging is less than half the price of biscuit packaging as in North America, my Aussie boss insists my Canadian counterpart named Daniel takes me to his biggest customer to see biscuits being packaged. So I head for Toronto.

Nearing the Nova Scotia's coast, we fly over many icebergs to touch down at Montreal, then to Toronto. Once through customs, Daniel waits for me, insisting I change my Dutch *guilders* for US dollars rather than Canadian.

"You are here for only tomorrow, Ric. If you want to tip the hotel staff, US dollars are fine. It saves a lot of queuing and fiddling for so quick a visit."

He takes me home for dinner, then to Toronto's Inn on the Park hotel. During dinner his two young sons are anxious for information on Australia. I ask the boys in which direction bath water swirls when draining. All four in the family scratch heads and follow the boys upstairs. I am able to report that south of the equator, it runs in the counter direction.

Next day Daniel drives me to Kitchener and I am fascinated at the speed of machines opening the folded square-bottomed bags, filling them with biscuits, sealing the bags, then packing them into cartons of a dozen. All from one of DRG's printed reels.

On my way to the airport next morning, I see the sky-scraping Toronto tower being prepared for its opening ceremony. We touch down at Detroit, then it is not far to Milwaukee. I call into the money-exchange office to cash a bank cheque and my Dutch surplus. In USA I have to, on the morrow, for the first time in my life, drive eighty miles on the wrong side of the road. It has me decidedly nervous.

Ah, the challenges of travelling!

~ * ~

Milwaukee and San Francisco...

Having taxied from the airport to Hotel Marriott West, I settle in, drink a beer at the bar then shudder at the prices on the dinner menu and again at the wine list.

Thinking back on my arrival in Duisburg, I had gotten quite a shock when at my first dinner in Europe, at the DRG table, a loudspeaker reports an incoming call for *Herr* Kevin Richardson. The caller is the manager of the company I am to visit here in Wisconsin. He is at the Fair and has a map to help me drive the eighty miles to their small town. We make an appointment to meet on the morrow at the DRG Display Stand. He giggles when I tell him it will be my first attempt at driving that 'wrong' side of the road.

After breakfast I have a cab take me to the car-rental site recommended by the hotel. Watching the cab driver, I note him look right for his rear-vision mirror and to my left, cars overtake me, a most unnatural way to drive!

"You simply have to hug that right-hand kerb," my conscience reminds me.

I ask for something small. "A two-door job is fine."

They bring me a two-door Chevrolet Caprice hardtop coupé, longest car I've ever seen…six and a half metres!

What could be even worse? Their exit gate is on to a freeway ramp!

There is no freeway on Karl's map! I've just got to get off this bloody thing and find the road he has marked, then follow it north to Fond du Lac, then turn right.

Of course there is no way of pulling up on the freeway to study my map.

Yet if I stay on it, I might find myself back in Canada!

To avoid trying to read the map at the same time as the strange names on the signs overhead, I decide to simply take the next exit and seek a gas station.

The guy there will surely be able to mark my map to get on to the road Karl marked.

I do it and find the countryside so delightful, feel somewhat disappointed at having to turn off at Fond du Lac. The map gets me to the little village of Holstein. I achieve what I want (usual for me,

I am beginning to find) from them and they take me to lunch in a neighbouring village.

"You head back that way," they say with a laugh as we shake hands on parting.

"No," say I, elated over my successful visit. "I now have enough confidence in my driving to follow this road to Sheboygan, then sightsee down the Lake Michigan coast."

"Will you then find your way to return your car?"

"No. I shall phone them from my hotel and tell them I will keep it overnight. They can pick it up, plus cash for the overnight, pinned to the key, at the airport tomorrow."

That earns quite a few laughs.

Head Office had recommended my four day 'reprieve' at the end of a round-the-world journey, to write up my report for Bristol be spent in San Francisco rather than after getting home, tired after the long journey.

"Best to do it before signing out at your last port of call," I am told, "and DRG has an account at the Sir Francis Drake Hotel. It's cute and comfortable."

"Cute?"

"Terribly British, dear chap, even the Sir Francis Drake doorman wears a Yeoman of the Guard uniform."

I confine my considerable sightseeing to daylight and my four evenings at my project homework. I quite fall in love with San Francisco; it has that holiday air about it.

Qantas then flies me home via Honolulu and Fiji.

Later, Maggie and I are to visit San Francisco, Hawaii then Fiji on several occasions, just to sight-see.

Two

Mags and I take long holiday...

A couple of years later, I have my 30th anniversary with DRG, which qualifies me for a three-month holiday on full pay. We plot on visiting Maggie's parents in England where she will show me around her native countryside.

On the way, we will visit two sights for which we share particular yens, the Greek islands and both want a second visit to Amsterdam. We book two weeks in each and I ensure Thomas Cook copies me confirmation of both bookings.

To leave herself free to take such a long holiday, and happy at having such a fruitful *casse* of trade shares, Maggie resigns from her job. She and a girlfriend will take up independent secretarial work between them, that each can do from home.

Flying 'steerage,' as I call economy class when I have to pay, we fly Qantas to Athens for a week of wonders; wonders of how, without mechanical vehicles, such wonderful architecture could be erected so many centuries ago. It proves indeed a land of wonders. In the early years of white man learning to write their language, Plaka had been the capital of Greece, the major city, along with Rome as rulers of Mediterranean settlements. It is now but a suburb of Athens, but remains deep in Greek history.

It has been careful in maintaining as many of its yesterdays as possible, particularly in Plaka. We spend our entire time all but mesmerised at how Greece has maintained so much of its grappling history. We fly to the Sporadhes, a small group of northern islands in the Ægean Sea, recommended as retaining considerable time-worn surprises. We have our own little cabin by a beach on Skiatos Island, envying families come dinner time, bringing meals into their outdoors to dine barbeque style. One night, a family waves us to join them. Even though they have but a slight touch of English and we have no Greek, it is a successful evening and they insist we eat with them every evening. We oblige by bringing foodstuffs and, while their children sing Greek songs to their father's guitar, we each night dance to it. That way we happily learn so much about Greece's countryside style of life.

We spend a glorious day on a small island where naked swimming is popular, then tour the Sporadhes' other two islands, Skopelos and Skiros, both with wonderful scenery. We depart both, delighted. I am particularly bemused by the sound of tide rising and falling to the clatter of small stones instead of silent sand.

"Sounds like Brighton beach," Maggie informs me.

Another major delight to enjoy in Greece is eating. And oh so cheaply! Wines are worthy enough and we come away convinced the Greeks have food down to a fine art, both large restaurants and roadside coffee rooms. We are intrigued that it is common for a restaurant to not have menus; customers go to the kitchen and point to what they want. Greek coffee is excellent, far superior to England or Australia, we agree and everywhere, coffee is 'bottomless': you buy one and they just keep topping it up.

We fly by Olympic Airlines (not as superior in comfort as some) direct to Amsterdam. Maggie had, in her earlier life, visited many European countries and had studied both French and Italian languages at school. She has both down to quite a conversational art, had even sung in a nightclub in Italy's Como for two years!

~ * ~

Amsterdam again...

We visit many museums, and on canals simply sit in passenger barges from which one gets wonderful views. Wandering the narrow streets is comfortable, for many are closed to cars. Bicycles are used by the million. Artists paint murals on walls or are on pedestrian-only streets and will paint you. Food shops abound, particularly in the 'walking only' streets and museums are aplenty. The Van Gough museum is closed for renovations, but we promise each other a further visit.

Again, I am mesmerised by floral displays and are reminded how many brothel shops openly display half-clad beauties beckoning passers-by to 'come in and be thrilled.'

Maggie and I never respond, yet both want to again visit Maduradam, the 'miniature' little city and spend an entire day there. It is great fun.

On our last night, we attend one of the city's several live sex theatres. This one is not hidden away in some back street but lit up with flashing lights opposite City Hall in the main square. We are amazed at estimating not only that the audience at about two hundred, but at their ages. Everyone must be at least twenty-one. Men seem mostly in their middle age or more and dress surprisingly formally. Many a wife chooses formal wear with diamonds aplenty. At one stage, four totally naked couples are at the extreme height of intercourse and a dozen or more singles form an 'arc' behind them, each performing solo what we could call self-abuse by some and solo pleasure by others.

All perform to measured music. Dare I admit that after the exhibition, the major performers mix with those of the audience who want to drop by the bar. We sit over glasses of wine chatting with one of the couples, the lady of which has enough French to comfortably converse with Maggie.

As it is our last night in Amsterdam, we leave the theatre, highly conscious of discovering such a unique form of entertainment. We had learned so much!

~ * ~

England...

We fly KLM but don't yet stay in London, just catch a train to Luton and phone her mother to come pick us up. At dinner we flip through the rough plan Mags had plotted for our tour. As expected, Edna and Arthur recommend things we can do together on weekends. Mags and I rent a car and set off to see the sights she knows I will enjoy. We reckon on two or three weeks.

Oh how nice being able to spend time on what we just 'feel like doing'!

We amble around the massive Cambridge University gardens, then via Saffron Walden for lunch. Need I say I find it all magnificent?

I don't know how Maggie manages to acquire gallery tickets for the *Last Night of the Proms* at the multi-galleried Royal Albert Hall, and good seats at that, when five-thousand people absolutely pack themselves into the theatre. The magnificent programme has stuck in my memory ever since. I write in my memoirs...

The shock of the moment is during Tchaikovsky's 1812 Overture when two vintage iron cannons situated within the orchestra, fire 'balls' simultaneous to near deafen the sold-out audience. The real smoke makes it utterly sensational.

Having lived in London for several years, Mags knows it well and introduces me to oh, so many extreme places...Buckingham Palace, Piccadilly Circus, Regent Street, Savile Row where my Gerard Rawes had his tailor-shop. We visit 37 Surry Street just off The Strand, what had been his home, but the entire Surry Street is now the Arundel Great Court. You can read about Gerard's amazing life in my book, *Gerard Raws*. He dressed Admiral Nelson, Lord George Byron and many historically known politicians.

Whole streets in Shoreditch where he lived in a second marriage are gone, levelled by bombs during World War 2. Sky-scraping apartment buildings now occupy that site. St. John the Baptist church in Shoreditch is, however, fortunately saved and we find his and wife's joint grave there. Since then, that graveyard has also had to give way to broaden roads, but I have my Kodachrome slides.

We tour Harrods where we buy nowt but a salad lunch in their expensive food hall to take across the road and eat in Hyde Park. After several magical London days, we drive south to Brighton with its ugly theatre and stony beach.

At Portsmouth we overnight in a B&B (Bed and Breakfast) equivalent to Australia's motels although smaller, often a single room in a private home. We see through major tourist attractions like HMS Victory, a 104-gun flagship from the Battle of Trafalgar in which the beloved Vice-Admiral Nelson lost his life (his costume tailored by my Gerard).

I spend most of the day walking about the ship, yet the ceilings are so low I must crouch. I depart excited and it is so late we decide to spend another night there.

Tomorrow is Stonehenge and those were the days before tourists are forbidden to walk around amongst the massive stone towers.

Further west, Plymouth has ever been a naval port, first for ships travelling north from the Mediterranean, a city totally levelled by Nazi bombers in WW2. It had to be totally rebuilt, spoiling it as an historical sight. Plymouth has remained a proud port since its mayor, Sir Francis Drake, in 1588 laid waste to the distressed Spanish Armada.

We overnight there and on the morrow look briefly around Falmouth, then drive through Cornwall to Land's End where the Atlantic Ocean laps English shores. We climb around the several rocky 'symbol' sites and drive east along the north shore to St. Ives where we spend that night. Then it is east along the coast to the top of the beautiful little township of Padstow.

'To the top', you ask? Indeed, for the entire town is vertical. No road, simply a series of steps with every little house-front a floral picture! We feel rested enough to tread the steps all the way down to a beach along which are many small workshops building boats.

Padstow is indeed a unique, beautiful little fishing village. On getting breaths back after the climb, we motor east along a coastline where many remains of earlier centuries' smuggling are retained... caves where saleable goods had been hidden.

The hundred kilometre drive to Bath is a countryside worth seeing, Bath City doubly so. Maggie's good advice is to stay a few days, for everything about Bath has sites both beautiful and historical. The scenery, to use a popular Pommy word, is 'smashing', as are the very Roman built baths which still operate!

The city's architecture is to be thoroughly admired. I indeed enjoy these for several days.

Nearby we have an invitation to spend a weekend with friends we knew in our Sydney days. Just out of Bristol, DRG's mother city, at Chipping Sodbury is Horton Court, a home built into the ruins of an old castle and an Open to View site two days a week. We had met Gabby and Stuart in Sydney and after marriage they returned to live in Horton Court's restored gatekeeper's lodge. In the castle part of the huge family home, it still has armoured knights arranged around the stone wall that rises to great heights. The hall is dressed as if ready for a feast. It is let out for wedding breakfasts!

From our bedroom windows we overlook glorious gardens with wild bird-nests galore, providing us with not only floral beauty but delightful bird-music aplenty.

Gabby gives us a booklet, *Historical Accommodation in England,* that from then on, we use to find the oldest overnight beds in whatever town we've arrived in. We find some delightful ones. If in Shropshire's Ludlow, try Feather's Hotel. That English town, Maggie tells me, has retained the most half-timbered cottages in all England. In Stratford on Avon, where everything is Shakespeare, we spend one night at 'The Stratford' and one at 'The Welcombe'. Both have furniture and fittings from his home.

We wind our way north through Worcester, where we lunch in a restaurant upstairs of the old marketplace. The entire building is, we reckon, some five hundred years old. I am in my element! We then work our way through Shropshire and Cheshire, to walk what remains of the latter's city walls.

West along the Welsh coast, we cannot resist stopping in Flint, a tiny town literally shouting 'History!' I cannot for the life of me remember the name of likely the most crooked house labelled hotel. It is two storied and once upstairs and one room along the hall are two steps down to a lower level to our room. Maggie plucks from her bag a half-empty water bottle. The floor of our room is so tilted from one wall to the other that she lets the bottle roll down, under the double bed, to finish at the opposite wall...and it rolls quickly. One wall is quite crooked. At the ceiling it leans out over the street some two feet or more. The wall between us and the next room has several patches. All walls are timber and what must have been just a hole, has a timber patch nailed over it.

Anglesea is interesting; most of the time we spend walking city walls to photograph interesting sights. Mags wants postage stamps, so a little way down the coast we walk into a post office and suddenly feel we must have something wrong with our apparel or stuck to our faces...but no, with a half-dozen men and women staring us up and down from head to foot, we are obviously just strangers.

Once outside, Maggie laughs..."It is obvious this town has little to boast of, for we certainly seem something dreadfully strange."

We find the town of Maconthleuth amusing because of its name. We break into laughter when realising each at the same time is likening it to hearing someone complain that their something is loose. However, we do shop there. We buy apples and bananas as a late lunch and next door is a shop for brass musical instruments.

"Just the thing to buy my son Paul as a souvenir," I reckon and buy a 'single curl' trumpet for him and for our house's dining room wall, a four-foot long one. Mags buys a decorative brass hair-comb for my daughter, Leanne.

After a picturesque drive through the centre of Wales, our next night is Breckon of Breckon Beacons fame. Next day we drive to Chepstow and espy atop a hill the remains of an ancient castle. I must go see it. Little is left, but we read that it is thought to be the oldest stone castle ruin in Britain. It had been badly damaged during the Civil War and Oliver Cromwell insisted that much more of it should be pulled down. I nevertheless find it fascinating.

Chepstow is the Wales end of the first motorway suspension bridge into England. We spend the night there, then cross the bridge to head due east to Swindon, then on to Oxford, Aylesbury and Luton...home!

In Aylesbury's little lake, still maintained on one shore is the dunking machine which centuries ago was the penalty for women who had stolen food...they were strapped in the seat of a great wooden arm and dunked in the lake for as many seconds as the magistrate had ordered, time after time for as many seconds as had also been ordered.

We arrive in Luton feeling somewhat exhausted, yet at the same time exhilarated.

Some of my favourite slides taken in many towns are of Morris Dancers...again left-over history being maintained. Groups of ten to twenty men dress in ancient style to dance in the village square to the rhythm of drums, trumpets and miniature harps played by others of their party. There seem no rules, for throughout the areas where we are lucky enough to discover them, several dance in rhythmic steps to musical beats one minute, then change to hopping and skipping, arms waving seemingly with abandon, with not too many in perfect time. So some independence is illustrated too.

I feel somewhat exhausted after nearly a month of such living, yet also thoroughly content with Maggie's chosen sights.

~ * ~

By mid-September, I feel the approach to winter. It is Australia's spring and I look forward to a surfing summer! In Amsterdam, the Van Gough Museum has completed renovation and on our way home, we want several days there. We choose KLM for, at no extra charge on flying direct to Australia, they allow a break if spent in Holland, no matter how short. We make admiring Van Gough's stupendous abilities in his shattered life last three days. On a high at that further experience, we lift off in a KLM jumbo, stopping to refuel at Bahrain and Singapore.

On that final leg, we are also lucky enough to find our favourite 'steerage-class' seats at the tail end of the jumbo. There are but two seats between aisle and window, rather than three. First stop in those early days, Bahrain is a long way behind its sudden modernity. On vacating the plane, we are directed to a lounge by soldiers armed with rifles nursed at elbow level, into a large room with hard seats, no open windows and no air-conditioning, no alcohol and only water at room temperature to drink. There are complaints galore, especially from upper class passengers. Many people, especially women, nearly faint in the heat.

All are happy when returning to the jumbo. KLM staff is apologetic, telling us that Bahrain is an Arab kingdom island squeezed between two Arab neighbour countries seemingly about to declare war on each other.

The further flight is enjoyable until, having crossed the Australian north-west coast and approaching the country's centre, an announcement interrupts film and music... "A First-Class passenger is victim of a seizure and requires instant hospital treatment. We have permission to land at Adelaide, where an ambulance is waiting."

Several passengers report that Adelaide has no runway long enough for jumbos. Recent news reported it considering making it a tourist set-down airport, but that is a long way in time yet. We circle it twice so the pilots can get a good view of where they have to land. The runways are not built for such big planes, yet we cleverly make it. Our seats are on the same side of our aircraft as the transfer is made and we watch the ambulance race off. Once his luggage is found and taken, we begin departure...

Being at the very tail, we can see that we are backing ever so slowly *over grassy lawn!*

When it stops, revving begins to increase until the plane is frighteningly shuddering.

"Bloody hell!" is what everyone must be thinking.

I reckon no one has ever heard a jumbo build to such a roaring take-off.

We make it. All around the country next da y, newspapers run the story front page.

Once in the air, our captain makes the apologetic announcement that having lost so much time and now in the very south of Australia, instead of landing first in Sydney then on to Melbourne, we will land first in Melbourne then to Sydney. There are lots of moans. Many have family or friends already waiting near two hours since initially due in Sydney. Sydney-bound passengers moan while Melbournians cheer.

Oh, what a startling *finalé* to our holiday! But then, this is travelling!

On arriving home and unpacking, Maggie declares...

"It wouldn't be often that a man gets off a plane with a four-foot horn!"

Three

Over the next few years, Maggie and I have three more exciting travel experiences, each with startling surprises.

In Australian law, employee annual holidays on full pay have increased from two weeks to three weeks.

Did that happen just before a Federal Election? Likely so!

Mags and I decide to take a three-week cruise, exactly twenty days afloat plus flights Melbourne to Sydney and back. We expect to find paradise and do, every day!

In Sydney we board P&O's Orsova, its largest liner. Both have worked at top pace, so with children 'grown and flown' we decide to make our holiday special by booking a First-Class cabin (bedroom, sitting room, dressing room, bathroom). First Class also has us dining at the 'royal' table. We don't want the early meal sitting, which happens to be the captain's table, but the second for which his table is hosted by First Mate. We prefer second so that dinner is longer for chatting over another glass of wine.

My Life, My Travels

Orsova departs late afternoon down Sydney's magnificent harbour. We awake to find ourselves sailing off Queensland's coast. After an hour for a Farewell Australia surf on an island, we cruise through more Great Barrier Reef islands, then veer hard to starboard on our way to New Caledonia's Nouméa.

Maggie doesn't swim, but knows my penchant for it, so every day I have an hour or so in the pool. Second night out and as First Class, Maggie and I are guests at the Captain's *Soirée* where we meet major officers and other boat-deck guests, a great honour.

Straight from breakfast, we dock in Nouméa. Maggie uses her French to find our way to the Maritine Museum to which she'd been recommended. It is indeed wonderful. Back in the city, we have a late restaurant lunch, then to *Orsova* for drinks in the bar which, fortunately, is but a dozen paces from our cabin door. We find it well attended and quickly make many new friendships, some lasting years.

Next morning, we wake to find ourselves docking in Vanuatu's capital, Espiritu Santo. Once ashore there is even less English spoken and Maggie's French is again a help to many. I'd been given recommendations to a restaurant and we enjoy a delightful part-French part-Polynesian lunch. Vanuatu however, is not yet up to Noumea's ready service to tourists...a new country still learning to please.

Once more using sleeping hours to cover island gaps, we have a day in Fiji's Lautoka. What we discover for lunch is the sensationally new taste of the *Luau*, since become popular in western countries., certainly in Australia.

Another night of 'sail' has us in the Fijian capital Suva where half the population is Indian. It is quickly obvious that the city population is 50-50 Fijian and Indian; the latter work while Fijians play, sing and dance. Shopping for souvenirs is a major pastime and after a full night and day and night again at sea, I fortunately awake early.

Every evening the setting sun in the South Pacific is 'magic colour stuff,' as the children call it, the slowly moving sky persistently changing colours to keeping scores of passengers along the railings, spellbound for an hour or more. Every evening, more are drawn to it, clicking cameras. Today I am to have as wonderful a sunrise, not of colour but of silence.

Maggie and I had danced in the ballroom until late and she slept in while luck had me awake early. I donned my usual shorts and T-shirt and went the one floor up with my camera. The sports deck is clear of building except for the funnels, so one has 360º scenery.

On this particular morning, we do not have ocean all around us but are heading west in a wide channel, the quietest looking coastline of beaches on both sides of us, as I've ever seen.

'Quietest coastline' you might ask?

Indeed. This is what I discover. Not another soul is in sight and it is the scenery on both shores that proffer such a silence. Only sound is the ship underneath me and the water it is churning all about. All the visual scenery is soundless.

We are in Tonga where one actually 'sees' the quietness around you, sees it and senses it. Nothing other than the ship's wash breaks the stillness. On the shore, nothing moves, no sign of man or beast, only here and there a tree. Not a person in sight. Even the thousands of birds whirling about seem quieted by the ship's presence.

I feel so much alone, enjoying the quiet until other early risers begin joining me.

We approach the tiny town of Vava'u where we have two entire days and I look forward to both…anxious to breakfast quickly as if that will get me to shore the more quickly, to discover the people who can love such unspoiled beauty.

They must be interesting people in every essence.

The only vehicles to take us from the wharf are buses that are old trucks with, on their open luggage area, long wooden stools. We are told these are for ladies to sit and men may decide to either sit on the floor or stand.

I love it!

It rattles its way to the beach over bitumen roads with more holes than it can avoid. One wonders, *Will the brakes work?*

Of course not! The driver simply turns off the motor and lets the 'bus' career over rough stuff into the sand until the wheels bury themselves. That is 'stop.'

I love it more and more, especially as the driver has a grin all over his face!

He knows he can easily get towed out.

That grin, I am convinced, is the epitome of this entire country's attitude to life.

One of the most intriguing sights when I get to see around their bamboo houses, are what must be graves of the family for centuries back surrounding them; no etched messages, just all around the house and encrusted into the dirt, coloured bottle tops and as vividly coloured food or beer cans as could be found, the more glaring the colours, the better. These graves quite encircle each.

We lunch ashore on salads and in the afternoon are taken (in a bus with brakes) to a field behind the school where older students hand out glasses of Coca-Cola and answer questions on their lives, habits and hopes.

Our group of visitors is fortunate enough to strike a lad of fourteen whose English is excellent. We realise that chatting with us is part of teaching him something of 'the world out there' and I guess, also to help him with the language. He is in bare feet and in answer to "Is this uniform?" he informs us no, that his 'slop sandals' had worn out.

He is quickly given enough coinage to buy twenty pairs.

As the sun goes down, we are treated to a magnificent seafood barbecue, Polynesian music and dancing. Tonga has little to offer in terms of spoken or physical welcome, yet the happiness in everyone is potently riveting. Their lives seem shared by joy and satisfaction. Giggling is the main habit and I come away full of envy.

Next day we go surfing in the morning and in the afternoon sail to Tonga's capital, Nukualofa. During the voyage, I admit to rendering a tear of two for the same reason I broke into tears when first leaving Holland.

Nukualofa is bigger and a more 'modern' city than Vava'u, so lacks its isolated advantage. In its harbour remains the wreck of a ship struck by Japanese bombs during the war. When I ask why it's left remaining there, I am told... "Moving it costs money."

I whisper into my notebook: "They simply don't need money. They are happy with their lives without the bloody stuff!"

I have never been able to forget Tongan's joy of life, especially in Vava'u.

Sailing to our last visit, we are again enchanted watching the South Seas Sunset... yes it deserves capital letters. Every evening before dressing for dinner, everyone holds the ship's railing to again be thrilled. The magic changing of colours is magnetic!

By then we have made so many friends that we never have a lonely moment.

The last is Pago-Pago in American Samoa, certainly one of the most attractive harbours of all, yet so USA influenced that it has lost ninety percent of Polynesian attraction. Everywhere is western clothing and family homes with television, natural of course in our day and age, yet lacking the natural happiness of Tongans and Fijians, in fact all Polynesians and Melanesians in outer islands.

Time of course, will change them too...sad but undoubted.

One thing I enjoy in Pago Pago is having a free afternoon to go surfing. I attend and Maggie has a 'Girls' meeting' to study making attractive native clothing.

Maggie doesn't swim but is happy to chat with friends while I surf.

Entertainment aboard is plentiful, something for everybody at every age at any hour. I get into chess games, Monopoly and even find a bezique enthusiast. Mags and I love 500 and there are always plenty of partners for that. Money games are frowned upon.

Our twenty days aboard is worth every dollar and next morning at work I do not find getting around business problems easy.

Mags and I both feel reborn.

~ * ~

Honolulu...

Sometime later, she has a phone call from sister Audrey. She and her next husband are having a three-day holiday in Honolulu, he on business.

"Come see us," she pleads. Mags wants to go.

"Come with me," she pleads in turn. I fiddle with dates on my office desk calendar, get Dale's nod, and go with her.

We cannot fit into Audrey's tiny hotel, so settle into one nearby. We rent our own car, for there is a lot of sightseeing and we tour the island from start to finish. On our last day, every one magnificently sunny, I park under their hotel but take our luggage upstairs to shower and change into travelling gear. On coming down to be kissed goodbye, the car has gone.

Audrey drives us to the airport in her husband's rented car.

I hand my keys in at the airport rental desk..."Sorry about your car, and the police didn't seem very interested, but here are the keys."

They don't seem to mind for they simply sigh...obviously it happens often!

"I left my camera in the car," Maggie mourns, yet quickly realises there is nowt to be done except get statements from the hotel and police, as evidence for claiming insurance.

We fly home disappointed about that, but Mags is happy for having seen Audrey so happy with her latest choice in husbands.

~ * ~

Yosemite...

Not long after that and I had been away a week touring the country on business, Maggie tells me her mother has contracted Alzheimers.

"I do need to go see her. Can you batch for a week or two? She is in hospital for a couple of weeks and I would like to be with my dad when she comes home."

"By all means," and next day when I arrive home, she puts a question...

"You've been flat out at your office lately and it's good that the huge problem with the unions you've had is over, but left you exhausted. I've two weeks before she comes home, so have booked myself a ten-day trip in California, taking in Yosemite National Park and Disneyland. I also want to see the San Francisco you've so often praised. Come with me?"

I again get Dale's nod and congratulation on winning the recent union war on salaries.

"Yes Ric, go and enjoy."

At home I find a grin on Mag's face. "The American end is sweet but my Qantas flight is full. I've booked you with United Air. I fly Fiji, Honolulu, San Francisco. You fly Auckland, Fiji. Honolulu, Los Angeles, then take a domestic flight to SFO. You leave two hours before me and I get in several hours before you."

I smile sweetly.

"And because we have reached the appropriate Hilton Hotel number of nights, for I have you booked into the Honolulu Hilton for two nights on your trip home, they offer you two more free nights. So I have booked you for those. They are not over a weekend, so DRG Melbourne will have to do without its boss for another two days."

She is such a good secretary! I wangle two more days out of Dale.

We put dog and cat, Tiffy and Piddles, into appropriate 'Animal Hiltons' and take off.

I find United Air thoroughly satisfying, on schedule everywhere; the service is good and the meals typical flight type.

Let's face it...the meals for this flight are made in Melbourne!

In SFO I pull out my city map with Mag's hotel marked, so rent my familiar coupé at the airport and drive straight to it. We have three days before catching a bus for Yosemite, so spend them with me showing her what I find familiar. She loves it, especially Lombard Street's curves and floral displays.

Yosemite National Park should be on the programme of every visitor to California. One can see the fall from so many different angles and mountain scenery is delightful. The coast road south had had a recent major landslide, so some was closed and we take the inland road. We get to the coast to overnight at Monterey and San Luis Obispo, then after lunching at The Biltmore in Santa Barbara (another worthwhile visit), drive on to spend a couple of wonderful days at Disneyland, staying in the Hyatt.

It is all wonderful stuff. Maggie flies east to take in a theatre on Broadway (she catches *Forty-second Street*), to then fly to London where she sees *Cats*).

I fly west for my few days in Hawaii, driving around Oahu again, buy a couple of sports shirts, get in some surfing at Waikiki Beach then fly to Melbourne via Fiji, New Zealand and Sydney.

~ * ~

Turtle Island #1...

Maggie and I have another memorable trip.

Wanting to be lavishly feted for seven days in the unique Turtle Island off the coast of Fiji, we pack very little. The resort is described by Britain's *Harpers and Queen* magazine as, "One of the 10 top hotels of the World"...the island used in the movie 'Blue Lagoon,' the hotel occupying its entire 500 acres with 12 separate beaches should any couple want to use one in private. Only twenty-four guests are feted by thirty-six 'front of house' staff. The Thomas Cook magazine describes it...

A refuge for reprieve from all the social pressures that besiege the rich and famous.

We are not of the 'rich and famous' category, yet once there, everybody is treated so. All are asked to be known only as a one-word name listed with photograph on a wall. Surnames and titles are taboo! It is a no dress-up holiday... guests spend their every day in bare feet for there are no floors except in every couple's *buré* (native hut). The hotel's only lounge has but three walls. It is the only common room. Even every magically prepared buffet meal of ample choices is served at a lone 26-seat table in sand under coconut trees. Every *bure's* refrigerator is daily restocked with your chosen wine, beer and spirit. The only other rule is that not a penny is allowed change hands. Everything is pre-paid when booking. If anyone feels like it, they are welcome in the kitchen to help prepare meals. In every respect it is a paradise over and over again.

Four

A multi-major event...

A major event in my several lives begins my 5th life.

My working life evolved around DRG and I accomplished the objective of successes in management. In 1982 I control a staff of 415 employees in one of Australia's largest printing-packaging industry and in that year top Australia in that branch of industry on a Return on Investment Basis. Even 'God' in Bristol telephones his congratulations.

However, events in Europe's business are far-reaching. European industries in general, including Britain, vote to establish their own Common Market at the expense of the wider world. A sensible move for them! However, most of DRG's investments are in the wider world than only Europe. In order to invest there, it decides to sell up all in the southern hemisphere.

Britain is to remain part of that organisation until retiring from it 31 January 2020.

In 1982 I hear a whisper that it had quit two operations in Tanzania, quickly followed by a small interest in New Zealand.

I phone my boss. "Is there anything afoot, Dale, that can affect my responsibilities?"

"Have you any morning appointments tomorrow?"

His office is close to my home so I get there early. His abruptness tells me it is serious. He begins by closing his own office door.

"DRG is selling up the entire southern hemisphere so it can invest in this European Common Market. You, me and the thousand Australian employees are to be paid off."

I feel stunned, yet no more than him. To save panic at the expense of our clients with whom we have contracts, until he has found a buyer, we must keep it confidential. He hires Maggie to do all his secret secretarial work.

Bloody hell! Once declared, what a shock this will be to everyone. It will turn the printing business in Australia upside down. And oh boy, the unions will come pounding on my door louder than ever.

Then I grin. *I'm to lock the door that has ever been open to all my people!*

For my company's last Saturday, however, I stage a farewell barbecue in the factory's garden for the family of every employee. There are many tears.

My eyes fill with them, too, when turning out the last light and closing the door.

~ * ~

Work goes Solo...

Expecting I should be able to obtain assignments that could keep me busy just two or three days a week, I establish my business in the industry's monthly newsletter...I advertise in eleven words...

Kev Richardson announces his advisory services in the Printing-Packaging industry.

I am immediately snapped up by previous contemporaries and long-term clients, to get handsomely paid. An Adelaide-based competitor now turns mate and despatches me to New Zealand's Auckland to find for him a small local packaging company prepared to consider a takeover. He wants to start going international. We agree on about a week, so he books me into Auckland's Sheraton Hotel. When the company I hook needs a day to consult with partners, I drive up the Tasman Sea coast sightseeing, and back by the Pacific Ocean coast. It is magnificent scenery, especially around the Bay of Plenty. A surprise is that along one coast, all the beach sand is white and on the other, black. Today I cannot recall which is which.

Rodney buys that company to start him off in New Zealand, to nail me down on a much larger exercise. He wants the 50% share of Woolworth's plastic checkout bags currently purchased from Singapore... 'Ric, please go think around your chances of winning that for me'. He explains how he has blotted his personal copy-book with the Woolworth's buyer, but has faith in me winning it for him.

"I've seen you pull so many strings in this industry. You worked wonders capturing that market around the country when it was paper, so know all the people involved. I've captured half your old Coles share now in plastic, and I now want Woolworths. Go see if you think it possible. If yes, you can have a desk in my Melbourne office teaching my sales guys in servicing it."

We agree on it taking a twelve-month trial, the Sydney Woolworth buyer my target, and he offers an attractive salary. My two days a week assignment leaves me ample free time to start work on family history study and writing my books.

"We both want to sneak back to Turtle Island," my Maggie hints.

"Yes, and this time for ten days rather than a miserable week!"

"Any chance of getting that *buré* atop the point again, do you reckon?"

"Do you recall the management byword, *'Never say 'No' to a guest request?'* Go ask them."

She laughs, "I've had whispers from your old employees that 'under cover' they call you, 'He who always delegates,' and now I'm a victim?"

"I know you can twist anyone around your little finger."

She does it.

"Yes, sir," she informs me, providing we move our date a week later."

"Okay, we go. But quit the 'sir'."

I know that she knows that in my factory even cleaners and apprentices had to call me either Kev or Ric. We were a close family!

~ * ~

Turtle Island #2...

We go again, joined by friends met on our South Seas cruise to again enjoy being spoiled in that most wonderful of holidays!

BOOK TWO

LIFE SIX

Alone Again
Feb 1989 – May 1992

Australia's Gold Coast
Greece
Turkey
Austria
Liechtenstein
Germany
Luxembourg
Belgium
France
Rome
Egypt
Thailand

Five

Dreaming when Dawn's Left Hand was in the Sky
I heard a Voice within the Tavern cry,
'Awake, my Little ones, and fill the Cup
'Before Life's Liquor in its Cup be dry.'
—*Rubáiyát of Omar Khayyam #11*

A solo sixth life…

With my two kids grown and flown, having won for Rodney Detmold his required Woolworth's business, Mags and my assets are cash in the bank each, a respectable investment share each, my beach-house in the Gold Coast's Broadbeach, our joint Melbourne home bought for cash. We can afford whatever future appeals.

However, there is a huge problem.

At 60 I want full retirement, to move away from Melbourne's cold winters on to a northern beach and to continue searching family history in English counties and Ireland.

In 1989 there is little such information in Australia for the latter, so I need be away many months of every year for some time and in each generation, each family doubles in number, not only in marriage but in the number of children each bear. And many move about their countries, so those studies can only be met overseas. My Richardson family already needs searching records in Northampton, Kent, Cornwall and Westmorland (now Cumbria)...three extreme corners of England and but one central. All will be very time consuming, enough to keep me away from home more months than at home.

And home must be at least on a beach well north of Melbourne.

Maggie's needs? Her business is based 100% in Melbourne. She doesn't swim, finds sitting on a beach's sand, 'abhorrent' and she hates the country's northern temperatures. Nor is she ready to begin spending her share of investments or leaving the friends she has made in the last twenty years. Her life demands that she remain in Melbourne.

Both are independently minded and neither wants divorce.

At this point, I begin university study in two correspondence courses.—English Literacy and Journalism.

For an entire year we talk on possibilities. If we separate, we will miss each other dreadfully. If we stay together, one must live a complete compromise to the other, losing all satisfactions in future life. For the first time since meeting, we face something on which we cannot agree.

"You have your investment at Broadbeach to move into and I don't want to have to clean this big house while still working for a living."

"It's joint ownership, Mags. We can sell it and split the spoils 50-50."

We do and are amazed at how much it brings. It happens at a high peak in a period of buying and selling and we make what both see as 'a killing.'

Both my kids are married and begun their homes out of Melbourne...Leanne faces her husband being persistently moved.

Paul and his wife build their home on Phillip Island south of Melbourne. I pay out his large mortgage and tell him...

"That's your lot, mate. My objective in life now is to spend my last dollar the day I die. You are now free to test your own life ambitions. Ask if you need help."

At least I have the knowledge that his little business is illustrating a strong future.

Maggie finds a smaller house. "It would be even better with a door between garage and kitchen for safer access at night."

I've ever been handy with tools. "I can build that for you."

Mags keeps the refrigerator/freezer, piano and what furniture she needs, and still sharing the marital bed, we move in.

After three months building the door, rearranging kitchen shelves and building storage shelves along an inner garage wall, we kiss, I jump into my car to drive the thousand kilometres 'home' to Broadbeach.

Two days later, coming on dark, I reach my Gold Coast house to find the tenant who should have moved out two days ago, still there..."I leave tomorrow," she tells me. "Do you want to sell the refrigerator?"

We settle on a figure because I need one with a bigger freezer.

"And the washing machine?"

To gain floor space I want an up-down washer and dryer so that is also a good deal.

"Pity you don't want those built-in kitchen cupboards, for I intend moving my kitchen around a bit," I tell her. She laughs and says she can move out with her purchases on the morrow. I take a motel room until my new items are installed.

In 1989 Charles Avenue Broadbeach's northern kerb has the Oasis Shopping Mall. Its southern kerb is residential and home owners anxiously await the day the Oasis needs to expand. So directly across my street I have several restaurants, the post office, three floors of shops, a huge supermarket and the city terminus of an elevated sky-train to the nation's biggest casino. I use the latter only when visitors come to stay and want to try their luck. I am anxious to write as many travel articles as possible. Studying family history doesn't pay a cent, so I want to recover some of my travelling costs as soon as possible, so life becomes a bit of each.

I work on a three-month plan to visit various European countries and Egypt. Whilst on this trip, I haven't time for Italy…I need a passport just so I can see down its west coast from the train as far as Rome, to fly from there to Cairo. I will start in Greece. The direct air route from Australia to Europe passes over it anyway. From background knowledge I know what I want to do and see there. My tongue curls at the memories of Greek food!

In March 1990 I have all passport stamps, and rather than Qantas, I'll try Singapore Air…differing airlines is gaining more travel knowledge and Singapore Air has a good reputation. It flies Brisbane-Singapore-Athens…lunch in Brisbane, breakfast in Athens.

Well so says the timetable!

It proves the most dreadful flying experience I am ever to have—58 hours from Brisbane to Athens!!!

A full jumbo flight has all passengers seated for a noon take-off, me in steerage class because I pay my own fare. At 1:30pm, I make my first note…

An hour and a half since take-off time and we are still on the tarmac.

After several promises that, "We shall soon be away," we are told it is a computer problem and we must go to Sydney where it can be "quickly fixed."

An hour later, in Sydney, no one can leave the aircraft because, "We will soon be happily away!"

Many complain having missed connections in Singapore. After having so far sat 7 hours, window passengers report a mobile staircase has moved to our first-class boarding door, and sure enough, First Class passengers leave the aircraft and fifteen minutes later, their luggage is taken to the waiting rooms.

A hostess appears through the curtain separating economy from upper classes and is besieged by several passengers."

"We have already missed our connections in Singapore!"

"And we have family waiting in Athens!"

I am annoyed yet my timetable is flexible.

Stewards replace the hostess and one raises his loud-speaker...

"We are very sorry but overnight accommodation has been booked for all economy passengers at city hotels where you will be given dinner and a four am breakfast."

Everybody is asked to take only luggage "to see you overnight."

All the rest will be secured aboard until another aircraft is available.

He has to stop, for no one can now hear him. Threats are being thrown, most women are tearful and men red-faced in fury.

I nearly am too, but in sympathy for not only those missing connections, but for those waiting for them in Singapore and Athens airports.

In days before mobile phones, nor can anyone get a message out to friends.

Unpleasant opinions continue being hurled at the helpless crew.

What a start to my three months of travel, yet I am likely the least inconvenienced.

I have but one piece of luggage so will not be leaving anything on board.

Further travel incidents worthy of mention?

Like me reaching Athens via Switzerland?

Singapore Airlines fails to get me even as far as Singapore.

The promised 4:00am breakfast at the Romada Hotel is served at 5:00am after which passengers are told to go for a walk and return at 11:00am. Sightseeing around the harbour of the city I was born in and grew up in I need like a hole in the head!

I hear a whisper that a Qantas flight due to leave has 20 spare seats to Singapore available for "those with all their luggage with them." First in, first served within the hour! Two old ladies already too late for their connection to Istanbul are anxious and I wish to help them. We share a taxi to Mascot and join the Qantas flight.

Nearing Singapore our steward informs us...the Greek airline Air Olympia has a flight due out of Singapore just two hours after our arrival. They have accommodation for the ten of you bound for Athens. You must first go to the Singapore Airlines desk and have your transfer approved."

Ah, at last some meaningful information. Why couldn't Singapore Air tell us this?

Getting to the Singapore Airlines desk, we pass the Air Olympia desk. I stop long enough to get assurance that they can fit us three once getting our tickets transferred.

"Yes, you have a half hour."

I catch up with the old girls who are at the back of some thirty noisy people battling for attention from the three Singapore Airline desk attendants.

It is a case of who has the sharpest elbows, so I leave my luggage with them.

"I will fight my way to the front. One of you try keeping behind me."

I grab their tickets and begin squeezing between those ahead of me.

There can be no gentleman approach here.

I like achieving in a challenge and urge my way to the front.

"No, "she snaps, "that flight is full."

Oh, you lying bitch!

"Just one minute ago they tell me they have seats for us."

She shakes her head. "You may each spend tonight in Singapore at your own expense, for we have already given you a free night, fly on to Athens on these tickets, at 2:00pm tomorrow. Or you can take a flight with us in two hours to the Maldives then on to Zürich where after a two hour wait, Swiss Air will take you to Athens."

She stares into my eyes. I can read... *"Yes or no and be quick about it."*

I strongly object having to pay my own costs, but this lying bitch is not going to barter. 2:00pm tomorrow? How many take-off times did this bloody airline tell us in Brisbane that we will soon take off? A lie after lie after bloody lie!

"Take it or leave it," she asks in a desperately rude voice.

Myra, the old girl behind me, nudges me in the ribs. "We have missed our connection. We will await tomorrow's flight."

The 'lying bitch' hears that and reaches for their tickets.

I'll not overspend on my budget before even starting and I'd like to see Zürich even if only from the air.

She stamps all our tickets with what I hope are appropriate stamps and wipes the sweat from her brow.

Myra and I fight our ways back to Elsie. I see that they get to the required desk of Singapore Air to attend them from here on, to then make my way to the loading queue for the Maldives alternative.

Swiss Air will be another new attraction for me.

I've a soft spot for the country that avoided World War 2 and maybe I'll get some great views flying up and down the Adriatic coast on different airlines. It can only broaden my travel experience.

As dark falls, Singapore Air flies me to the Maldives. With few passengers, I have plenty of space to make a comfortable bed and quickly fall asleep. I vaguely realise we have taken to the air again until awakened for breakfast and have glorious views as we… yes, as we fly over Greece en-route to Zürich!

One cannot help but smile.

I take lots of photos of the Adriatic sea's east coast, all delightful sights one after the other…Albania, Montenegro and Croatia.

At the Zürich check-in desk, I find that the promised two-hour wait before taking off for Athens is yet another Singapore Airline lie. It is a four-hours wait.

Have they been trained in lying?

~ * ~

Zürich…

My unexpected visit to Switzerland is brief yet in a little way, dramatic.

Four hours? It is yet some years before 9/11/2000, and visas for flying around the world are flexible. I arrive in Zürich mid-morning and with no visa for Switzerland, I ask at the arrivals counter where I show my passport and the complicated mess of my flight tickets Australia to Greece.

"With four hours to spare, any chance of me looking around Zürich?"

I show him my recently received Australian Journalist Licence...

Yes, more formal execution since retiring, but essential if I want access to strange incidents as subjects to write about.

He opens a drawer in his desk and tosses my passport into it. "If you want to just view part of Zürich, take a train into the City station then tram to Zürichsee. There you can buy food and ice-cream and just sit and watch how Swiss people enjoy themselves."

It sounds great and I enjoy, from my train and tram window seats, the European style of architecture that has always been a magnet.

At lakeside I buy lunch and thoroughly enjoy seeing folk of all ages also enjoy the wonderful sunshine by a spectacularly large lake. It all adds up so nicely, especially with trains and trams being free. Only years later did I discover they hadn't been free.

How was I to know they had machines to drop your coin in, to get your ticket?

The harbour views down the Zürich Sea are indeed worth the visit.

After my enjoyable break I have a window seat in a spotlessly clean little aircraft. I thrill on taking off into spectacular mountain ranges. The scenery leaving Zürich is sensational, stark mountains topped with snow, absolutely enchanting.

We follow the sparkling Italian coastline south until veering east over the Adriatic Sea, to then follow Greece's Pátraikós and Korinthiakós Kólpos's (beautiful waterways) to land in exciting Athens.

After Singapore Airline's rudeness, I am happy to have such an enjoyable flight. I vow that once home I will publish my experience as a travel articles for Paul. I doubt he will use it, but it will give him a giggle. In fact, once home I gave my written report to my local Thomas Cook office. They know me well, for they had helped arrange my whole three-month journey.

"As coincidence has it, Mr. Ric, our boss is here right now, making her regular visit around our several offices. I am sure this will interest her."

I am able to show her photos of my many-changed ticket.

Only after Thomas Cook copied my report in their monthly newsletter to Travel Agents all over the world, am I contacted by Singapore Airlines. They write with apologies, offering me upgrades in all future travels.

I don't reply.

~ * ~

Greece in 1990...

When Maggie and I visited Greece, we concentrated on islands. I have since read up on how Plaka retained more of old Greece than other areas, so I make that my target.

The airport hasn't improved. Greeks remain ignorant of queuing and still push and shove. Maggie's impression had been…"I don't know whether they've learned this habit from Italians, or vice-verse."

At the time it reminded me of her living in Italy for two years.

Fortunately for 21st century readers, Greece has since made itself a new and efficient airport, but its people haven't changed. Bedlam ensues and one learns how to love and hate Greece at the same time. Love its fabulous history, its pride in restoring what time has won from its past, its wonderful food, yet one wonders how they can make visitors so welcome by being so ruthless when amassed among strangers.

Or are travellers at fault? We come, realising that their habits and style of living will be different, yet too many of us lack the ability to sway with the different breeze, fail to pack that flexible attitude.

In the arrival's hall, a surprise greets me. My single piece of luggage has indeed followed me. At the baggage carousel, I see the two tell-tale bits of white cloth stapled into the look-alike black luggage.

Singapore Air has at least got this right.

I recall how Maggie and I found, at the very foot of the Acropolis, a basic little hotel. I can even recall where to catch the bus to take me there. I feel anxious too, to test the few words of Greek I've learned since then and have brought my *Berlitz for Travellers* guide, the tiny book with answers to every question in a traveller's mind as he or she arrives in a strange country. In fact, I've bought my Berliz's on this trip for Greek, German, French and Thai. If you carry it with you, you are never stuck for getting your message across to anyone in their language. You can point to it.

After changing my money, I take the aircraft bus into the city to find Greek traffic hasn't changed, only city in the world where buses take off on the change of lights with a screech of tyres (I hadn't yet seen Cairo!).

I take the Plaka bus, strap-hang alongside a couple of American backpackers booked into the Plaza Hotel. I recall it as all but next door to my Hotel Phaedra, so have them follow me.

The Phaedra does not serve meals, but I recall a dozen little restaurants scattered around it. Rooms have water that sometimes runs when wanted, even a bathtub and a phone on the wall that reaches only to the front desk. All is again scrupulously clean. From my bed I can gaze all the way to the Acropolis!

Constantin, bell-boy, manager and owner, is at the desk.

"Is there water running in the bathtub, Constantin?" I ask as he hands me the key.

"Oh, I thought I knew your face. You must have been unlucky last time."

I reckon he answers that to every such complaint.

I take the lift and after my 58 hour journey during which I had little sleep, any bed would look as inviting as the one greeting me here. I miss dinner and sleep until morning.

On Odos Kidathenona, a street with many a café, I breakfast on omelettes, bread-rolls with jam and bottomless coffee for $4. The lass asks if she may correct me on language and I assure her I will breakfast there every morning.

I change my mind about starting with several days inspecting the Plaka in detail. Since moving to Gold Coast, I find a morning swim washes away many a life's smudge. I here attempt to ask in

Greek where I take a bus to the beach. The café lass corrects my errors, then points out the required bus-stop on my map.

It is a stinking hot day and I am keen to see down the Apollo Coast. Travel in Greece is ridiculously cheap. For 80 cents, I sit by a window on the coast side, watching hundreds of fishing boats and many sportsmen out on water skis.

One of the most important things I must tell anybody visiting Greece, to save lots of trouble and even danger, is when a Greek answers, 'Yes,' the head is waved from side to side. When answering 'No,' they nod it up and down. So take care!

I leave the bus at Varkitza and walk one block to the beach. After a quick swim in what they sadly term surf, I trudge by sand further south. Despite that litter is ever present in Greece and tends to spoil the joy of the Aegean Sea's brilliance, in a pretty little cove I see how the purple of the water slowly progresses in depth as one looks out from shore. It is indeed a unique colour.

Offshore is a tiny rock island, not too far to swim but being Ozzie-bred, I've an instinctive fear of sharks and this beach has no life-guard on lookout. I realise big sharks know better than to come inside breaking waves, but then small sharks also get hungry.

I instead spend several hours enjoying sea-birds wheel and screech.

In my shoulder pouch is fruit, bread, cheese and a bottle of *Fix* (delightful Greek beer) so I lunch about 3:00pm while trudging in the heat back to the bus stop. A tout drives up in his sedan seeking passengers to share the price to each of their homes. I cannot understand such conversation made so quickly, so offer the recommended *Dhen Katalaveno*. The driver asks in English where I am from and of course, as is the case in millions of families here, he has relatives in Melbourne.

Having lived near twenty years in Melbourne, I quickly learned that when Australia opened its doors after World War 2 to homeless Europeans, Greeks flooded into Melbourne. It sits on the same parallel line south, as does Greece in the north, so quickly became the 2nd largest city of Greeks in the world. My Melbourne suburb of

Malvern is a neighbour of Prahran, in which the Australian population became outnumbered by Greeks! Walking down Commercial Rd., you hardly see a sign in English. All is in Greek.

Maybe that's why I now find it not too difficult picking up a little of their language?

The taxi driver wants to talk with me about Melbourne and insists I take the seat alongside him. Along the way, he picks up two more passengers, so in the back, three people sit on the knees of the other three. He had already been paid by our four, so only charges the newcomers. That sort of thing is not a problem in Greece. There are no laws on which to abide, so anything seems possible. I gather this is just common.

Back in Phaedra, I'm again looking forward to bed. Tomorrow I will, straight from the hotel, begin my climb to the Acropolis summit and Oh my! How does even a professional writer on tourism do as much justice as that pinnacle demands? It is perpetually being restored to as near the original temple as possible. Thirty years later I read that the building as such is completed, yet much of the etched hieroglyphics must surely take another generation. Or more.

I buy food for the morrow. I'd been on Greek ferries and the food they serve is cheap but uninspiring, and if one leaves his seat, someone claims it. I always take lunch with me and try finding a window seat on boarding. My lunch is juicy peaches and nectarines, bread, cheese and bottled water. All over the middle-east, tap water is suspect.

My plan for an early night comes dreadfully unstuck when Constantin recommends a garden restaurant just two blocks away. Greeks eat late, so short of 8:00pm they are still setting tables. Because my ferry tomorrow for the island of Paros leaves early, Constantin advises me to catch the 6:30am train from Monistiraki, some five hundred metres from the hotel, which takes me to Piræus, the Athenian portside.

So I pack ready before dinner, then make my way to the Erato, recommended by Constantin. I arrive to find many already there and spot a small empty table outdoors. My neighbours on the right are noisy Germans and, on the left, four young noisy Frenchmen.

Oh oh, flashes in my mind, *Germans and French trying to out-do each other as usual.*

It is a delightful garden…the entire overhead is wire latticework for grape vines and right above me is the arm of a massive fig tree. As I begin tucking into a delightful looking meal, a large fig falls to the cobble floor, breaking open. It also gives the young Frenchmen frights. One gets up, picks up the fig, his other hand scratching his head. He shrugs shoulders and turns to me as if seeking help.

I have enough French from both my school and Maggie days to be able to make myself understood…*"C'est un figue,"* I tell him and reach out a hand, palm up.

He puts it into my hand. I halve it with a knife, plop one in my mouth and hand him the other. He eats it and turns to his friends with *"Ah, Magnifique!"*

A waiter brings a small-headed rake and shakes down several figs, giving some to the French and German tables and some for me. It prompts the Frenchies to invite me to their table and the waiter helps me move.

Despite the vast difference in ages, it is to start a friendship to last so far into 2020.

The evening turns into one of gabbled conversation in Frenglish and Englench which soon has us toasting each other with another glass of wine. They question much about Australia and tell me they are part of a local football team, have lived in the same small village all their lives in France's Bretagne. All four work together in Nantes. None is yet married, although Christophe and his lady, who I am told is talented in English, expect their first child soon. Of the four he has the best English. Dominique (1) who enjoyed the fig has a few English words. Dominique (2) has none but is almost engaged to be married…the 'almost' explained as 'because he cannot afford the engagement ring.'

I daren't ask how he can afford a holiday in Greece.

Eighteen-year-old Pascal has no English or girlfriend, all others are nineteen.

"When loving seems looming," explains Christophe, "Pascal gets cold feet."

Each one's chances of an early marriage are toasted in turn, for they prove as partial to Greek wine as me and it seems they are anxious to best the noise of the Germans.

I have a riotous evening and when the Germans give in and depart, we toast that too.

We are, in fact, by just after midnight, the last of the scores of diners that evening.

When waiters begin setting tables for breakfast and present us with an almost unspeakable bill, we split it five ways. When both Christophe and I each throw down a respectable sort of tip, we are proffered an amicable farewell.

They are particularly happy when, on marching off, arms around the next guy's shoulders, I am able to join them word for word in singing at the tops of our voices as we ply the Plaka streets, *Les Marseillaise.*

Coincidence has our respective hotels only a block from each other and I am at least sober enough to know the way to mine. I have told them I leave on the morrow and expect to be in France in two months. They insist I visit them and both Christophe and Dominique$_1$ pen addresses and phone numbers. Fortunately, my travel has provision for change, so I accept. I am still in touch with all and on my last two visits, have been houseguest of Christophe and his lovely Edit, still unmarried for reasons I never question, but on my last visit they have both son and daughter.

~ * ~

Paros...

Come morning, with a somewhat clouded head and not even a cup of coffee, I make the metro at Monistiraki and train to Piræus and oh, what a busy port it is!

I buy my ticket at the gangplank, cheap indeed, a six-hour trip for 1,764 drachma ($14). Whilst waiting to depart, I settle in the lounge and devour several coffees.

Leaving port is a game…ferries jockey for position to beat each other into shipping lanes. If two or three have the same port as first stop, first in gets first birthing. Others must wait. It is a race all the way with whistles and hooters proclaiming victorious moves as any ferry passes another.

Greeks call them ferries, yet it defies the description as Aussies use the word. To me they are ships of 5,000 to 15,000 tonnes with several passenger decks apart from vehicle decks below and even private sleeping berths (expensive). Ferries are far from luxury, yet facilities are adequate.

I spend hours at the stern, simply gazing at the colours of such a magnificent ocean. *Aegean* blue, they call it, the most unique but majestic of blues, near purple. In the snowy white-wash behind a ship it proves to me little short of magic to behold.

Stuff sitting inside just looking out a window! Here I am enraptured!

After conversations with many a fellow traveller, we win the arrival race into Parikia, the main port on Paros in the Cyclades group of islands.

All Greek port-towns have a sameness...not a boring sameness but their beauty is infectious in one way or another. In the main, barren islands lack green-ness yet are ablaze with white walled houses bunched together with blue terra-cotta roofs all draped with bougainvillaea, hibiscus and oleander vines. Here and there a bright orange paint is used as relief. Being surrounded by the ocean's deep blues makes it all spectacular. The closer one gets to the Mediterranean's eastern shore, the blue sea really does merge to purple. All is a captive sight, indeed a massive mixed rainbow.

This ferry is to go on to Naxos and Amorgos islands, but Paros is my home for several days. I plan to then take an overnight ferry to Samos.

Spectator sport on any island in Greece is watching the turnaround of ferries. They reverse in, stern to wharf, their massive doors thump down on the dock where thousands of people wait to board. The roars of motor-car, coach and motor-bike engines burst into impatient life on departure, becoming deafening. Passengers wheeling pushbikes and wheelchairs begin to disgorge. Despite every attempt is made to deter people from boarding whilst the ship vomits up its entrails, there is a melee of push and shove, those departing the island anxious to claim choice or vantage points as are those arriving to be first into buses or tourist offices to claim a bed in the most desirable hotel.

Traffic, both motorised and afoot, becomes instant mayhem.

Greece is one of those countries where it seems mandatory for drivers to lean on the horn as conscientiously as on the accelerator. Traffic policemen blow whistles non-stop yet seem to have little effect on traffic attaining goals on streets built for plodding donkey carts and wheel-barrows. Goals are any small space, and swirling dust mingles with exhaust fumes to near suffocate all. Here and there are screams either of pedestrians knocked down in the crush and trampled on by those behind, or of children in the stampede, separated from parents.

All so entertaining!

I travel light, ever only one bag, one star up from a backpack, sufficient that I can either pull it along like a dog on a leash, for it now has light wheels on rugged streets, or toss it over my shoulder as a backpack. Or in an instance like this, wield it in protection.

Having battled my way to the tourist office, I am told there isn't a bed to be had in all Parikia. In the oppressive heat, and bemoaning the fact I drank so much with such convivial Frenchmen last night, I wander the town door-knocking, to maybe chance on a small hotel or pension or private house with a spare bed. After two hours...hot, tired and bedraggled, by which time all the buses, people hanging out of doorways and even windows, have departed to hotels and camping grounds, there are fewer about. The cars and motor-bikes streaming off the first ferry have in the main, also departed.

The next ferry is reversing in, so the melee will repeat.

Accepting that I must sleep on the beach under the stars and risk being robbed, I notice across the square, a panel-van with 'Apollo

Hotel' emblazoned on its side, pull up. In stumbling Greek, I ask the driver would his hotel have a room and he asks in turn, thankfully in English, if I am English.

"No, I am Australian. All I…"

"Australia? I have a brother in Melbourne!"

"In Prahran?"

"Yes. The hotel has no spare room but my mother will kill me if I turn away an Aussie from Melbourne. You can have a bed in our house."

"Where is that?"

"Right on the beach just down the road where you see that flag flying."

"How much?"

"11,000 drachma."

I don't mind making him see I have no intention of being made a fool of.

"Five thousand," and I pull out my wallet.

"Six."

"Okay."

"And you must pay in advance. How many nights?"

From seeing how many people Paros must have ashore, most of which seem tourists, is not what I seek. If I am to report, I must see quiet sides of the island. It cannot all be like this. I'll give it two or three nights, have a good look around here tomorrow, then go see other parts.

"Three."

He looks disappointed, but that's in my favour. Maybe his mother will be more helpful…if she speaks English.

When I meet her, she hasn't a word!

His name is Dimitro. He drives me down what would have been a fifteen-minute walk to a modern house. He leads me into a pleasant room, tells me it is his room and he will sleep elsewhere. He takes a few clothes from his sad looking wardrobe and shows me hooks on the wall I can use.

His sister arrives from high-school and I simply cannot understand the name he tells me, just too long and too quickly. They chat in Greek for a moment then, still at work, he drives off. The lass has reasonable English and shows me the bathroom, gives me a fresh bath towel, coffee, then leads me to a modern sitting room where we sit and talk.

"Can I swim at the beach just here?"

"I learn the English in school," she whispers, "and yes, neighbours swim here."

"When finished school, will you work with tourists?"

"I hope so. Do you have holiday?"

"No. I write about travel for airline magazines."

"You write nice things for Greece?"

"I will be happy to say I like Greece."

We talk for a time and she hands me a towel for the beach and a key. "Do not take valuables to the beach. Your room has a lock and only family has keys."

As I unpack, I check my ferry timetable and yes, three days from now is an overnight ferry to Samos. I choose it because it is a green island, one of the few in all the country.

Paying so much for rent here puts me behind in my budget, so I must somehow catch up before leaving. When travelling, budgeting should not be treated flippantly.

At 6:00pm, people are still spread out on the sand, disported in all possible postures, or playing ball games, or drinking Fix or Metaxea. A hundred or more are in what they call surf. I frolic for a time, then sit on the beach watching others.

On all Greek islands, it seems there is the 'old town,' a part remaining as the original BT (Before Tourism). Today's visitors love seeing it, yet still want modern hotel comfort that is available in only modern areas. I love comforts, yet I also want to see how the people live in an area they can afford. I need a bit of both. The best of restaurants are lodged in the upper class area, yet small ones dot both. That is how I've so far found Greece. Sometimes one chances on a cheaper one with excellent food.

A regular island sight I love is watching a mother or housemaid on her knees on the cobblestones in front of the house, scrubbing clean the cobbles from the shit of the postman's or milkman's donkey. It is common everywhere.

Tonight, in a taverna by the beach, I eat a simple tzaziki and *koriahteeki salada* with a glass of house-wine...an ample meal, but after my repast with the Frenchies last night, sensible. As I eat I watch moonlight twinkling on the ocean, plotting my programme for the next few weeks. So far, Paros is a disappointment, yet today's experience could be just catching it at a seasonal peak. I should not even consider it for yet a few more days.

This taverna however, scores highly...a little village to remember, on a quiet beach, bazoukis playing, chatting women watching their men dance together.

Tomorrow I will quit the daily noise here to go see the other side of Paros. On Dimitro's wall is the island map and I see a free beach within walking distance of Naoussa town.

There I can be hopefully away from the hordes of tourists... hopefully with people who share the natural side of life.

Tomorrow, laden with drinking water and fruit, I strap-hang in the bus all the way. Naoussa is a modern town, no ancient Greece about it, yet across the magnificent bay at Monastiri is an ancient monastery well worth a look. Beyond it is the free beach I seek.

The monastery is certainly interesting and the free beach is well sign-posted.

As I find a shaded spot, I see some fifty or more of all ages, drink up this solitude.

Once in the water, one gets to speak with others and I greet a German, his wife and teenage daughter. They invite me to come sit with them under their beach umbrella. Close by is a French family with a toddling babe and an Austrian couple who drove here, towing their speedboat all the way, from the Bodensee (Lake Constance) in Switzerland. All are seeking refuge from the hordes, and envy my olive skin. Even under a scorching sun however, so long as I don't overdo it, it doesn't blister. Others have to be more careful.

I have a most enjoyable quiet and lazy day. What it teaches me is that this part of Paros lives without the daily rush that so saddened me yesterday.

For a peaceful holiday, it lacks only fresh water.

On the way home to Parikia, I gain the last empty bus seat alongside an old woman nursing a restless chook. I eat in the part of the old town that has a few eateries at a local price rather than tourist, one learns about these things so long as you take the risk now and again. Where locals eat is usually a good choice.

My cheap day out has brought me closer to budget and I spend the next with camera in the old part of town. In it I find The Albatross, a worthy restaurant under canvas with delightful breezes rustling their ways between tables. I return to it for a wonderful dinner, especially the *baklava* dessert. I have them give me their personal recipe and still use it.

Last day on Paros I spend wandering the old town with the French couple of my 'free beach' day to find an area currently filled with old homes. Alternate houses have walls bedecked in flowering magnolia or bougainvillea and all over freshly white painted walls form a spectacular sight. Gardens here are well tended. I have a satisfying day and again eat at The Albatross.

On my last day, I rest feet in sand and lunch on fruit. There is considerable amusement watching two ferries jockey for position. Neither is mine, so I've plenty of time to chat with others, two young German brothers to have but two days in Samos from where they head home to Bavaria's Kempton. Penny is English, travelling with Peter, a Brisbaner studying in London to be a solicitor. Brian of Toronto is a taller streak than me and is also travelling alone. Nouella and Neville, a middle-aged couple from Australia's Gold Coast hinterland, are backpacking the islands 'on a sixpence.'

Having enjoyed such convivial conversation, we decide to stick together once aboard. Being near the front of our queue, the wait proves its worth and we hurry to the upper deck because inside many ferries, there is no air-conditioning.

It proves a funny night. We spread our benches fanwise so heads are close for easy conversation as we stretch out, grabbing patches of sleep so the night passes quickly, and we can talk together quietly. As morning dawns, we dock at Ikaria and are joined by yet another Aussie, Bernadette Jansen from Melbourne's St.Kilda, who prefers to be addressed as Bern. She is on her way to Turkey. She writes poetry and is en route to read her work in Zürick, then Paris, enjoying this travel on her way. She left Turkey but two days earlier to work her way through Greece but 'finds it too expensive,' so is returning. Nouella and Neville, Penny and Peter are also bound for Turkey.

"Why not come with us?" they ask of the German lads, Brian and me.

The Germans fly home tomorrow. The Canadian jumps at joining those for Turkey. I had given no thought to Turkey and remain keen to see more of Greece.

One island isn't enough to give me an honest impression for writing articles. Also, I particularly want to look around this Samos 'green island.'

After breakfast we lose the race into Samos and must wait aboard several hours. Those for Turkey must wait until mid-afternoon in any case. I set about finding myself a bed for a few nights, so we all share names and addresses.

Tossing my bag over my shoulder, I make for the tourist office.

"There is no bed to be had in Samos. The few left was taken by those of the early ferry. Other backpackers are on the streets looking for what we call B&B."

Pity I did not make prior bookings but now pay the penalty.

I find that all offices close midday to 3:00pm so I cannot leave my bag. I must lug it. I search for a *Enoikiazontae Domahdia* (*Room to Let*) but in street after street, I fail. I call into a small hotel in the hope some guest might be leaving today...No luck.

When I get footsore and my pack seems heavier by the minute, I return to the wharf.

Outside a bar drinking beer are my fellow travellers and I receive a hearty welcome.

"Do I need a visa for Turkey on my Ozzie passport, Bern?"

She assures me I do not, so I depart Greece. I shall bus down Turkey's coast then take a ferry to Rhodos and work north to see my Dodecanese Islands.

Six

Kussadassi, Turkey

After the size of Greek ferries, we have quite a tiny one for fifty people, several motor-bikes and lots of traveller luggage. There is no downstairs and its small glassed in lounge quickly fills. For those who sit adeck, there is no protection. It's a one-hour trip.

It doesn't rain, but with a rough sea and the journey at full speed, we end up drenched from wind having blown the bow-wash into our faces.

Entering the harbour we pass under the lee of the ruins of an ancient fort, to soon make landfall at the customs house. They do not change Greek drachma.

"Oh, the bloody hate between these two countries has been on for centuries," Neville tells us. "Every new generation finds a further difficulty between the Greek version of Christianity and Turkey's Muslims. Both have experienced more war with each other since Christendom was founded, than peace."

"Don't change more than money you need," Bern warns us. "If you go back to Greece, it will not accept Turkish currency."

I travel with only $200 cheques so I've no option but to change that much. It brings more than a half million lirasi, handed to me by the armful. It will not fit in my wallet and I doubt I've enough pockets. I manage, but look a lot fatter.

I swoop out to where the others wait...

"I've suddenly become a millionaire," and am answered with giggles.

At least I won't want for anything here. But will I be able to exchange lirasi when arriving in Vienna? Germany? France, Italy, Egypt? Thailand? Australia?

With no alcohol available, we drink apple-tea, which I find delightful.

"I'm one for saving dollars," Bern says to me, not endeavouring to hide what she has to say from others... "but next week I have to face much more expensive countries for more than a month. I need to squeeze every penny before taking the train to Zürich. I left a perfectly comfortable guest house just up the hill from here the other day. Rent for a couple is half the price each. If we become a couple with twin beds, Ric, can you keep your hands to yourself?"

It brings a load of giggles and I give her top marks for guts and common sense. And trust.

Having experienced occasions of living on a shoestring, I have learned what it can be like, but that was when a kid after my father died. But one doesn't forget hardships.

I promise to avoid nature and achieve applause from all. So we tote our bags up the steep cobbled hill to The Golden Pheasant, where they treat her like a lost daughter.

I bet they wonder how she got a partner so quickly, yet now wants twin beds???

We let them stew. But yes, everything is neat and clean and with shower and toilet.

At 40,000 *lirasi* a night ($20), breakfast is not included, but Bern knows a nearby café that serves adequate breakfasts.

Whilst Greece and Turkey might not get on well together, it seems they share the same plumber, for there is very little water for showering. So far, that is the only disappointment but nothing serious.

Another good fortune is that we are within a five-minute walk to a bazaar, a shopper's paradise.

"In the middle-east," we learn from more experienced tourists, "never pay more than half what they asked and then, if you turn to leave, the price is dropped further."

I find soft leather clothing is particularly cheap. Bartering hard, I indulge and come away extremely pleased.

For dinner, our contingent meets as arranged and with everyone in a camaraderie mood it becomes a hilarious, delightful dinner. For tomorrow, Bern recommends Deni's Restaurant, where I devour one of the most enjoyable dinners anywhere. My share is 18,800 lirasi, ($9.40) including wine.

In Muslim Turkey, few restaurants serve wine, and pitiful wines at that. When parting, it is unanimously agreed that the quality of service for tourists is poor, that Turks are still learning what Christian travellers seek.

But the cheap price of everything and quality of food are huge attractions.

On our next full day, we all go see the city's major attraction, the Ephessi ruins, an awesome 3rd century city! Crowded buses bring tourists galore. When we arrive, there is a queue that fortunately moves quickly and inside the walls there is ample space for comfortable viewing. It is indeed wonderful and I am so glad I came to Turkey. Even the sparsest of Ephessi ruins have been retained, yet some likely had help to remain in much their original condition are the library and museum...wonderful to admire, startlingly 'real.'

A further startling exhibit is to sit high in the bleachers of the amphitheatre, looking down at the stage where thespians performed seventeen centuries ago. Some twenty levels up from the stage, we sit on the very stones on which ancient audiences sat.

What an honour!

Some tourist scholars are right now playing parts, sprouting in some unintelligible language and the acoustics are amazingly clear. A few of us go down and await turns for short performances in such a theatre of nature. Bern delivers some of her poetry, Peter quotes from *Merchant of Venice* and I reel off my favourite 'when young' stanza....

Myself when young did eagerly frequent
Doctor and Saint, and heard great Argument
About it and about: but evermore
Came out by the same Door as in I went
—*Rubáiyát of Omar Khayyám #XXVII*

Other tourists indicate rapture as much as ours, applauding enthusiastically.

I am engrossed in the cleaning women. In scorching heat, all are nevertheless dressed Muslim style head to toe, faces masked in *ashmaks*...dozens of them with short-handled brushes, bend with hand-brooms sweeping the score of terraces. They swish dust and litter down to the next level then move down one, to do it all again. Tomorrow they will start at the top again.

For lunch we queue to buy the biggest peaches ever seen.

While devouring one, Bern takes time out to tell all that "Ric snores."

More laughs of course!

All of Ephessi is adventure. We hook onto the tail of an English-speaking guide and learn about the surviving buildings and, for 500 lirasi (25 cents), a guide shows us a rock spring which he claims has never in all these centuries, been dry. We drink some and it is clear, sweet, cold and refreshing.

The weather is so hot I, who cannot abide hats, buy a handmade straw one for 50cents.

If touring in Turkey, I recommend that before leaving home, practise long on using the public toilets throughout the middle-east.

Draw a 20cm chalk ring on your bathroom floor, stand over it and shit in it! You need to practise quite a lot!

Ephessi's toilets are free but if you need to clean up after yourself, you must pay a woman at the entrance 10c for five pieces of toilet paper. Remember this before entering!

Next day, Peter and I decide to ease the exertions of our holiday by chancing the celebrated *hammam*...the Turkish Bath.

At least it is given by a man, not as I later in life discover in Paraguay, by a mountainous woman!

The *hammam* is indeed an experience, almost sadistic the way the beefy masseur 'attacks' you. We emerge still shaking from fear, wondering what contortion he will put us through next, yet our bodies are thoroughly refreshed.

Come dinner, the seven decide to save costs. We buy bazaar fruits, bread, pickles, a couple of tomatoes each and a bottle of wine each. We bring along bed-sheets, bathroom towels, etcetera that we can spread on sand at the harbour beach for an al-fresco meal.

The sun is setting, the time of day locals come out to perambulate...entire families. It is their time to be together before eating or before any of the family goes out to whatever evening pastime. We draw quite some attention.

Have they never seen anyone bring a meal to a beach?

We are soon joined by those with a mouthorgan, fiddle, zither or any sort of instrument...our seven quickly becomes a dozen. We eat our hearty meals to happy music with several score of onlookers not only watching but singing to the music. It is a most enjoyable evening.

Tourists in your fancy and expensive holiday hotels around the world, we reckon, go eat your bloody hearts out...we are having real fun for a few cents!

To picnic on a beach, we feel as we retire, might well have sparked a new tradition for Turks in Kussadasi.

Tomorrow reduces our seven to two. During the day, all but Bern depart to bookings elsewhere. She and I spend it lolling about reading, then wander down to the beach for a swim, and in a café drink Turkish coffee. We find it exciting, simply watching the passing parade and generally having a lazy, lost day.

Together we go to our respective Turkish Baths for *hammams*, me 'shouting' her for being such a great travelling partner, and I see her off to Greece on its European border, for her train west. I then spend a quiet, early night alone.

At the bus depot on my way to Marmaris on the south coast, a strange thing ensues.

I ask..."A single to Marmaris please."

"When you go?"

"Now."

He stabs a whistle in his mouth to blow a shrill blast that nearly bursts my eardrums. Outside, a bus already in transit, jerks to a dusty halt.

"You run quick," says the ticket officer pushing a ticket into my hand.

I hurl my bag over a shoulder and run.

I haven't paid, I think as I go. *Surely then, I must be able to pay once aboard.*

Sure enough and lucky enough, I have a spare window seat. The bus door closes and we move off and I pay a conductor 20,000 lirasi ($10) for my 4-1/2 hour bus journey.

Turkey is a cheap country, all right, and with great food but little wine. For much of my trip the country is indeed barren and dry, just like Australia's deserts...red dust and shale and one seldom sights good soil. I find it strange getting frequent glimpses of Aussie eucalypt trees, the only tree to survive such a sun-baking heat.

I find Turkish buses far from the comfort of those at home. No road I experience is worthy of the name 'highway,' for it is narrow, winding, bumpy and dusty. Aboard, free iced water is available and commercial soft-drinks are for sale. The countryside people seem poorly clad and the one train I see, for Turkey has few, illustrates what the guide books advise...*Turkish trains should be avoided!*

Ah, maybe that is why Bern was keen to take a Greek train west?

Coming into Marmaris, we descend from the heights and are treated to spectacular scenery, a magnificent southern coastline.

~ * ~

Marmaris, Turkey...

As we enter the sleepy and pretty little tourist town, I am unaware how dramatic a time I am to have leaving here; one to ever remember....No, please read 'suffer.'

We arrive just on mid-day and booking touts wait in droves, clipboards in one hand, their other snatching at our luggage. He holds on to it while pushing his clipboard with photographs of a flower-fronted house under your nose. In excellent English he tells me it is clean, nice and only 20,000 lirasi ($10) per night, just two streets from the ocean front.

There is nothing lost by seeing it, I guess. I am totally ignorant of life in Turkey so it could be interesting.

I accept and he carries my bag. He has a little but ancient Ford Prefect and my mind quickly tosses over the possibility of being snatched somewhere to be robbed.

But no, there are simply too many of his kind here to meet my bus.

It is a short drive and the little house is indeed swathed in gardens with colourful flowers. The family...grandma, mummy, daughter and three toddlers with thumbs in mouths and questioning eyes, lead me down the hall. The door is swung open with almost a '*Voila*, here it is' type of flourish and all stand back, bidding me enter.

Oh my! The room is hardly big enough for such a crowd, yet sparklingly clean but a-clutter with plastic flowers (my pet hate), several vases of them. Gaudy plastic picture frames dot the wall with film-star photos snipped from magazine covers. Lace doilies cover the dresser, curtains are ruche and the carpet is pink.

It is not for me.

Yet I'd be foolish to refuse it until sure I have another. I accept the smiles and bows that are on the increase, and the key is prettily strung with freshly ironed pink ribbon.

Having used the bathroom after the long coach trip, as prettily decorated as my bedroom except with twice as many plastic flowers *(as if they are going to expel bad odours)*, I walk into town to try the small hotels along the front.

For $12.50 there is a tiny room three floors up a narrow staircase, basic in the extreme (not one plastic flower) yet with a 'bathroom' down the hall. Paying in advance, I take it.

'Bathroom'? I measure the walls with my hand...exactly a square metre! When sitting on the toilet, my knees are under the wash-basin and above my head is the shower!

Thank God that back in my room I have my battery shaver and mirror.

The hotel's advantage is that it is right on a beach driveway. A skinny beach of sand means I close my door and am in the water in but a couple of strides.

I walk back 'home' to my 'flower room' to pick up my bag. As I return to the kitchen, their smiles fade. I shrug, explain that I am leaving, realising that none understands a word. The smiles return however, for when handing them back the key, I have a 20,000 lirasi ($10) note folded into the pink ribbon loop.

I quickly learn that in Turkey between 2:00pm and 5:00pm. no one shops or uses banks or business houses. All close. But then, shops and bazaars are open until midnight. At 2 o'clock, locals disappear from streets and one can fire the proverbial gun, hitting no one except tourists. So shop morning or night and save afternoons for sightseeing. Even taxis and all motor traffic seem thin. The afternoon heat, though, is oppressive.

Consequently, cafes are popular on afternoons. Ceiling fans move the hot air about, and outdoors rafters are hung with grapevines and clematis. From the towers of distant mosques one hears people being called to prayer.

I have late lunch, grilled chicken with salad, a beer and Turkish coffee for $4.75. I am back to budget and can quit my cheap digs on the morrow to find a decent hotel for my last couple of nights.

The Bamboo Café I'd found serves adequate meals, so having added Turkey to my budget, I've learned a lot more with it costing within my budget.

It is a delightful harbour, incredibly large. The far shore is almost the horizon and the harbour heads are out of sight. On my third day, I take a harbour tour. It skirts the western shore and drops us off on a glorious little beach for a quick swim. An excellent idea comes to mind as we approach the home beach...it will only be a matter of days before I make for Europe where I will not need so much summer clothing, swimming gear, beach towel etc. From here where prices of everything are so cheap, I shall despatch home by postal mail by sea, all the gear and the souvenirs I have purchased. I do not care how long it takes...*(it takes four months)*.

Being a decent hotel, it provides me wrapping paper, and I pack it up ready for mailing. Tomorrow I am early on the beach, have my swim, then, happy that I won't have to tote it all over Europe, post my large parcel. For a time I sit outside the café with an apple tea. I say 'happy' because I have a front seat to an outrageous occurrence. The entire square is decorated with colourful dangling canopies. With siren blaring, a fire-brigade with long ladders atop bursts from a street into the square. Decorations are so dense and so low that by the time the engine has reached the square centre, its path is blocked from above...it is dragging all the decorations behind it. It can neither enter any of the streets leading from the square, nor reverse.

Every policeman arriving seems to have a different suggestion of how to quit the obstruction, so the fire engine continues with its siren despite everything and everyone is already alerted. Traffic is as stranded as the fire-brigade, none can move in any direction. I record the distressing picture on my Philips and camera and but hope other fire engines are using different approaches.

After a quick dinner with a middle-aged English couple that joins me because the square is so packed, we are almost squeezed together. Struggling through the square best I can, for decorating rubbish is everywhere, I have an early night. I want to rise early to get a seat on a ferry to Rhodos. Little do I know how unlucky I am in choosing tomorrow.

At dawn on 2 August 1990, Iraq bursts through its border with Kuwait, bombing from the air and firing from tanks, followed by a mechanised army of a half million, guns blazing at all personnel in sight.

On the dot, Turkey closes all borders. Not a soul can move in or out until individually vetted. Oh, what a day to remember...It seems to me and those around me, only children are exempt. Everyone must deliver his or her passport on demand or be simply clubbed, handcuffed and dragged off by the thousands of police arriving from everywhere. Wartime law is enacted against every adult soul, particularly foreign.

As the sun begins blazing, more people faint. Children scream either that their parents have been taken away or they had simply been separated into the melee, to be lost. No help is given the aged, pregnant women, children, anyone needing a toilet, in fact anyone without their own drinking water (e.g.: thousands!).

Even I am near to swooning in the glaring sun as it heats more with every hour. No food is available and no shade. Few, even if trying to aid family or disabled, can move far from where we are packed. An aged woman in a wheelchair becomes a victim over a sunshade someone has given her.

Just after 4.00pm, we (me and those around me who have somehow become a large family) notice names being called. Passports are being handed out...'handed out' means handled by a score of people passing them back over their shoulders to the mob, not even seeing who is claiming it. Many languages are involved as a thousand or more shout their names. As it darkens, no effort is made to change the 'system.' It is frightening.

My passport arrives safely for I can shout loudly and am allowed to board the ferry for Rhodos which will leave 'within an hour or two.' I learn only when boarding that I must surrender my passport again.

At least being boarded gives me hope of getting out of the melee.
No passenger is allowed in the glassed-in lounge. It is where

Turk personnel study each and every passport. Only when the ferry pulls out from the wharf and begins its journey of only fifty kilometres to Greece, but obviously not being in any hurry, do a few of the interviewing men begin walking around calling out names from the handful of passports they carry, and carefully ensures the face of he or she who claim ownership.

All of us watch carefully, of course, wondering about our immediate futures. However, when a passenger has claimed their passport, they are taken indoors and the male, if it be family, is sat at a desk opposite an interviewer. He and they, if passed, are moved to another guarded part of the lounge. I see no one yet handcuffed, rather than just moved to the scores already waiting.

My turn arrives an hour after having anchored outside the massive 'welcoming arch' into Rhodos *(to use their spelling)*. Fortunately, the ocean is calm for there are still many to be interviewed. I am lucky enough to be able to show my fellow, about my age, my journalist wallet. It seems to satisfy him about all the visas for entry during the next two months.

"Why is your visit to Turkey only been an afterthought? It is so recent."

I explain about failing to find accommodation in Samos, so decide to try a little bit of Turkey and return to Greece from Marmaris. The little smile he gives me is one of the most relieving incidents of my life.

"We find Australians are in the main, honest people."

He picks up a rubber stamp and gives me my clearance from Turkey.

It's quite dark and I am very hungry. I wonder how long I have to wait before being let ashore.

~ * ~

Rhodos, Greece...

Almost a new me is delivered through the Rhodesian arch by a motor-boat along with a German family of five, an old Maltese man in a wheelchair, a Swiss couple and an American movie director 'trying to work on a fuckin' film.'

I am in for quite a shock, for homework I didn't do. Not having intended visiting Turkey made me aware that Rhodos does not have a Greek background, but Islamic Ottoman. Turkish lifestyle still overshadows this Greek island.

Consequently, Mandraki has two faces, the 'old town,' surrounded by its mediaeval walls enclosing yesterday's Turkish life, whilst the 'new' spread outside the city walls reflects a modern way of Greek life.

At the tourist office I am severely limited as to what is available. I am directed to Hotel Afrika and for 5,000 drachma ($40), whereas in Paros I'd paid 10,000 drachma for a small room without facilities, I here have a large room with a private balcony over-looking the ocean, with telephone and private bathroom. And the plumbing works!

Rather than go on to Crete, and being so tired after the day's dreadful hours in such exhausting heat, I decide to rest here a few days and reconsider touring several small islands with one-night stands. Rather than exhausting myself, I need to be sensible.

No sooner have I begun thinking of a pleasant, quiet dinner, the wind comes up, doors slamming throughout the building. The wind-storm develops into hurricane proportions and over on the beach people scatter and tents and umbrellas go hurtling into the distance. Of a sudden, the previous invitingly calm ocean whips into a cauldron, small boats tossing about such that there must be panic aboard. One yacht loses both sails, shredded to ribbons in an instant.

Minutes later, the calm returns as quickly as it had attacked.

The force of this wind for only a few minutes on the beach area is exactly what I experienced in Holland's Scheveningen. Am I going to experience yet more such strong sudden windstorms before reaching home?

Come 7:00pm, along with many other obviously hesitant people, I take to the streets. Seeking history, I make for the old town, finding quite a mob doing the same. Finding restaurants are still preparing for dinner, and passing the Berlin Bar, I decide on having a Fix. I quickly find myself chatting with people from Germany, Switzerland,

England, Finland, Sweden and of course, America and Australia. It is quite late when many decide to eat, so all together we retire to a restaurant and enjoy wonderful food yet with mediocre wine. Some even then retire to another bar. My watch says 2:48am.

Late next morning, in the town food market I buy fruit for my room and drinking water for my satchel, a serve of *moussaka* to eat cold with bread, cheese and a bottle of *Demestica* (Greek wine).

After last night's expense, I would eat dinner in my room.

Having deposited my purchases, and after a swim, I sit on the beach, reading, then walk through parks, around the casino, spotting and noting major hotels, then climbing down a cliff to a beach on a far point for another swim. I return to near 'home' and sit with a Café Frappa before retiring for my 'in' dinner and early night.

Rising next morning I find under the door a surprise notice asking me to vacate my room by 10:00am. The desk clerk is most obliging, checking the register, for I tell her I have booked for yet another two days. I cannot read the register she shows me, which seems a mess of erasures and scribbles. She insists today is the day against my name and that the room is already relet. Whilst I wait for her to find me a similar room at the same price at another hotel, a busload of Finns arrives and in conversation with one she says they have just flown in and must wait for rooms being serviced. I wonder if my being ejected may be a deliberate 'mistake,' for there are two beds in my room. However, I am booked into Hotel Astoria. They drive me with luggage to what I find satisfactory.

Armed with camera, I again walk to the 'old town,' now not so far.

Rhodes (as we spell it) has a long history. Founded four centuries before Christ, it was the major commercial centre of the Aegean district. The apostle Paul brought Christ's teaching in 43AD and in 395AD it became part of Byzantium. In 1306 it provided refuge for the Knights of St. John in religious wars with the Saracens, to hold it two hundred years before being vanquished by Ottoman Turks. Taken by Italy in 1912, all Dodecanese Islands are ceded to Greece in 1948 as compensation for World War 2.

The historic Mosque of Suleiman and the Palace of the Castellan built in the 16th century dominate Hippokratous Square from which cobbled streets spread like spokes of a wheel into the rest of the old town. I find it tremendously exciting walking streets that people over so many centuries trod, to lean on walls they leant on, and to sit in a café on squares where women drew water from the communal well, toting ewers of it on their heads along lanes I've walked. I note that for tomorrow, the Turkish Bath is also just off the square.

Falke (Falcon) Tours provide an excellent full day tour down the east coast. In the quaint Koskinou village are picturesque pebble courtyards set in Rhodian style. At Faliraki is a beautiful white sand beach, uncommon in Greece, with a huge crowd. It also has a 'free' area for nudists. Pick of the tourist sites on that coast is Lindos, another picturesque village nestled at the foot of an ancient Acropolis, converted by the Knights into a fortress...intriguing to visit. Time is available to climb to it, so with several others I hire a donkey for the steep ascent. Once atop, the complex has a number of ancient buildings. Up a further unique ancient stairway is the Propylaea (5th century BC) sanctuary of the goddess Athena and close by, to further boggle the mind, hovering on a cliff edge is a temple dedicated to her, built in the 4th century of 'our' time.

Today's Greece is certainly a land of legend.

On the way home I pick up a new novel, food to go and wine to take with me on the ferry to Athens tomorrow, purchasing my ticket at an agency...3,865 drachma ($30.90) for the 20-hour journey.

As daylight wanes, I shower and shave and head for my *Hammam*. Only once my body is steamed to exhaustion I am thumped unmercifully, twisted in unkind contortions, pummelled and beaten until again exhausted, then tumbled into the showers before being wrapped in towels to be left in peace until returned to normal. It makes one quickly feel so relaxed that I fall asleep. An hour later I am woken.

It is already getting dark, so I am off to the old town yet again (Oh my word, it is so inviting!). I sit over a Fix on the big square watching chairs and tables being set up on the cobble street, wondering which one is going to be mine for dinner where I am to be joined by several of today's fellow passengers. Flowers and lit candles are set up on each chequered cloth and waiters busy themselves setting up trestles for *morgasbord* fare. After my *tzaziki* I will eat *a-la-carte*, for when reading the menu, *kohkoras meh krassi* (chicken braised in wine) catches my eye. I choose it served with okra and zucchini. Few Greek wines are really to my taste, yet a dry *Hymetos* is palatable, so I have that, followed by a small platter of cheeses with Greek coffee, which is always excellent.

Some see out the evening with an hour at Valentino's bar run by an English expat. It is a great fun-crowd, but then it is back to a welcoming bed.

Up early and having paid up my hotel, it is a snack breakfast in the marketplace.

By 10:00am it is a case of borrowing from Greek culture. I elbow my way aboard a long-distance ferry, keen on finding a window seat on its port side...port because we travel the long way to Athens, north up the Dodecanese Islands each of which has its harbour on its eastern shore, facing Turkey. Remember, all these islands had mostly been Turkish until 1947, and this ferry calls into most on its way to Athens.

I want photographs yet daren't leave my seat. Beds aboard Greek ferries are expensive. Certainly, few Greeks can afford the private room and they are the majority of passengers. It would be cheaper to fly, but there are no air services to such small islands. If I've a window seat, I have something to lean against and for photographing but it means during twenty hours I must want to visit the toilet and disturb everyone between me and the aisle. If I can be lucky enough to gain a back-row seat of a block, I can climb over the back of my seat.

So yes, I am desperate to be one of the first on any deck. I just hope there are not too many old ladies ahead of me.

To sum up, all I can write about the Dodecanese islands is, that of a hundred and fifty with names, only twenty-six are inhabited. They have limited soil and limited rainfall. Surely that makes growing food difficult. How people live simply cannot be assessed from the ferry.

Most of the shoreline is either rocky cliff or small sandy beaches, the latter visible from the eastern ocean is either resort hotels operating or being built, hiding whatever is behind them. I find it disturbing that absolutely every hotel has its beach-borders with neighbours barbed-wire fenced! So there is local friction!

Let's face it, mixing Turks and Greeks calling the same islands 'home,' cannot remain peaceful.

There is considerable wondering by the passengers I can talk with, what any of the islands can have to offer tourists but the remnants of historical buildings. With no trees, can there be birds? With little soil and little water, can there be edible animals? Can the only natural food be fish? Living there must heavily depend on importing from other islands...none of which are like the Greek islands I visited years ago, promise of an enjoyable revisit. But again, this history has been more Arabic than Greek.

As it turns out, my window seat is not boxed. If one has luggage enough to stack clothing on it, making it obvious it belongs to someone temporarily absent, one can move about for short periods. It is essential, however, to befriend as many neighbours as possible, that if any one of you must leave your seat for not too long, they will help protect it for you.

We make many stops, but on every occasion, more passengers arrive than depart.

Sleeping is a shambles. There is undoubtedly not enough clear floor-space for all passengers to stretch out either inside or on open decks. It is sad to report that particularly Greeks, by far in the majority, expect right of seats before tourists. Some tourists acknowledge their right, but many do not. Nasty words are exchanged in my hearing.

Sad but true, especially when recalling memories of the fun overnight I had ferrying from Paros to Samos. On this occasion, though, as the sun rises, tempers ease and I am careful to wait near last before departing and taking train and bus back to the Phaedra and Constantin. Dare I hope he again comes up with a lucky last room?

~ * ~
Athens again...

"Ah, welcome back, Mr. Ric. You are lucky, I have one room left, not a single but a double room, so must ask just a fraction more."

"Thank you, Constantin. I am happy to see the Phaedra so sought after."

I pay 4,000 drachma ($32).

It is a Tuesday morning and I'd had little sleep on the ferry, yet from the bright side, had many conversations with sleepless neighbours. My foresight dinner indeed helped stem the dysentery I'd developed over the previous few days. If you plot long journeys, here's a worthy tip...your last meal before departing should be one of bread and cheese. If not flying but by boat or train, take with you as well, fruit and wine or water...maybe the exception is if on an overseas cruise where not only suitable meals are provided but you have ready access to toilets. Of course, if flying on a long journey, especially overnight and if travelling 'steerage' class, do not leave your toilet visit until close to arrival...the bigger the aircraft, the longer the queues.

But that ain't the case for me in Greece. My next flight is Athens to Vienna and for an Aussie, that's but a short hop.

Also, one of my hints on travel is on postage of letters or cards. In many countries, letter-boxes are coloured red, and in others, yellow. So without your care, in some countries it can mean your missive is not going to reach anywhere but a garbage unit.

~ * ~
Back to at last inspect the old areas of Plaka...

Entrance to the Agora is a worthwhile 400 drachma ($3.20). It is open daily, 8:30am to 3:00pm and is a must for photographers. Well laid out, its history is told in many languages. It dates from 150AD and I'm shown the meeting places and even the actual rocks on which philosophers expounded their theories, encouraged and taught students, and about libraries where graphs and tales, weapons and tunics are illustrated.

In Omonia Square on every corner are shoe-cleaners. I sit before an old man from whom I take no change from $2. He'd taken 30 minutes over my leather thongs, polishing them as if an historic treasure (they very nearly are!) and when I rise to leave, he grabs my hand and shakes it warmly as if I am a prodigal son returned for blessing.

From the centre of the modern city where litter, graffiti and choking exhaust fumes abound, I wander back through the exciting hubbub of Monistraki to The Plaka where history draws one like a magnet. It is hot and dusty and I find a quiet little spot (unique in the Plaka) with an inviting kerbside café. It is the Square Pateiamitrolis, flanked by a delightful little antique church and the Café Metropol. With a *café frappa* I sit under an umbrella to rest and enjoy the passing parade. With locals and visitors dressed in such an array of preferred costume, I actually feel I am living through centuries.

My final night in the middle-east, I want to celebrate all the wonders when travelling on such an ad-hoc programme, so make for what Plaka claims its best restaurant, *Diogenes,* small but upmarket by Plaka standards, yet with an attractive ambience.

With its candles and statues, its garden is particularly inviting, part of an archaeological excavation site. At 9:30pm and at last cool, diners are beginning to arrive. By 10 o'clock, waiters are rushing about setting up more tables because arriving patrons are forming a queue. I stick to my favourite *tzaziki* for starter, followed by lamb *siskabab* with salad and a half *Demestica*, topping it off with French *profiteroles*, cognac and coffee, all for 2,950 drachma ($23.50).

Summing up the Greece and Turkey of 1990...love and hate, disappointment, delight and loads of such extremes, yet an adventure for which I am thoroughly grateful. Both leave me longing to see more, for in each I could see but small parts...a lesson in learning how different are lifestyles abroad, each within themselves.

If one is careful to pack the right attitude, he/she can learn a lot from visiting each.

Seven

Vienna...

Air Olympia carries me over the conspicuously green countryside of Yugoslavia then Hungary. After Greece, the Vienna airport is sparklingly clean, yet watching the increasing price of my taxi on its dashboard dial, I shudder. I cannot but help feel I am being robbed, yet a quick mental summation tells me taxis in Austria are still cheaper than in Australia.

Yes mate, but as expected, I'm virtually no longer saving money on anything. No wonder Europeans choose the near east for holidays.

When booking my hotel from Athens, I make sure of having written confirmation.

Vienna immediately begins proving as beautiful a clean and tidy sight as expected.

On checking into Hotel Urania, a brochure on the desk advertises *Das Wiener Mozart Orchester an Konzerthalle*...I cannot understand the rest. Mozart is my favourite composer so already I have my first 'must see' on my Vienna programme.

My Life, My Travels

"Thursday night, sir," the desk clerk explains in excellent English, "and this is but Tuesday. I can book from here if you like. We are given gallery seats at stall prices."

I book. He hands me a tourist map of the city.

"I will have your theatre ticket for you come breakfast, sir."

The three 'My things' of importance...My hotel presents time well. It was built in 1685 and I admire its etched wall designs, chandeliers and carpets... 380 schillings plus 40 for shower ($47) per night. Like its city, one can admire the way it presents itself, sedate and gentle.

My room is comfortable and the map tells me it's a long walk to city centre. Seeing new things is what travel is all about, so that doesn't worry me. The little *Berlitz* helps me understand the city map he's given me. My programme is to spend only three or four days here, then take the scenic train journey to Germany's Lindau, then Liechtenstein.

For what is left of today, I take in some city sights. With a map of Vienna's efficient quiet tramway system (all rubber-lined wheels) so noiseless, I begin both wandering afoot and using the tram to take many photographs. The map leads me to Kettenbrucken-gasse and the Franz Schubert house/museum. Next door is a recommended Café Reiner Kunstlerklaus with a marvellous atmosphere, plush tapestries, studded lounges, brilliant chandeliers and interesting Victorian clutter. To suffice until dinner, I order a sandwich-snack and it is so huge, I make it dinner too, so order a litre of beer. The notice I'd read claims this place rocks late at night. I can sense it but am very tired. This afternoon, I have nearly walked my feet to exhaustion. Strange bed or not, I sleep well.

Wednesday is a free day, 'free' in that I've no particular place to seek except to see the Danube River and Mozart's grave. I hail an empty horse-carriage with an 'English spoken' sign and ask to just get taken on a tour of Vienna's most interesting sights. In a city of so many historical statues, I'm sure I see all, my 'driver' imparting the history of each as we pass, like the Opera House and the Royal Palace with its 2,600 rooms!

What a wonderful way to sightsee! And the old horse only shits on the cobbles once.

Having enjoyed last night's hotel dinner, I ask the desk clerk to recommend a period café where I can have a light dinner. He directs me to Café Landtmann, which I highly recommend, eating early then going to see a movie in an English only theatre. I see the early Australian black-&-white movie *For the Term of his Natural Life* made in 1927.

I again enjoy a typical German *Frühstück* (breakfast)...ham, cheese, mushrooms and hard-boiled-egg topped with several cups of decaffeinated black coffee with honey.

Thursday has me first going to the Hauptbahnhof to validate my Eurailpass for tomorrow, the pass that gives me first-class rail travel throughout Europe within thirty days. I pay extra only if requiring a sleeper. Having accomplished that, I begin my plotted tour and I start falling in love with Vienna...palaces so grand they put most of England's to shame and I discover Mozart's statue in the Volksgarten, the garden at his feet in the shape of a treble-clef. After a light lunch and two beers at a café in the city's central mall watching people perambulate, I head for the oldest part of town where flowerboxes bedeck streets and buildings, and note more flower-bedecked horse carriages taking tourists sightseeing.

To ease the day's tiredness in readiness for my *Konzert*, I take in the Roma Sauna on Passauer Platz, then taxi home. Dressed as formally as my wardrobe permits, I dine lightly opposite the Konzerthalle, and Wow! Seated in the café's large street window priming myself for an evening to remember, I watch hundreds of people dressed exceedingly well entering the concert hall.

My gallery seat is front row and almost level with the stage front, ideal for sighting every member of the orchestra. My programme informs that the entire second half will be my beloved *Eine kleine Nachtmusik,* the most wonderful of Mozart's masterpieces.

The concert is magic. A huge welcome is given the conductor as he appears and takes up his stance centre stage, the sole waiting instrument a Mozart's period pianoforté. Gasps go up from seemingly everyone as all male musicians enter, clad in period costume even to white wigs of curls, every garment of the Mozart period, white stockings and buckled shoes with gems aglitter. Each carries his instrument. They receive a welcome from every member of the audience, standing and clapping with vigour.

First half is extracts from *Don Giovanni*, the *Ouverture & Arie des Graf* from *Le Nozze de Figaro,* then many others. At one stage, with most of the presentation yet to be played, the conductor walks off the stage leaving the orchestra to its own resources...and it never misses a beat. When he returns, the audience proffers more standing applause.

After interval where I chat with several people, all comments honour the wonderful performance. The entire second half is *Eine kleine Nachtmusik,* all of which I tape. Its Allegro is strings...no drums, French horns, piccolos nor flute.

With not a microphone in sight, acoustics prove wonderful as the performance has us all near tears. It receives a standing ovation not just the first encore, nor the second but the third when the conductor pleads relief for his musicians.

That in itself brings applause that seems to never fade.

I am in seventh heaven.

~ * ~

Leichtenstein...

The *Hausmeister* at Hotel Urania as I book out, recommends Bregenz as my best 'resting' point for visiting Liechtenstein.

"You will find it an interesting city in itself to overview what the Swiss call Bodenzee, Lake Konstanz, but I'm sure your Atlas calls it Bodensee. All three countries share it."

It is good advice. A very early train takes me the western length of Austria to where Bregenz joins it to both Switzerland and Germany at the Bodensee's most easterly point. Again, I have to run so fast I jump into a second-class carriage, to wait for our first stop before changing into first. I make my change at Linz and find a window seat. Looking back down the train as we round a curve; it is more than twenty carriages in length.

Next stop, on the German border, is Salzburg, where I am anxious to see the Mozart Museum. Particularly after last night and it being his city of birth, the opportunity grabs at me. With my rail pass so free and I have until dusk before the next Bregenz bound train is due, I decamp for those few hours.

Sadly, the museum is closed for repairs and renovations... *Clouds of Maggie and me when heading to England, finding the Van Gough Museum in Amsterdam closed.*

It gives me time, however, to see something of Salzburg.

A big advantage in plotting travels is preparing a flexible timetable and Salzburg is a city with much more to honour it than seeing where Mozart was born...just so much beautiful Baroque architecture, wonderful views of the rising mountain ranges that extend to Switzerland and France and the tense atmosphere that the Tyrol imparts. Only six years later, UNESCO rightfully lists the city a World Heritage site.

Scenery west of Salzburg as I train out is magnificent. I am quickly conscious of climbing at a great rate. We stop here and there for only a few minutes for passengers to depart and others to board. Rain begins falling and I can make out in the distance on a neighbourly mountain, a cable-car rising up into clouds.

I leave the train at Feldkirch, last stop before the Swiss border, and change to a local train to Bregenz, arriving late afternoon. Fortunately, there is no rain and I find Hotel Central on Kaiserstrasse, recommended by my Vienna host, is but a short walk.

Bregenz is indeed true to the recommendation for it is a unique small city.

~ * ~

Bregenz...

Hotel Central is modern. I have a private bath and can have laundry done overnight and shoes cleaned for free. It serves breakfast but neither lunch nor dinner, as I'm finding common in Europe. I simply follow the path taken by most, soon to realise every way is up yet more mountains. They dominate everything in sight!

With all restaurants displaying menus outside their doors, I suss out two or three and decide on Das Gossbrauhaus for tonight. Large and busy is always a good sign and the heavy air promises rain, so I am quickly inside.

The table alongside me is a couple speaking French, who ask where I am from.

"*Est-ce que vous parlez Anglais?*" I enquire and fortunately both have a little, so I am in a similar situation as with the Frenchies I met in the Plaka. We struggle along with *Franglaise*. She is French, he Turkish and I tell him I have recently arrived from Kussadasi and Marmaris.

"I know Kussadasi well. I lived there for a time..."

Suddenly his tale is chopped short... Screams rend the air, several people drop cutlery with a clatter and my heart nearly stops...never have I heard such a clap of thunder so loud... the very tables tremble and it doesn't stop, it just keeps resounding to meet its own echoes. It reverberates throughout the valleys around us, bouncing off this mountain on to that and back again. Lightning flashes, brilliant streaks light up the night outside and more thunder crashes and rolls through the mountains.

A waitress comes by and laughs. I gather her remark, in German, is explaining that this happens often, that we should not be alarmed.

As had happened in Greece, the Frenchies invite me to their table.

The echoes continue reverberating...disconcerting to say the least, so conversation is consistently interrupted. A little rain follows but the thunder and lightning continues.

The meal is a huge serving, roasted wild boar with vegetables, a new taste sensation and magnificent. For dessert I choose a pile of baked cherries with a mountain of whipped cream, then coffee. Along with wine, the cost is $40 and I hope Austrian dinners are reflective of all Europe.

At the breakfast table I am greeted with many a *Morgen* or *Guten Tag* and we share conversations on topics of the day.

Breakfast, typically Arryan in style, mountains of sausages, cheese, hard-boiled eggs, a selection of breads from grain and rye to heavy, black jams, treacles and wonderful strong coffee.

I walk through the town. There is no sign of last night's storm, in fact it had quite blown itself out, or did it blast itself out by the time we leave the restaurant to walk our ways home?

Today, a Friday, I am off to Liechtenstein and need to take two trains and a bus. Travelling from Austria into Switzerland and back again, passport control takes more time than I spend in Verduz, Liechtenstein's only town. And it has no 'countryside.'

The little duchy is quite surrounded by Switzerland and so tiny one can almost be out of it if leaning too far forward from any lookout...or that's what they claim! There is no passport control with Switzerland, yet their own postage stamps contribute highly to their export market. They use Swiss currency, but I find all shops and restaurants readily accept German and Austrian, even ask what currency I prefer in change.

It is certainly a pretty town and in that my friends around the world are hardly likely to ever get mail from here, I buy postcards, scribble a short message and post them.

Fortunately, rain holds off and I walk much of the attractive town. There are but a handful of streets for very quickly from anywhere, one is climbing steps. All views are up and on top is the Grand Duke's palace *Schloss Verduz* which seems to just hang on a cliff face. The clouds above it move at an amazing pace.

I lunch on *bratwurst* and beer in a little café bedecked with bunting, including the Dutchy flag and those of its three neighbours.

It seems a well-to-do little society for houses are large and all in pristine condition with pretty gabled roofs, shuttered windows and blooming flower boxes. Every car with local numberplate is new, and I note Porsche, Mercedes, BMW, Audi, Jaguar style, even a Rolls Royce. Affluence is everywhere.

All from postage stamps?

~ * ~

Back to Bregenz...
Outside the hotel on Saturdays is a mall where chess and draught games are well attended. Street theatre is popular with everyone, laughing and applauding. I understand little of the dialogue yet easily the intent.
I must study up on German.
I wander in a different direction from last night, straight up, for it is the only way and am delighted to find a castle/home complete with portcullis straddling its road to the modern city park. This is what had been the original town with only centuries old houses walled in. All houses are half-timbered and thatched. It is indeed a pretty area within its little square, colourful gardens and trees.
I enjoy my walk until rain returns, venturing out only to eat.
I am short of local cash but as I leave in the morning, am loath to cash another travel-cheque...a good reason for choosing a budget dinner. I had noticed a backpacker eatery, so hurry there through light rain. And oh, what good fun it is with several languages adding to the camaraderie in seemingly every breast.
Then it's back home to say farewell to Austria...a most satisfactory visit, a country offering ideal hospitality, backed by attractive prices for Europe.

Eight

Germany...

Today introduces many more highlights, another part of the world to enrapture me, another to extend wonderful welcome.

My train skirts *Die Bodenzee* for less than 2km by which time we are in the German island town of Lindau. The train doesn't cross the spectacular causeway and a half hour is spent changing trains and adding a second engine. Meanwhile we are treated with generous views of a picturesque old town, its church steeples and lakeside villas.

At every stop we seem to shed a carriage until we are at the pretty town of Kempten, where live the German lads, part of our group on the Greek ferry to Samos.

When left with only two carriages, it is a sign that we are very near the top of the Tyrol.

We wind up through fields and valleys of *eidelweiss*, every house in every village and every farmhouse with window boxes ablaze with floral colour.

Surely this has to be Bavaria at its best?

I am impressed with trains here. In every one of my three so far, there is no sign of graffiti or vandalism, either in trains or on platforms. People seem as proud of their public transport here, where they use trains and buses where we use motor cars, as they are of their villages and houses. A train station is a focal point in any town and there is obvious competition to outdo others with flowerboxes, tended gardens and fresco walls.

And without any sign of graffiti!

Every pair of seats in this train has a litter bin which attendants empty frequently.

We wind across the border back into Austria where at Reutte we again change trains for two smaller carriages for the yet steeper climb. The little village of Mittelberg is spectacularly pretty and past Ehrwald we cross back into Germany and pass its highest mountain, Zugspitze.

At Garmisch-Partenkirchen, we again change trains for the yet steeper climb. I am now in a single car motor-rail with snowplough. In the winter season, Garmisch is the end of the line, snow preventing anything further. At each village I remain tempted to leave the train, for I feel it the prettiest, most inviting, yet.

Mittenwald is indeed tucked in a fold of valley. Mountains tower all around it. I'm told on three sides of us, the Austrian border is but a kilometre distant. Here in this valley I am already higher than the tip of Kosiusko and the only view I have is up and further up into mountains soaring out of sight into clouds. The Alps of Ober Bayern and the Austrian Tyrol meet here and it certainly is a magic part of a world new to me.

I am enraptured enough to not even ask price but seek the most appealing of hotels in a town of pretty hotels and pretty everything. Even the town bank has every wall frescoed, its balconies wooded and every window hung with blooming flower boxes.

My hotel, in the main street, is Die Alpenrose, which doesn't fail me. It is the centre of the little town, spitting distance from the very golden cathedral and but fifty metres from a workshop of manmade violins. Every window in the street has blooming flowers and every wall is frescoed in some historical feature.

Inside Die Alpenrose, the atmosphere is no less traditional: women in Tyrolean blouses, short skirts, legs in white stockings and long hair in pigtails. Men are more formal in black tie and waistcoats, yet still in short trousers and stockings. The three-storied hotel is seventeenth century, ceilings low and heavily timbered, hung with forged iron chandeliers, wooden floors polished to a gleam and every hallway adorned with stag-head trophies. My room is as traditional as the public areas of this little hotel, quaintly comfortable. I marvel at how some of these centuries old hotels manage to incorporate modern bathrooms seemingly without pipes? My window, too, has shutters, and a well-attended flower box of impatiens affords a view of not only the wooden-tiled roof of the shop next door but along the street with flowers blooming from every window.

The German word for Flowers is Bloomen...oh how apt.

Everywhere upwards are towering peaks, tops lost in wisping cloud.

I spend what is left of Day 1 wandering about the little town, getting my bearings.

Oh what a wonderful introduction to a new country.

I cannot but feel—what with everywhere illustrating such devastating pleasure—lucky.

Tomorrow I will return with camera and notebook. Tonight, I will eat here, for the menu is a tease. If their food is as dramatic as everything around me, I daren't deny it.

And what a sensation it proves!

The dining-room is open to the public and is obviously well patronised by gentry. Its curbed timber ceilings are as frescoed as the walls. The entire room is heavily timbered, the street-side wall an incredible half metre thick! Each wide sill has regulation window box and windows have shutters both inside and out. Furniture befits the décor, traditional and intricately crafted. The hotel is run by the biggest butcherly *frauleins* imaginable, the type you would hate to meet in the dark! I am sure either could fell me with a single blow.

Anna is a classic, looks like she came with the building and been here ever since. She is obviously an owner and the brochure claims the hotel has been home to the family for centuries. She is built like the mountains that surround us and indeed looks a character in her Tyrolean costume. Her 'friend' I dub The Spanish Princess, even bigger and more the butcher, blouse stretched across her more than ample bosom far too tightly, heavy necklaces dangling to her waist in front and thick black hair which she keeps swishing about, at back, to her waist. Large bejewelled hair combs adorn the crown. They both must be in their sixties but, 'my God! they don't just move about...both waitresses taking orders and delivering them to table, they run. Many patrons are well known, for the hosts have them in fits of laughter.

I begin with Willsupper and find it nowt short of magnificent soup. I follow with the Stroganoff, recommended by the Americans with whom I had talked during the change of trains at Garmisch. Yes, they were spot on!

Anna serves my dinner on a spitting platter, a mountainous helping. I am in no hurry, for the atmosphere, like the food, is most enjoyable. Anna rules her domain like the tyrant she looks, shouting directions through the heavy doors to the kitchen, and *toqued* staff come running with whatever is called for. It is great entertainment.

A dog whimpers close by me but under the table, a reminder that animals are welcome in any European restaurant and this one is severely rounded on by its owner for having made its presence felt. It is a large and noisy group in that alcove and it isn't until they later get up to leave, that I see it is two big dogs which had so quietly spent several hours better behaved than any patron or staff member.

It seems there is some celebration in the house, for as the evening progresses, laughter and merrymaking in the kitchen increases. Each time Anna and The Princess return there, it becomes noisier and their absence from serving becomes longer.

Patrons begin getting testy as they are kept waiting, and lasses from behind the bar begin to appear with trays of food and most often serve it to the wrong table. After further noisy laughter from the kitchen, Anna appears, brushing fallen coiffure from her face, to busy around customers. It is obviously a token gesture for the situation deteriorates. The girls behind the bar continue to fill the gap, illustrating both goodwill and embarrassment but get little co-operation from the kitchen from where the noise has developed into raucous frivolity.

I reach the stage of calling for *"Die Rechnung bitte"* for I have given up waiting for my cognac and coffee. Several would-be diners have given up and walked out.

The lass returns from the kitchen, acknowledging with a nod, and I wait and wait. Eventually I go to the bar and ask that it be charged to my room.

"No," she insists apologetically. I must have a *Rechnung* (invoice).

Shortly Anna appears with it, trying without success to do up her apron and brushing back further fallen hair at the same time, pissed beyond belief.

Having enjoyed the farce of it all, I finally get to bed.

At breakfast, The Princess, looking much the worse for wear, is on duty and there is no sign of Anna. I learn that yesterday had been Anna's birthday.

In town, highly elated, I sit in a kerbside café with a glass of wine and stare up at the closest mountain, watching the cable car go up and down into the clouds. I then take a walk to become further enraptured. For those who enjoy visiting baroque churches, some of the world's most intriguing are in Oberbayern. The pick is in Rottenbuch, Wieskirche, Ottobeuren and Mittenwald, the latter named the *Pfarrkirche*.

The frescoes on many houses, sometimes entire streetscapes like on the Obermarkt on which my hotel stands, are a photographer's paradise, despite streets being so narrow and twisted, it is often difficult to find a wide enough angle.

Also on Obermarkt is *Geigenbauer-Werkstatt*, the violin maker's workshop where you can go in to watch the craftsmen lovingly fashion their world famous instruments. I spend an interesting hour there, he explaining in broken English, some of the more difficult parts.

Tomorrow I take the cable car into the clouds...and beyond?

At the top I stroll through a pedestrian tunnel to where one has gasping oversight of the valley between Germany and Austria. Even without field glasses, I can pick out scores of hikers dressed in traditional hiking gear climbing tracks on adjoining mountains.

I have afternoon tea in a café up there where travel information is there for all to inspect, in English, explaining how for only three months in any year, the tunnel is blocked by snow and nor are hiking tracks open. Over coffee and cake, I chat with American, English, French, South African and Portuguese tourists. Tomorrow I leave for points north and, to help with budget, tonight I eat at a little self-service snackery also just a few doors from *Die Alpenrose* and sup on sausage and *sauerkraut* with a quarter litre of *rhotwein*. It is but early in my time in Germany, so there is ample opportunity to get back on budget, but I have not a moment's regret over what I spend in Die Alpenrose, especially the first night's dinner...worth every bloody cent!

~ * ~

Schloss Linderhof and Romantische Strasse...

I take an early train to Oberau and just miss the hourly bus. I book my luggage in at the station and repair to the Gastof Brauhaus (pub). Finding no one about, I wend my way to the kitchen where I ask for coffee and they serve it on the lawn under a sun-umbrella. I spend hours just walking around the district, coffee in hand, for I regret having to leave it.

Then it is back to the bus stop, and along the road we pass through Oberammergau where the famous annual Passion Plays are held. Like every Bavarian town, it is abloom with flowering window boxes and general tidiness.

Schloss Linderhof is a smaller 'showpiece' castle than Neuschwanstein in the next valley, the better known 'fairy' castle of the mad King Ludwig, yet is as spectacular in its furnishings and eye to detail as are the gardens and fountains. It is a Schloss (castle) he built especially in order to personally enjoy and spent most of his life here. Particularly stunning is the dining room. I find it as gilded as any room, yet walls of mirror are especially contoured such that when he sits to dine, the mirrors give every impression that the table is not only many times longer than in fact, but as far as he can see in any direction, other Ludwigs are sitting side by side of him! It does seem like magic and is a stunning example of seventeenth century intellect and science.

Linderhof is the ultimate in opulence and ostentation. For $4.80 it is a worthwhile tour in a choice of languages.

Most beautiful of the villages we pass through on the road back to the train is Ettal. It is difficult to judge when all fall within the 95% barrier, but in Ettal, even streets are hung with cascading blooms. If visiting an Oberammergau play, I recommend staying in Ettal.

North from Oberau the train tumbles (comfortably) down the mountains and by the time we reach Weilheim, the countryside has well unfolded. It is approaching dark and my bible, the Thomas Cook European Rail Timetable, which no sensible roving traveller is ever without, tells me that at the next stop, Starnberger-See, I change trains for Augsberg only 3 minutes later. Trains being spot on, I overnight in Augsberg and from there the next day, bus up the Romantischestrasse.

Lo and behold, as I emerge from the Augsburg Bahnof, the Hotel Riegele that Thomas Cook recommended is blinking its neon at me from across the street. They have a room. It is expensive at $76 per night, but saves me tramping the streets close by and my Europabus departs right outside the train station. Meals are at a price to send me walking up the street seeking something cheaper.

By then, rain is falling, so under an umbrella proffered by the hotel, I scamper around the corner to the recommended Palace China Restaurant. Its doorway menu promises pleasant dining, and upstairs I am greeted by glass ponds of terrapin ranged all around the walls. One must watch where you walk for as some terrapins are picked up off the carpeted floor by anyone, to plop back in any pond, others are climbing out. Children in the big crowd are having a wonderful time.

The staff is most attentive and serves me fried wontons, fried rice, a unique variation of sweet and sour pork, Chinese tea after which I sit over a beer, all for $24.

By morning, with laundry I left at the desk overnight waiting outside my door, I breakfast at a kerbside Kinditorie on pastries and coffee.

I've time for a walk to discover that every block of centre city had to be rebuilt after WW2. It is a major rail intersection linking Munich with Germany's industrial heart in the north-west, so it received quite a pasting from Allied bombing.

Fortunately, this is far from the case of the three tour towns we visit, Nordlingen, Dinkelsbuhl and Rothenburg-op-der-Tauber. Each claim to be the only German town unscathed by war.

Today one sees the magnificence of mediaeval history. Apart from a few motorcars and many TV antennae, there is indeed no change from the middle ages. Buildings remain picturesque in the extreme, further paradise for camera clickers.

Europabus covers all forms of travel except by air or train. For a fixed period, one can jump aboard tram or bus anywhere in a chosen city. You can buy one for several choices of time. Eurailpass covers train and bus between cities. Once purchased, the number of times it is used depends on the time factor purchased.

For the Romantischestrasse during the tourist season, two buses run daily in each direction, one between Frankfurt and Fussen, the other between Frankfurt and Munchen (Munich). The whole is a twelve-hour journey with plenty of time allowed for wandering around the three major centres. One can disembark anywhere along the route and catch another bus. Between towns, passengers are given brief histories in several languages.

Nordlingen is the first, and entering it through its old wall we get our first sight of how this entire little 'rainbow' town is authentic for its age…a world of yesterday. The bus drives slowly to the town centre and we have an hour to wander at will and photograph at leisure.

Dinkelsbuhl is even a more colourful example, such that the bus stops long enough for us to choose where to buy lunch. Again, all buildings have been unspoiled except to emphasize the emblazoned colours that seem as new as yesterday. With several of my bus companions, I lunch kerbside at the unique Der Golden Rose Hotel dining room outdoor on the roadway. Several declare they want to stay the night and catch tomorrow's bus.

In Rothenburg-op-der-Tauber, I take time out from walking the city walls to partake of a beer on a hotel rooftop. They are sold only in litre mugs (1.76 pints) and the laughter around the rooftop illustrates many have imbibed more than one or three. It is the larger of the three towns and its complete wall to walk around and peer into so many back yards and magnificently carved front doors of the ancient houses are wonderful eye-openers. I particularly note all the timeworn hollows in every stone doorstep.

Oh, what an intriguing experience for all us modern travellers.

The *Romantischestrasse* is indeed a wonderful experience.

~ * ~

Gottingen…

Jurgen and Emmi are expecting me late afternoon.

As with the Frenchies in Greece, this German couple had been tablemates in Turkey with whom to strike up a long-lasting friendship…a matter of: "Whenever you get to Germany…"

Jurgen is a university medical doctor and Emmi teaches high school English in the university hospital. We had talked on the problems of teaching the new generations that there is nothing to be proud of during the Nazi period, that it had been an unfortunate hiccup in the county's history.

"That is what we teachers are told to assure the newborns."

I phone them from Mittenwald and they expect me Saturday night. I call from the station and Jurgen drives in to collect me. I bring wine and we talk long into the evening. They are amazed to learn that, during the war, I was in my teens and kept diaries on Australia's part in it. They had not even been born!

But it is interesting to hear how Allied school students of the time saw the war.

On Sunday they drive me to Berlin. "Next time you come, Ric," Jurgen explains, "we shall take you south to see some glorious countryside. But you wishing to visit Berlin in the present circumstance, you could face a barrier at the East-West border..."

"I checked this with the German Consul before leaving home, Jurgen. He says okay."

Once over the East-West line however, every sign of advancement and new construction of battlefield ruins in the American and English west is instantly missing here in the east. The countryside between that border and Berlin still lies in shambles, barbed wire fencing everywhere around many buildings and lookout towers lying rampant all along its length.

I am anxious to see eastern Berlin. The Russians are reported to have deliberately left its sector in ruins.

As we drive through the Russian sector approaching Berlin, I can certainly see how all the countryside has been left abandoned.

I wonder what these poor bastards had been eating during these cold-war years?

~ * ~

Berlin...

My journalist title sees me through some areas denied a normal visitor, yet Jurgen still does not dare try a shortcut into the British Sector. It is a huge city but he uses only highways. The American and British sectors illustrate considerable rebuilding and the French less, but at least some. The Russian sector? None!

I like their son Gunter. He has two jobs, teaching English at a junior school and between hours making jewellery.

"No diamonds but various brightly coloured stones."

He jests that he is delighted to show me Berlin sights if I respond by mentioning the particular jewellery shop that buys his wares. I promise to recommend Wissenschaft Juwelier on Kurfurstendamm, one of the major Berlin highways.

And yes, there has been considerable rebuilding. The entire British and American sectors look like a brand-new city. On the Kurfurstendamm, the startling ruin of the Kaiser Wilhelm Memorial Church has been left as a forever reminder of the futility of war. All that is left are blackened ruins of the magnificent cathedral in a picture posted by its door.

On my map, Gunter outlines a large area of Berlin in which it is safe for me to wander and photograph. He proves an excellent guide and with the wall coming down, he is allowed in what had been the Russian sector. While western areas by now have excellent roads, modern shops and hotels, the eastern area is best described in one word...derelict.

We bounce and bump unmercifully on what the Germans call Redback Roads...the broken bitumen under tramlines has still never been repaired in East Berlin, so tram travel is painfully bumpy. Commercial buildings stand empty, windows broken and doors nailed shut. Even buildings being used still have broken guttering, fallen downpipes, paint worn and flaking. Abandoned cars are common sights, obviously left where they died. Weeds grow around them, the car bodies home to feral cats or dogs. While West Berlin sparkles, East Berlin is a sad sight. I think of the beauty in Mittenwald and wonder what East German resorts must look like.

At the renowned Brandenburg Gate, tears form in my eyes as I watch a father holding the hands of his little son trying to hold a heavy hammer to break concrete walls that kept East Germans from families in the Allied areas. Meanwhile, his mother collects chips to take home as souvenirs. I am to remember that little scene forever.

I am to soon find out, for we call in to sightsee the once proud Potsdam Palace. I can now call it, simply 'derelict with a capital D.'

We drive back to West Berlin where colour and order greet us. We park in Kurfurstendamm and go upstairs in Berlin's most elegant Konditorei, *Leysieffers*. It is where matrons and divas come

My Life, My Travels

to be seen, where East Berliners peer in the window and wonder, for they cannot afford such luxurious fare.

Visiting from the eastern end of that very boulevard are Turkish gypsies who lie on blankets with their babies. Now allowed into the western end, they beg alms of those peering in shop windows at clothing and jewellery that none can afford. Gunter buys us a bachelor type dinner of grilled beef, baked potato cakes and frozen peas. For dessert I go back to Leysieffers and queue up to buy an elegant *tiramisu* then next door a Pino Noir.

Tomorrow, Gunter has no school, so while he works on jewellery I return to the city by tram for more sightseeing and stroll street after street. All about me, the new Berlin is building...I wonder where the money is coming from...but modern equipment is used for digging holes clean of broken buildings and laying foundations for new ones.

That night I ask Gunter what chance I have for getting photos of the squalor in East Berlin?

"Ric, tomorrow is your last day and I don't want to see you disappointed."

I name things like the broken bitumen under tram lines, the street-fulls of shattered buildings that have remained ignored since war ended, some sad looking houses and buildings East Berliners have had to call home for 45 years.

He nods, scribbles some notes and we then watch football until I fall asleep.

He wakes me and helps spread my 'mattress' on the sitting-room floor.

Come morning I make him an Aussie breakfast of cereal, fried eggs on toast, but he balks after the first bite of the Vegemite I carry with me in single serve packets made for motels.

I just smile and eat his share as well as mine.

When next morning I have my photos, I ask if we can return to the Brandenburg Gate train station by the East Berlin U-Bahn. "I want to photo its squalor and tape its noise on my Philips, also to return by the Western U-Bahn with its cushioned fabric seats, carpet, piped music and everything clean and tidy. And its smooth track."

"Then where do you go?"

"I've a yen to visit Cologne, Gunter, another city critically reduced to rubble during the war, yet one with a theatrical history that is rebuilding its pre-war past as it was in 1939."

After getting my photos, I collect luggage from the Central Station holding area, then mount my train for Köln.

~ * ~

Köln and the Rhine…

Getting back to the real new Germany is not comfortable travel. Between Berlin and the East-West, German fences still must be faced and certainly in 1990 it still has wooden seats and bumpy tracks and all fencing is still barbed wire. Even lookout towers remain that no one seems anxious to take down.

From Hannover however, it is a comfortable ride to Cologne, although being through the Germany's industrial centre lacks the delightful countryside of the south. Instead of wineries and flowers, it has mines and chimney smoke.

Walking from the train station to the hotel I'd booked, a strange thing makes me halt and wonder…

How can this possibly be a hotel?

On my way to what is called Old Town, ie: before the war, I cross a street to stop and stare…

A pub squeezed into a 3-metre-wide building?

Sure enough, the sign reads *Die Timp Hotel!*

And it's been rebuilt like this?

I look up to see it has four floors.

Utterly curious, I have to see more!

The reception desk is in the small room off the street, its desk doubling as its bar. It is, except for a tiny kitchen, the only ground floor room.

Small as it is, I am to find it is also the breakfast room, lounge and dance floor.

Let me explain...This tiny hotel, I am to slowly discover, is the city's 'top drag-show' theatre, a gay establishment from way back. In fact, this fourth largest city in the country is one of Germany's gayest cities. Hotel Timp has but two single bedrooms and a shower 'stall' on each floor. I am on its second floor and pay $38 including breakfast. It is so recently the only spare room that the bed isn't yet remade and the room service guy is the desk clerk, chef, housemaid and owner named Hermann.

I'll trial it tonight. If I can make it a few days, I can quickly get back on budget.

All rooms have single beds because bigger beds cannot fit. My tiny room also has a tiny desk with a three-legged stool and a few hooks on a wall.

By the time I fit my six-foot body in the room, my bag has to go under the bed. The shower room is free, so I shower then go for a walk to see what is nearby. I start with the cathedral. I had read that one of its two towers was the only thing left standing in the city centre and it is only around the corner from Die Timp.

I shower again while Hermann remakes my bed. On arrival downstairs, I find him scratching his head. His ledger is on the bar that triples as his desk. Fridays and Saturdays he has permanent bookings and this week he's miscalculated. Unfortunately, he will find me another hotel for those two nights. This is Wednesday and I hadn't intended staying through the weekend anyway.

Come 7:00pm he asks if I am ready for dinner, for he will be busy later, so I eat and the meal is basic but adequate. I am the only one eating here. Come 8:00pm, a crowd arrives, gay screamers all, flapping and carrying on a noisy treat, toting boxes from a panel-van. They set up lights and bunting and from under the stairs comes a collapsible stage which is erected and the sides are draped with cooking foil. So the bar becomes even smaller. The stage is pushed into what is the dance area to make room for the DJ, so there is no space for dancing.

And this happens not every day but every night?

The stage is in so the DJ is okay, but there is no room for people at the bar, nor to dance. Again, I can but shrug and wait to see what happens next.

Oh, it has become so noisy with 'screamers' rushing about, all but two or three on the sidewalk. I am utterly intrigued.

Come 10:00pm, guests start arriving and I try sorting gay guys from straight guys, for dress and make-up are confusing, especially as some are as old as me, with wives. And I'm getting squeezed against a wall. The crowd, now outdoors, continues increasing, dressed in denim, leather and lace. Once jam-packed, the entertainment begins, dancers using the sidewalk. Noise and cigarette-smoke is stifling and sitting in the gutter I chat with a couple in their sixties.

"We only come Wednesdays, for Fridays and Saturdays here are just too crowded."

Hearing is difficult because the Andrew Sisters are at an ear-shattering level and by 2:00am when the show starts, when people are dancing on tables in the street, I hear a boy's voice whispering in my ear...

"For 100 marks, I am yours for an hour."

Somewhat bemused, afraid yet quick thinking, I whisper back...

"I'm afraid I am already booked by a big man who should be here any time now."

So he struggles to move quickly away.

The show is a riot. A red velvet curtain is hung in the doorway and through it the stars appear, so that all others are pushed into the street, the music changes and for the size of the stage, several dancers kick too high and slide into the crowd. All is simply bad drag and even worse mime. I give up giggling and fight my way to bed, finding it delightfully clean and comfortable, but the noise even with my window closed is unbelievable.

At breakfast, Hermann does not look well. He has not been to bed but is cleaning the bar, to then face breakfast. He brings me bread rolls hot from the baker's oven and pours coffee. Having served others, he realises my boiled egg still boils. It is rock hard but he digs it out with a spoon and plonks it on my empty plate and asks what I had to drink last night... "So I can make up your *Rechnung*."

I pay the horrific bill and make sure I eat, on the house, a monstrous breakfast before taking to the streets.

Oh, what a wonderful day I face after such an excitable night.

But at this price I'll give it another night.

So much of the city is so centred that just walking around a few blocks one is amazed. So much centres on just this very area.

The Cathedral of St. Peter and St Mary is, in itself, a day's study! History books tell that three-quarters of Köln city was flattened in air-raids in 1944-5, yet the cathedral was fortunately left partly standing. One of the twin towers had crumbled to a sad pile of rubble, but is being restored even as I watch. It stands right by the River Rhine, next to where they are also rebuilding the Old City, of which Die Timp is a part. The new bridge across the Rhine is already in service.

Köln traces its history back to the 1st century AD and right by the cathedral is the Römisch für Angewandt Kunst Köln...During World War 2 when a bomb shelter was being built, a Roman villa was uncovered...after the war it was fully excavated and rather than try to move the huge centrepiece, a beautiful Dionysus mosaic, an entire museum was simply built around it. I visit its Treasure Chamber to view precious objects, ancient reliquaries and manuscripts. It will take several days to see all the *Adoration of Kings* from 1440! To see artefacts specialising in glassmaking is mesmerising...the single most valuable piece is the 4th century "Köln cage cup" bearing Greek lettering reading, "Drink, and live well forever."

My personal sentiments are at last proven!

The city centre is a maze of cobbled malls. Along the Cacilienstrasse, the remains of many Roman walls, bastions and watch-towers have been carefully preserved...streets are literally built around them so they become features of the streetscape.

Sightseeing cruises up and down the Rhine attract me, but I am conscious of outstretching my budget, so decide to enjoy the same views by taking a train down the Rhine's east bank. I will remain at the Timp because at the price it is a most central city site. The two days Hermann botched his bookings, I can use to visit Mainz and he has pushed my luggage under his own bed, so I do not have to lug that around with me either.

After a Bratwurst lunch in the station café, I take my train and walk through until finding a window seat on my right and there are many island castles on mini-mountain crests. My plan is, once over-viewing Mainz, return by river steamer, viewing some of the castles from their opposite sides.

At Mainz, the rain bursts and clouds indicate it will remain all day so I buy an anorak. Seeing what had been totally flattened areas during the war being rebuilt in their historical baroque image, gives me considerable joy. Rain increases so I'm in another museum, and learn Mainz was home to Gutenburg, founder of moveable type to be known as the Father of Printing. With my background, I find this quite a bonus.

At the river-steamer office, I find travel is closed.

"Had I not heard of the drought?" There is insufficient water in the Rhine.

I cross the river and take the train for Koblenz. We pass cottages with their blooming window boxes and up the hillsides ashore are many vineries. We pass villages similar to those I had so admired in the south, cobbled streets and baroque houses, tiny but pretty.

One in the extreme, Weingud (Good Wine) grabbed me and it is one I should have jumped out to inspect. With the rain stopped and me being me, at the next stop I jump off and catch a bus going back south.

"*Hält der bus in Weingud?*"

"*Ya, meneer.*"

In Weingud I had seen a little *Kneipe* on the cobbled square, a German place I am never sure is a bar come café or vice-versa, so I bus back and find 'mine-host' an amiable fellow with reasonable English. I tell him I am a travel journalist, that stories of where I travel get published in airline magazines, and order "a local dry red, please."

As I finish it, he lays a different one afore me. "On the house, *Meneer.*"

He watches carefully and on seeing my smile, tells me it is one of his own, so we chat about the various tastes of dry reds. I realise he had misunderstood my claim on writing about travel for airline magazines.

He thinks I write about wine for airline magazines.

"I have something of real interest for you, *Meneer*, come with me."

He locks his shop and physically pulls me to his car.

I'm convinced this is not another offer that for a hundred marks I can have him for the next hour, but I'm to learn something new about wine.

In his comfortable Audi we drive but a hundred metres up a steep hill of vineyards.

I am to sample a *Spatlaser* from his vineyard, "That is renowned throughout Europe," he insists. "I know you have excellent red wines in Australia, so you will enjoy it."

Ah! He thinks I write for Australian airlines.

He forces two on me and when I congratulate him, he gathers up a bottle of each and presses them into my arms.

I don't want to disappoint him so I nurse them as we get quickly back, for the next train north is due and he must reopen his bar. He gives me his card and I promise to copy him the article I write on his wines.

Oh how happy I am that, without any lies, I have made his day.

I had noted a restaurant named *Athens* and being such a sucker for Greek food, I dine there, happy at being met at the door by *bazouki* music! I splurge on *tzaziki, calamari* and galaktabouriko, a half litre of Greek wine, Greek coffee and *metaxa*.

Despite the ravings downstairs at Die Timp, I sleep soundly and dream about this almost unbelievable little hotel. With everybody pissed and laughing, it has proven such a rare sort of experience.

All in all, I depart *Deutschland* with a happy heart and two bottles of wonderful wine.

Nine

Luxembourg...

I change trains at Koblenz, where from the rocky cliff alongside the railway station hangs the ruins of some ancient building. This is where the Moselle River flows into the Rhine and for so long I gaze from my window seat into the picturesque valley that brings us to the tiny country surrounded by Germany, Belgium and France. On the German side of the Luxembourg border, steep valley hillsides rise from its twists and turns in the valley floor, all arranged with orderly fields of unending vineyards.

Little villages of stone and half-timbered houses cluster here and there to break the otherwise endless green.

Come harvest season, the mountainsides are undoubtedly alive with itinerant pickers.

We cross the border at *Wasserbillig*, a delightful introduction, for this station is yet another ablaze with flowers. The German crew departs and we are asked to present passports, an annoying introduction when I'd rather be looking 'out there.'

Despite being so small, it is the country where all Europeans meet to confer. It is headquarters of the European Court of Justice, Parliament and Bank. Placenames are German, language French and currency Belgian. People also represent a delightful mix... German order, Gallic *joie-de-vivre* and Flemish detachment, yet it enigmatically exudes its own identity. It has a history as ancient as its neighbours, the physical evidence of which is preserved in the city heart where nostalgia seems to slumber behind the throbbing pulse of European commerce.

All this rushes around my brain as I tread the streets of the fascinating little city.

Across the road from the station on Place de la Gare is Hotel Alfa of imposing appearance, typical of mid-European architecture and exceedingly large. After Die Timp, my comfort is ready for a decent pub.

Why it quotes in French francs I've no idea, but for 1.600 ($62) with *petit dejeuner* (minor breakfast) I have a twin room with bath on the fifth floor. I set about washing 'smalls' and sorting other gear to deposit in a laundry. I find it strange to suddenly recondition my mind to again think in French. The city is divided in two. I am in *Gare*, the suburb across the twenty-five arched viaduct Passerelle over the deep Petrusse Gorge. On the other side is Central.

For whatever is left of today, I wander Gare streets and espy in a shop window a long-sleeved soft cotton shirt with an amazing mix of brown and black design like tree-bark. Even at $85 I buy it, to hand-wash and iron it for thirty years. I still wear it and love it.

People here have adopted the French habit of eating late. In Hotel Alfa at 9:00pm, staff is near finished setting dinner tables. I discover a restaurant named Royal Garden that begins serving at 8:00pm and not only is its food excellent and moderately priced, but it has a sit-up bar where one can drink excellent Belgian beer and chat with others until called to your table...excellent meals for $28.

Next day I cross the inviting Passerelle and find it difficult to stop camera clicking. The green valley is the deepest I've seen and I feel I am in the most scenic of cities east, west, north, south or down. It lies where the Petrusse and Alzette rivers meet, super-entwining their torturous narrow path 'way down there.'

Everywhere are ancient fortifications, ramparts, bastions, dazzling views of ancient Europe. Strolling in Central offers a succession of delights: the chic boutiques in Grand Rue, and the Oberweis where Cartiers, Tiffanys and Rosensiels beckon, the picturesque Cathedrale de Luxembourg, La Place Guillaume with its impressive Hotel de Ville and statue of William II, King of the Netherlands and Grand Duke of Luxembourg. As in much of the city, all is hung with weeping flower baskets, a blaze of colour beneath the myriad Duchy flags.

Around the corner on Marche aux Herbes is the fifteenth century Grand Ducal Palace. Mid-day finds me browsing in a bookstore looking for a history of the Duchy, when the lights suddenly dim. The store is closing for lunch. In Luxembourg, restaurants excepted, all commercial enterprises close noon through 2:00pm.

I choose to tour the Corniche, a planned promenade around the plateaux along the route which provides the best Luxembourg has to show, to then move about unescorted. Despite their history beckons, I refrain from descending into the lower suburbs for I begin feeling footsore. Back in Gare, I treat myself to coffee and pastries in the chandeliered ambience of Sheer & Aarens, watching matrons 'take tea' and gossip no doubt about friends.

On Rue J.Origer, I had noticed the inviting restaurant of Le Papillon and come dinner time I attend the husband-wife run diner. My dinner is a semi-litre of house rouge wine, *escargot* and fillet steak, which is superb, and after café and cognac, it's but $35. I am invited to the bar as their guest, to be plied with several liqueurs of a local vineyard.

I have thoroughly enjoyed my several days in such a tiny country and undoubtedly lack of time denies me much more. I phone the French friends of that hilarious night in Greece to ask them if it is okay for me to revisit their corner of France. Christophe settles for Friday of next week and there is a train from Bruxelles to reach Nantes around 5:30pm. We could all then travel together to their little area of Nort Erde.

With that fixed, I add more wine to my shopping list.

~ * ~

Brussels...

Paul of London, he who buys my venue reviews, had given me the name of Edwin if visiting Brussels. Before leaving Australia, I arrange to call him a week or more in advance. His work shunts him around Europe and Britain at short notice so I phone my programme from Köln. He lives in a government building in which he can arrange a room for me.

"I translate at meetings," he explains. "At a moment's notice I am called here or there. I translate between English, French, Dutch and Russian, so seldom know where I shall be, even tomorrow. Taxi to here, and others will be worded up to find you a bed."

When I get to the huge building, I go to room 536 and he is there. I phone Christophe, who advises that if his mother answers their phone and hears a foreign language, she immediately hangs up. "So when you phone me, Ric, you must speak French."

From Luxembourg it is but a 2-1/2 hour train journey to Brussels and of a sudden there is a dampening of the high spirits I'd enjoyed. Belgian trains, compared to Austria, Germany, Holland and Luxembourg, lack style and comfort. I find them untidy and drab. In fact, my general impression of Belgium is unpainted houses, poorly kept farm buildings and a noticeable lack of the more affluent motor-car.

On arrival he insists that I call him Ed. He is in his thirties and as do his companions here, finds life too hectic to start families, so very few are married.

"But for a few years yet, the payment is excellent," he informs me. He introduces Beryl, who shows me to my room.

"I'm the German and Swedish speaker in our group," she tells me, "and I must get back to our meeting now, but all will properly welcome you later. If not, breakfast is at 7:30 on floor 2."

She gives me my room key and hurries off. It is indeed a comfortable apartment of three rooms and bathroom. I set aside a bottle of wine for Ed.

It is late afternoon and spitting rain, and an umbrella hangs on the back of my door. I have no problem changing money, for it is Belgian cash I've been using. Within a block on Rue Nort 42, is Restaurant Ill Perugino where I will eat tonight and retire early. I walk around the block and note some streets have underpasses which helps traffic on narrow streets. It is dribbling rain and on a street-corner is a massage parlour.

Yes, just my feet and legs need a massage.

As a young woman massages my feet, a fellow with strong fingers tends skull and shoulders. When the feet are finished, she departs and he has me strip to undies and for the next hour, pummels my thighs and back, all with soft background music and chatter in reasonable English, on the unsatisfactory state of the world.

I come away thoroughly fresh and retire to a bar for a Pilsen, then am an early arrival for dinner. After a Dubonnet is Scampi in a delicate serve of garlic. After a wait during which I appreciate its after-taste, my fillet steak is so tender I ask *madame* for another fork and return the knife and she is obviously pleased at such a compliment. *Pomme-fruits* follow and I am thrilled to find they stock Bisquit, my favourite cognac. Dinner is a delightful splurge but costs 1,560Bf ($52). I begrudge not a cent.

Petit-dejeuner in this part of Europe is regulation croissants and bread, jam, cream and bottomless coffee. Breakfast in small hotels is always chat time and people tend to chat rather than see you sit alone. Right now, I am the only Aussie present at breakfast, so receive lots of questions. With eight at our table, we end up in lots of laughter.

I take the metro to Centro, to stroll downtown. Train carriages and windows are dirty and untidy, the upholstery raggedly sad. The colour of Belgian trains is an uninspiring dark green with buff trims, a sort of bilious khaki.

But at least they have no graffiti!

Grande Place is magnificent, a large four-sided square which every morning is a flower market. On each side, cafés with colourful umbrellas dispense food and wine from breakfast to late suppers. In the background on all sides are fairyland baroque buildings, centuries old. Restoration work on walls and rooftops is under way and much gold leaf glistens in the bright sunlight. The square is the hub from which the spokes of cobbled streets fan into the greater Bruxelles city, canopied against inclement weather where fruit and vegetable markets, butcheries, confectioneries and patisseries abound...a veritable warren of culinary goodies. Galleries du Roi is a delight, a cavernous gallery of food and clothing boutiques, sunlight glancing through its leadlight roof.

In many areas of the city, despite the time approaches 11 o'clock, many stores have not been long open, irrespective of which they will close at mid-day until 2:00pm and then not to close until tonight.

Belgian lunches are generally served 2:00pm to 4:00pm and dinner from 9 or 10 o'clock.

Around a corner from Grande Place is the famous Pissing Boy fountain, smaller than imagined. As I watch, they dress him in a costume commemorating some world event.

Such is the old part of Brussels. Its many gardens are a delight. Opposite the palace gates, a columned walkway leads to a large fountain around which people sit and chatter.

Belgium has a confusing mix of languages. French, Flemish and Dutch, and even street signs are printed in both the latter, as are names on railway stations. English is seldom seen. By mid-day my feet are exceedingly tired, so I am anxious to do further travel by the unpleasant train. A major advantage of Eurailpass is ability to jump aboard trains at whim. I recall the Japanese fellow I talked with on my train from Vienna to Salzburg...he holidayed in Europe for ten days and never once slept in a bed. He used his pass as a makeshift hotel. When hungry, he jumped off a train to eat in a station café, then board another train to anywhere.

I warn him that food is always more expensive in railroad stations.

I visit Ostend on the north sea, from where England is 'just over there' to find a nice surprise. It having been so long since breakfast, the name "Capricorn" makes me homesick. It is a large seafood restaurant so popular I must wait for an empty chair at any table. The atmosphere is jocularly noisy and as led to a table, I order mussels-on-ice. It is served in Champagne buckets with a plastic pale beside me for shells. The table to which I am guided is all fishermen who recommend I follow with Sole, which I find excellent. The restaurant is decorated with fishnets, anchors and floats and in particular a veritable gallery of nostalgic photographs of Ostend's part in the war. In no hurry to be back on my feet, I sit long over lunch then have a beer and several coffees, all for $22.50.

Absolutely wonderful food and tablemates!

Back in the city and on Thursday, after another day of foot-slogging, I call into my local metro to check the times of my train tomorrow morning. I am off to see the Frenchies and it's a full day's journey via Paris to Nantes on France's west coast. I find the directory covered with a blank white bed-sheet. At the enquiry desk I am told...

"*Non monsieur, il n'ya pas possible demain.*"

Railwaymen have called a twenty-four-hour strike. No train runs tomorrow.

Shit!

Back at my free accommodation, I call Christophe but *Maman* answers.

"*Je voudrais Christophe sil vous plaît?*"

She lets several thinking moments pass then adds,

"*Il n'est pas ici M'sieur. Peut-être qu'il huit heures.*"

I tell her I will call back after eight and she promptly hangs up. I have my answer, so it is back to my present situation...

Ed is a great guy and all his mates are anxious to please. Beryl tells me she wishes she were 30 years older, so I am among helpful folk. Between them they have fourteen languages, so I shall have one explain about the train strike to Christophe. That way I'm sure he gets a clear answer rather than Christophe's English leaving me only hoping I've made it clear.

It all works well except that the four Frenchies have already bought five tickets for a Saturday cruise up the Loire, Frances longest river, sighting ancient ruins and *chateaux* galore. Instead, Christophe will get a refund on my ticket and we will meet the same time as agreed on Saturday evening rather than Sunday.

So I have a further day to see more of Brussels, but I spend Friday reading up on my French. Rain continues but I get out long enough to buy vitals for dinner.

~ * ~

Bretagne...

Crossing the border, I am asked to show my passport. France remains the only European country that so far does not require a visa from Australians. Visitors to France however, should not expect any language but French. Like the English, they continue to believe they are God's chosen people and the rest of the world should realise it.

I find English and French people so alike in that respect, yet neither believes it possible they could be as arrogant as the other.

Any wonder the two were persistently at war over so many centuries?

But I continue to love both!

All I see of Paris on this journey is the underground metro from Gar-du-Nord to Montparnesse, and even at the information desk of this major terminal there is no English, nor at the reservation desk. Reservation is essential for France's newest 'baby,' the TGV, Europe's first very, very fast train which is absolute luxury. Air conditioned, comfortably furnished with carpet, reclining cushioned seats, everyone at a table complete with table-lamp, it is so quiet and smooth one is not aware the journey is under way until everything outside begins gliding backwards.

We cruise at 250kph and at times pass 300. It is true that one can lay a coin on its edge on the table when the train speeds at its peak, and it remains on edge until the train takes a slight turn. I am amazed.

We stop only at Le Mans, and at Nantes, a reception committee of all four Frenchies...Christophe, the two Dominiques and Pascal... are waiting.

In two cars we drive some 30km to where, because all live with their parents, they have me booked into the inn at Nort-Champ-de-Foirs. Dominique I is obviously well known there and as I am yet to discover, he is known in most local inns. Madame has no English, but shows me to a pleasant little room with its own bath, opening off a veranda: Ff9($90) per night including breakfast. I am able to tell her in her language, "Thank you, it looks quite comfortable."

Over beers we reminisce on the fun night in Greece, our laughter such that onlookers must believe we have been friends for years. We enjoy a fun meal in the village over several bottles of wine and they insist that as a visitor, I am their guest tonight. Because I was denied yesterday's ferry trip, they made the trip and videoed much. I can rest up during days and each night they will show me the videos. One evening we visit Christophe's home at Nort-sur-Erdre, where I meet the *maman* who would have hung up on me had I not spoken French. Next Saturday, because Dom2 and Pascal play football in the afternoon, Christophe and DomI take me to Nantes to see its history.

Le Chateau des de Bretagne is a magnificent castle on the Loire. Begun in 1466 by Francis II, Duke of Brittany and finished in 1491, it had ever been home to Dukes of Brittany, a fortified castle with massive walls and a prominent wartime history. Today it is the city's museum. We spend many hours climbing stairways into the garrets, descending others into dungeons. We visit the Jules Verne home/museum...that intuitive man of vision and teller of grand tales spent much of his life in Nantes, and his home is now a museum with manuscripts, diaries, personal effects and his own models of the fabulous crafts and machines his imagination dreamed up.

Back in the village football club, we help enjoy the celebrations. There is much carousing then we motor back to Dom2's home in the tiny village of Les Touches.

At Ancenis-du-Loire we dine at 9:30 in Le Grillard which I highly recommend. I choose Les Huites Naturelle (raw oysters) and a magnificent steak in a 'magic' sauce they call *Bertrant*. We drink copious bottles of wine and mine-host eventually joins us and produces a further bottle of wine 'on the house,' after which we head for home.

En-route, Christophe asks, "Is it true Australians spend Christmas Day on a beach?"

I explain that some do, that I had done that with friends only last Christmas.

"A BBQ on a beach?" To which I simply explain, "Either that or a picnic lunch."

The four fall into a hurried *tète-à-tète* so fast I could not understand a word.

Christophe puts a hand on my shoulder:

"We will come!"

Yes, even Dominique 2 who still cannot afford to buy an engagement ring!

They drop me at my lodging about 2:00am and we bid each other farewell. In the morning they must catch a 7:15am bus for work in Nantes. I will leave later, to take a train for La Rochelle.

~ * ~

La Rochelle...

Since I was a lad enraptured by the adventures of d'Artagnan and *The Three Musketeers,* I have wanted to visit La Rochelle and its fortress island Ile-de-Re. It is but a two-hour run and I can look forward to a few 'quiet only' days.

After that, only big event on my programme before going home is Egypt.

The tourist accommodation office recommends a hotel to suit my needs at a modest price. l'Hotel de l'Ocean is on harbour's edge and extremely central to tourist requirements. Whilst the huge harbour holds many large seagoing yachts, its minor branch holds a hundred or more small vessels, all directly across a cobbled court from 'my' hotel. Next door to it is La Rochelle Musée Histoire. A few doors to the left is an entrance to a market and on its right, a string of *al fresco* and indoor restaurants. At its northern end is a large ancient fortified tower. Across the narrow mini-harbour entrance is a smaller ancient tower, both flashing beckoning fingers to my inquisitive mind.

Behind my hotel is the city shopping area, all built in the 10th century.

It's the centre of my every need, all for Ff260 ($54) including full breakfast.

I am in French history's very centre!

I need to change a traveller's cheque and the nearby bank is closed for lunch and beside it, of all people, a coach-driver of a visiting English tourist party is an excellent guide to things I want to see, exactly where, for instance did *The Three Musketeers* fight their battles. He marks them on my map.

"La Rochelle these days," he tells me, "is more French than Paris."

I gather he means La Rochelle chose to retain more of its history than has Paris.

Cash in hand, I make for the dominant Le Tour de Chain built in 1382, its brochure giving me its stunning history. A hundred metres away is the smaller tower La Tour de la Lantern in which I spend worthy hours. Also near my hotel is Rue Son-Cheryl-de-Peron with many restaurants, all with menus on doorway display. La Toque Blanche (The Chef's White Hat) appeals and alongside it is a restaurant serving crab Chinese style...all wonderful food awaiting me.

I hie back to my hotel for a cat-nap and at ten o'clock decide on beef-steak...every French steak I had eaten has seemed even better than the last. La Toque Blanche is packed out. I am promised to wait no more than ten minutes and they serve me a Dubonnet on the house to ensure I do.

An elegant restaurant to be sure! The dinner does not belie the promise. A seafood terrine in a sauce *d'homade* is delightful and I have a steak tartare, not mixed at the table as in Australia, but they ask what strengths of capers I prefer. Served with a simple green salad, it is superb. I find French dry red wines 'heavier' than the Penfold 389 I enjoy at home, yet tonight chance on *Chateau Meintelgris*, a *Cote-de-Bourg* wine from near Bordeaux which has me drain the bottle with consummate ease. Profiteroles complete a sumptuous meal and a *Bisquit* with my coffee tops it off...for Ff277($57).

I am really starting to fill an article for Paul, just on Eating in La Rochelle. All is wonderful stuff, and wines from Bordeaux are proving a new magnet area for me.

But I do really need to ease the pressure on spending. Maybe I should make my next visit Bordeaux rather than Provence?

At breakfast, two dear old spinster sisters from Ludlow Shropshire are at my table.

"What will you visit today?" they ask.

"I take a ferry to Minimes, from which I can photograph the pair of towers guarding the harbour entrance from that angle...the very visage British invaders experienced."

"Ye'll no get to Minimes this mornin'," says Ray in an unmistakable Humberside accent, "tide's out, mate. Ain't no ferries when tide is out."

I am to discover the tidal height here is extensive. When the meal finishes, I cross the road and instead of the Atlantic lapping on the breakwater, I am confronted with a sea of mud some six feet below me. Behind me, the little yacht harbour is safely secured behind loch-gates.

"There is an excellent aquarium there," says old Dulcy of Yorkshire.

I note it in my diary but first visit Le Tour de Chain which on Thursdays anyway, opens at 9:30am. It is indeed exciting. Brochures are available, only in French so I learn only some things. Its history, however, is told of how suffering prisoners were held in the dark dungeons that no daylight or fresh air could enter, by scratching names and dates in the stone walls...over several centuries. There are however, for those intrepid enough to make the winding climb to the tower top, stunning views of the entire city and surrounds.

In a small café I find the two old sisters, inoffensive in the extreme, at lunch. I cannot but be amazed at how adventurous they are, driving their little Ford from Yorkshire to Dover, then shipping it across the channel, to then drive it here. And they tell me they also often go to St. Malo. I note that.

After a small lunch I take the bus over the 2.9km bridge-way to Isle-de-Re, the other major site marked as *The Three Musketeers* territory.

In their day there was no bridge. They had to cope with the huge tides, to row across.

Then the island was well fortified against the British but unfortunately the ruins today guard nowt but a quiet little harbour for fishermen.

I wander through the sleepy town which I reckon has hardly changed for centuries.

Back in La Rochelle, I walk a different direction to find not large, yet with many half-timbered buildings at crazy angles where foundations had slipped or floors have rotted. All obviously remains habitable. The cobbled square is where Alexander Dumas's Musketeers had their dramatic swordfights with the cardinal's guards.

Musée Historique de La Rochelle right next to my hotel has brochures in English. It is an exceptionally well-presented display, enhancing the significance of the town's many adventures. Le Jardin de Chine serves giant crabs cooked in a piquant marinade. Clients are supplied with liberal quantities of washers and towels to clean up as you eat, for it is a fingers and fork meal of exotic taste. Every table overlooks the floodlit garden with its fountain and waterfall...indeed a gourmet's delight.

By late morning, the tide is sufficient for small ferries, so in beach gear I am off to Les Minimes. Passing between the two great towers sends wonderful little shivers down my spine. The sun shines brightly and I take my photographs of the two towers from the sea approach to the city. The two old dears had made no understatement about the quality of the aquarium. I spend an easy, few hours enjoying it, then to the beach...first time on to a beach since Greece and I enjoy it immensely. The Bay of Biscay provides a reasonable surf yet mid-autumn this far north has me shivering. The sun, however, remains soporific.

After a modest dinner as early as I can find one, I head for home.

I've enjoyed La Rochelle immensely. Its very atmosphere instils a vacation mood and everywhere service is tourist oriented, except maybe not enough English brochures explaining many sites. Everywhere one finds attentive and happy-hearted staff.

I am booked to fly Rome to Cairo on Sunday and that timing is not flexible.

Today is Wednesday and I'd love to visit St. Malo. It had a strong pasting leading up to D-Day and basically flattened but, like La Rochelle, it has a great history.

I am again amused at European trains, the numbers of dogs and cats, all restrained, behaving so well all the time. Some even have booked seats.

It isn't far to Nantes, then a train, not the smart and speedy TGV, but nevertheless comfortable, to the north coast.

~ * ~

St. Malo...

This last visit in Europe has me changing trains at Rennes. On its platform is a bookstand with a fine selection of novels in English. I purchase one. I had got into the habit of leaving finished novels on train seats or offering to strangers over breakfasts. The last daily train between here and St. Malo on workdays is a 'shuttle' commuter stopping at every tiny station to deliver working people to and from jobs, so I have lots of little villages to make notes on. Soon, however, I espy the English Channel and we draw into the St. Malo railway station.

As one steps outside, he is confronted by a huge circular garden around which runs a road and even so late in the day, it sparkles in floral colour. Opposite is the Hotel Arivee.

I am highly conscious of the fact that on Saturday I must leave very early for my train to Paris, so a hotel 'across the street' appeals. My host has as much English as my French and he finds me a room with my own shower for Ff220 ($46) including breakfast.

I had eaten so well last night that I seek a five-&-dime eatery, always a place to watch backpackers and their usual strange habits. I find one, have a satisfactory meal at a satisfactory price, then book my sleeper on Saturday's GTV Napoli Express from Paris.

It is no problem booking it, but I must train from St. Malo Saturday morning at 6:55. I can breakfast aboard that train.

Friday after breakfast I bus into the city, to be dropped alongside a stone wall of incredible height that stretches several hundred metres out to sea.

Is it part of an ancient city wall? Or just part of an old prison which the board-sign nominates? Or both? The sign merely refers to it as 'An Historical Site.'

I see parts of buildings atop it but it is still early, and despite several doorways along it, all are still closed. Maybe I am simply too early?

I cannot walk around it for modern buildings block further passage. I just keep walking and quickly find huge photographs illustrating how this particular street looked before the Allied bombings prior to D-Day when every coastal city of France was bombed. It illustrates the timely past of the city, every building obviously centuries old, nothing like the rubble now so unimpressive.

Yet even more than forty years since war's end there is still work in progress.

My Life, My Travels

I then find parts of the original town wall also under restoration, so realise St. Malo has been just a long way down the country's list of post-war restoration.

The little island Le Forte Nationale is teasingly inviting, what with a ruined castle and the tide so far out that in bare feet I can walk to it. I do so and get so thoroughly absorbed in searching that I fail to notice the tide returning. I have to quickly join others in making the best of not having to swim. And who knows which way the strength of the tide heads, directly ashore or sideways to some other neck of land? At least I don't wear jeans but shorts that even then get drenched as I wade as quickly as possible to get safely ashore in time. I add yet another strange rule to travel in safety...keep an eye on tide levels in this north coast of Europe.

Last purchase before dining at a modest café is a small padlock and chain. I leave tomorrow for Africa and have been warned that all sensible people need to take care of even bags slung over shoulders. This time my main travel bag will be handled through eastern hands before being placed on Cairo's luggage carousel into mine. I will then chain it to my wrist.

So it is back to the pub for a beer before settling my account, then to pack my bags.

~ * ~

To Rome...

At Rennes I join the TGV fast train to Paris, stopping only at Le Mans. Again, I am reminded of the tidiness of French farms. In Oz, despite how affluent might be the farmer, rusted car bodies, patched and broken farm machinery and fences are the norm. In Europe all is neat, tidy and no visual pollution to offend senses. Every European farmyard I see illustrates pride in the farm.

In Paris one can never avoid crowds. I had been sure to get myself a map of its metro for no one can travel the city except by rail. Rather than clutter traffic by buses as does London, every close Parisian suburb is connected by underground train. Today is all I can give to Paris, for my TGV for Rome departs 8:56pm and has no dining car until Torino in Italy, for breakfast. I need to be at Gare-de-Lyon at 8:30am, so before we take off, I can assure my luggage is aboard.

Seeing Paris in a few hours will be like trying to visit all of Australia in a weekend, so I carefully plan over my map. I dearly need to walk the Champs Elysées so make a half-run into the Place-de-la-Concorde. One side of me is the grand Champs Elysées and on the other, the towering Egyptian Obelisk. I turn to the Obelisk...such an amazing thing, and I shiver when realising that within a week I will be seeing its twin in its rightful home, Temple of Luxor in Egypt, where they were built three thousand years ago.

Oh what a feat it must have been, getting this obelisk prone then shipped here and having it reassembled!

To stroll up and down the Champs Elysées can take a day just noting Head Offices of many world-renowned perfumeries, jewellers and the like. With its tree-filled islands, its breadth must be the greatest in the world, leading down from the Arc de Triomphe to where I stand. I leave that thrill for another occasion and take to The Tuillerie where hundreds of people already perambulate while listening to Strauss waltzes orchestrated from somewhere.

I know there will be no dinner aboard the train, so face the difficulty of choosing in which of the garden cafés that abound around me to eat. On Rue Royale I find Le Tour Mandarin. Waiters setting tables take pity on me and feed me early.

The metro takes me quickly to Gare-de-Lyon, where I am hustled by people seeking alms. The Napolie Express is the slower of the daily sleeper trains to Rome, but I choose it because it hugs the Italian coastline of Liguria and Tuscany. The train is indeed comfortable and I have a private sleeper for Ff863 ($180) for the 17-1/2 hour journey. I bear in mind my Maggie's tale of how, when she lived her two years in Italy, aboard her overnight train there, girls had handbags stolen as they slept.

The lock I bought is on my luggage, a light chain to my wrist. It is dark as we leave, right on the promised minute so my last views of Paris are metro walls.

My Life, My Travels

Aboard the TVG, I awake at a quarter to midnight as we pull into Dijon yet am soon again in slumber. I sleep well on trains. On the dot of the 6:00am in the timetable, I awaken on arrival in Italy's Torino. The sun is already waiting for me as are the customs staff to stamp my passport, then I enjoy my only breakfast in Italy. I again see tidiness in every village on every farm, and the coastal city of Génova is so tidy it seems manicured.

I chat with the few English-speaking passengers in the lounge, all impressed with the magnetic scenery of little islands and rugged coastlines, the ocean sparkling under the morning sun like a million mirrors on the one hand, and of enviable cottages and their gardens amid a range of castle ruins on the other. On many occasions we burst from long tunnels to where vistas of houses and resorts in orange brick and terra-cotta roofs, cluster around little beaches.

Besides Génova, we stop at LaSpezia, Pisa and Livorno.

As we pull into Rome, the amiable carriage steward puts his head through my door... "Keep hands on your wallet when in *Roma*, M'seur, it is renowned for pickpockets."

My time in Rome is but to take a subway train to the airport, clearing my way through departure and buying duty-free wine for Islamic Egypt where choice and opportunity will be limited. So I need some *lira* cash. Fortunately, the conversion rate is simple, near enough to 1,000 lira to the $au.

At the station, money windows are closed for siesta but the money touts descend as we emerge through the barrier. I expect their offer is extortionate, but they do not accept Australian dollars. I must give them a $us Travel Cheque for which I get 250,000 lira which I find reasonable enough. I come away satisfied.

The entire transfer being underground, I have seen nowt of Rome.

At the airport, making the second of my only two transactions in Italy, I really find myself being cheated! At Gallaria Duty Free, my purchases come to 62,000 lira. To help quit my small currency notes, I hand over 3 notes, a 100,000 and two 1,000. I receive in change, 32,000 lira. I raise my query with the cashier, a middle-aged man who suddenly loses all the English he had been using with the lady ahead of me, to confront me with a gaggle of Italian which he knows is lost on me. However, I stand my ground and insist on a further 8,000 lira. He continues arguing in Italian until the fellow behind me puts a hand on my shoulder. He claims, in English, how he had watched me select the 102,000.

The cashier overcomes his sudden lapse of memory and I get my 8,000 liras.

I buy some pastries and when sitting to eat, that Englishman sits by me. I share my pastries with him and he repeats the need to always in Italy, count my change.

When called to board, I recall Maggie's comment in Greece about Italians also needing to be first aboard. Here is indeed a stampede. I have my seat ticket in my hand so wait and watch the snatching attempt at so many joining the queue.

Then still a smoker and used to aircraft boarding passes marked either Smoking or Non-Smoking, mine reads 'Smoking.' Aloft, Alitalia proves no more efficient in this three-hour journey, than in the duty-free store.

When I light up, I am told I cannot smoke, that this side of the aircraft is No Smoking. I show her my ticket clearly noted 'Smoking.'

"I am sorry but you cannot smoke on this side of the aircraft."

A chorus of travellers also realise they have the same problem and especially the Arabs aboard, who are many, come to my aid. The flight attendant has workmates come to assist her handle what is becoming a mob in the aisles, wanting to change seats. Yet others insist they want the view on their side, as they had ordered, and refuse to move. Somewhat further behind me, two men, I think Italian, are in fisticuffs.

Suddenly several male stewards come pushing their way quite roughly, to see to it, and just ahead of me on the other side of the aisle, a stewardess has a woman trying to nurse her baby, in tears. Two seats ahead of me on my side of the aisle, another stewardess snatches a cigarette from the mouth of a man who, like me, has a ticket marked 'smoking.'

I just wonder if this aircraft might just turn around!

Rather than encourage more unpleasantness, I return my cigarette to its pocket holder yet remain amazed at an aircraft crew taking such a rude negative stand. None tried to pacify confused passengers, simply insisted they cannot smoke.

While the little I've seen of Italy is remarkably beautiful, and its history legendary, in the few hours I've been here, its people are sneaky robbers and now this disgraceful exhibition. I am happy I shall soon be quit of it.

I doubt if I might ever feel I want to return to a country of people with such attitudes.

Twice in two wars they changed sides. Where are their spirits of mateship, honesty and guts?

Ten

Cairo…

 Touching down in Cairo, dawn is barely breaking so I've yet seen nowt of Egypt…not only a new environment but a new culture where history is more ancient than anything in my life so far…an intriguing challenge.

 Nor have I to yet again find myself arriving somewhere new and having to seek out where to abide. Insight Tours will meet me here and take me to Hotel Marriott. I am booked to attend a three-day seminar in the Cairo Museum and on my third night join an eight day tour group to upper Egypt, sharing accommodation from then with another gent. All that is prepaid.

 A great advantage of travelling alone is changing my mind on a whim and having none but myself to consider, but for the next eleven days, everything is planned for me.

 Insight Tours however, blot their copybook at the first benchmark. With luggage in hand I emerge into the airport arrivals

My Life, My Travels

hall and when finally through customs, seek out the Insight rep... with no success.

When the crowd has dispersed, I have the awkward dissatisfaction of having been 'stood up.'

I've no option but to find my own way to Hotel Marriott, but first need currency.

At the Thomas Cook Exchange Window I cash a travellers' cheque and it is a happy coincidence that the Egyptian Pound is exactly 2:1 to the $au. The clerk tells me it matters not in Egypt where I change cheques, be it at a bureau, a 5-star hotel or any bank. A fixed rate is struck daily and everywhere in the country is bound to it.

Oh, if only all countries would adopt such convenience to travellers.

When turning from the window, it happens!

My luggage is whipped from my hands.

A dozen or more fellows, all *gallabaya* clad and many wearing turban, jostle and shove, each proclaiming in a gaggle of languages that they have for me the cheapest taxi in all Egypt. A tremulous little old lady would, in such an introduction to a country, find it both frightening and intimidating. In the moment, I feel it too!

I tug at my baggage. "No you bloody don't!"

He lets go and the others let me push my way to where I hope is a taxi rank. There is and I ask the price to Hotel Marriott.

E£25. I've no idea if $au12.50 is good value or bad, but must learn as I go.

The fellow seems all right.

With a half-smile he reaches for my bag, his spare hand waving away all who had trailed me and locks it into his boot, then opens a back door for me. As he takes his seat, he introduces himself as Abdul. Alongside us at the red light is a laden bus which, as the yellow appears, and seconds before the green emerges it revs up and takes off with a noisy skid.

Abdul follows it, but without the screech. With the dawn still breaking and driving at what seems like a hundred kph, he assures me in excellent English that Hotel Marriott is the best hotel in all Egypt, like his taxi, is the best in the world. He offers me the cheapest hour rate in the country, to take me sightseeing around Cairo over the next several days. He spends the entire trip with his sales-talk.

In all my working life as a salesman, then teaching it, I would give Abdul high marks.

At the next corner, I ask if he learned to drive in Greece's Athens.

When we reach the hotel, he places his arm around my far shoulder, giving it a gentle squeeze. He pulls it away only to get my luggage and wheel it to the hotel doorman who is already approaching. I reckoned he is well worth the E£30 I pay him.

I am to find that The Hotel Marriott with 1,250 rooms is not only the largest hotel in the entire Middle East but in all Africa. It is shaped in the form of a massive flat-bottomed 'U.' The horizontal part of the U was built in 1869 as Gezira Palace to house Empress Eugenie at the opening of the Suez Canal. Gleaming brass chandeliers, some 350 of them in the public rooms alone, are polished daily by an army of cleaners. Antique paintings and restored French furniture dating from the 17th century, exquisite Persian carpets. Marble sculptures and fountains abound throughout the lounges and elaborate ceilings range in influence from baroque to traditional Islamic.

To a new arrival, the forecourt and building itself, all desert pink, is indeed imposing.

Resident rooms are in the modern twin towers comprising the vertical members of U.

Reception is not expecting me. I unfold my booking copy from Insight Tours and present it, clearly affirming my prepaid rental as of this date. The clerk scratches his head and summonses the desk manager. They then refer to the Insight booking for the eight-day tour. It affirms that I am on that schedule.

The manager, in Egyptian, obviously instructs them to quickly find me a room. He picks up a phone and telephones the Insight manager at her home, to then turn to me...

"She will ensure that you are on her list for the date on your copy."

Again, I remind other travellers to always get a copy of hotel bookings and have it in a pocket or purse on arrival.

They find me a room in the south tower, as comfortable as everything else indicating first class. The hotel brochure introduces everything available to guests including a garden map showing a large swimming pool and a huge outdoor dining area.

This most elegant hotel offers three breakfasts, a-la-carte, smorgasbord and for tour groups, a mini-early-smorgasbord. If required, any can be delivered to rooms. Being up early for my seminar, I am given leave to join the tour breakfast group.

It is affirmed that two nights are private, then I share a room with the tour group.

The three-day seminar spelling out Egypt's amazing historical buildings even before the wheel is discovered, is yet another experience to forever hang in memory. In many ways, it prepares me for the wonders of my next week's tour.

During the three days, the gentleman and his son, both formally attired in Egyptian garb sitting to my right for the seminar become so friendly that I am invited to dinner in their home once the tour is done. The father introduces himself as Ali el-Haq Da'oud, Sudan's Cultural Attaché to Egypt and his son Amr. Both speak English and French as if their natural language. Nineteen-year-old Amr has just finished university studying laser technology. Our relationship strength proves so instant that when the seminar closes at midday on its third day, Amr takes me on his motorbike, showing me parts of Cairo so close to local habitat as never included in official city tours...habitat such as the quarter where the uneducated poor people live.

"It would be dangerous for you to come here alone, Mr. Ric," Amr tells me, "but they know me. I help them get food and medical help, so they accept you as my guest."

When later sitting at their dinner table, it is explained why, when living in such elegant surroundings as their house on Gezira

Island in the middle of the River Nile in Cairo Central, I would be interested why Amr did that sort of work.

It is to bring tears to the eyes of he, his mother and very nearly too, his father.

"I am Sudanese," the father my age explains. "Egyptian law rules that every child born in Egypt automatically takes its father's nationality. Egyptian law also states that foreigners cannot take salaried jobs. So Amr, well born and well educated and even with an Egyptian born mother, can never work here in his home country. You may not know of the sad current situation in the Sudan. Any day now, it could explode in civil war and if Amr were to visit his family there again, or go there to work, he could be assassinated purely for being his father's son. Because of its political instability, no other country in the world will allow visas to Sudanese. If one person is allowed in, there would be a stampede of millions."

And, they declare, the insecurity of Sudan ensures no visa will be afforded to foreigners, even diplomats. Amr then tells me he would love to become British and raise children who are not declared Sudanese.

It is then that I see the tears in all their eyes.

Shit, what a useless future for an educated lad to look forward to!

My award-winning *A Soul Forsaken* published by Wings-ePress USA 1st July 2015 tells the entire tale, but suffice here simply say that once home I seek Australia's government to allow me to bring the lad to Australia to present him to the British Ambassador in Canberra…that as Britain held both Sudan and Egypt as colonies before granting them independence after World War 2, he at least, on a humanitarian basis, be allowed to present his plea for a visa into Britain and work there in that needful laser technology industry.

It takes a year, but I do it and win it!

~ * ~

My Egyptian tour…

My tour begins at dinner on the day my seminar finishes. Cal, an aged Johannesburg guy who will be my share-mate during the tour, is an excellent type. We meet our tour guide, Farass, a male guide with excellent English, so excellent that I name him in my airline magazine article on the tour. His knowledge of the country's history, tact and diplomacy in cultural differences are astounding. Our tour group represents Australia, Canada, South Africa and USA. We depart by train for 'upper' Egypt, 'upper' of course being 'down' south...*yet another discrepancy in our wonderful language.*

Just driving around Cairo, I am so glad I am not behind a wheel. There is not a word of English in any street name, driving direction, rule or signal. First stop is the Egyptian Antiquities Museum where I had spent my three-day seminar including the museum tour, yet I am thrilled at seeing it all again...there is so much to see and one's mind can only hold so much. The museum is again packed with visitors.

"Stay close," warns Farass to all in our group. "Keep Ric and Don in sight, for they are our two tallest."

Understandably it is the richest museum of Egyptian antiquities in the world, with 'pharaonic' treasures up to (or down to) 5,000 years old. High on the list of tour 'musts' is the Tutankhamun Gallery, its entrance flanked by man-sized statues of ebony with priceless golden skirts, footwear and head-dresses. The legendary Golden Death Mask of the Pharaoh is a highlight. The gallery is generally too crowded for comfortable viewing, yet from upstairs in the public gallery, an overview is recommended.

To describe all the museum's delights would take a book of its own, so for pretty well all the major sites of Egypt I will leave description to the many publications available. Or better still, go see them!

We drive west through the teeming city of fifteen million, the vast majority of whom live in squalor. We keep windows shut because fumes from the streets of more than seven million exhaust pipes, let alone industry, are suffocating..

West over the Nile to Giza, the first sight of 'the' Pyramids is but a haze through smog along the Shari El Ahram Boulevard. They enlarge as we get closer, yet dirt and dust in the air in which people live, is annoying. Houses and people all seem the dirty pink of the desert itself and squalor is obvious everywhere. Every house seems unfinished. On flat roofs are jumbles of tents and lean-to canvas awnings. Farass tells us Egypt is ever in trouble with accommodation for it has one of the fastest growing populations in the world. One of the reasons for flat roofs is so any family can simply build another atop the top...most often only so ignorantly built that it collapses in the next windstorm.

At the entrance to the pyramid site, we start in a bazaar/restaurant complex with a salad lunch. The three great pyramids stand proud, tempting yet forbidding. Cheops is the largest, then Chephren and Mycerinus. We visit Cheops, even explore its interior.

"We are one of the last to do so," Farass tells us. "As early as next week, Cheops will close for all time they say."

I reckon that in a future generation it will reopen once restoration is complete. It is simply too beckoning as a monument to lay dormant. Surely it has to be that there is deterioration of the interior. Being exposed to fresh air, it is surely expected that passageways must fall into disrepair.

For those wanting to inspect pyramid interiors, Mycerinus is to open in lieu. Farass stops the bus for those who want to hire camels for the approach and the Canberra family and I opt for the opportunity, for E£25. I am excited at climbing aboard a ship of the desert to approach the very essence of desert history.

It is simply so awe-inspiring to approach the sole survivors of the Seven Great Wonders of the Ancient World, particularly when aboard a lumbering camel.

We approach Cheop and I ensure that in my photographs of it, my camel's neck and ears are in the foreground.

Cheops is 137m high, 230m along each side and comprising 2-1/2 million mammoth blocks of granite, all raised without the sophistication of machinery or wheel. Once afoot again, we clamber up several of the block 'steps' and enter the tunnel single file, often having to crouch lest our heads receive a painful bump. We clamber up ramps and rough steps, bent double for in some places the passage roof is but a metre and a half in height. All about us is loose wiring and ladders where workmen are already tearing out lighting that has guided tourists for decades.

What sort of lighting could they have had when building it?

Eventually, thankful that my claustrophobia is ringing warning bells, we are in the tomb itself. Empty now, it is buried so deeply inside countless tonnes of granite it presents nowt but a sinister quiet.

I fail to find more words to describe the awe of being there.

From the pyramids it is but a 'hop' to the Sphinx standing amidst the still being excavated ruins of the ancient town. It is said that 3,733 years before Christ, her body lay hidden by sand, although her head gazed out over the desert and Nile. In the 15th century BC, Tuthmosis IV cleared away the sand and in 1905 the great paws were excavated. The body stretches 45metres and her paws are 15m long, her head 10m long and 4m wide, yet the Sphinx is small in comparison to the vast hulk of the pyramids behind her. A *Son-et-Lumière* (Sound & Light Show) in several languages is conducted around the Sphinx every night.

Back at the Marriott, I make for the pool for the temperature hangs around the 36c mark yet feels like 46c. It is stiflingly hot and the pool surrounded by garden lounges is indeed inviting. After a swim, I settle with a drink and am soon joined by group members and swim again until the kitchen sets up a poolside BBQ. As dusk descends, we decide to eat outdoors. It consists of delicious lamb kebabs with salad and rice and before retiring for a needful early night, several beers help its digestion.

My day has been almost as exhausting, as exciting!

At breakfast on day 3, I am told by fellow members they had taken Farass' advice to dine last night at Arabesque. They recommend it so wonderful that I should name it in any article I write for travellers.

~ * ~

Saqqara, Memphis and Horrenaya...

Today we are off to three ancient cities. In each of Saqqara and Memphis, excitement is high when informed they are the world's oldest surviving manmade edifices.

Saqqara is a remarkable concentration of tombs, pyramids and mortuary temples, the most significant being the stepped pyramid of Zoser, oldest still standing building in the world!

Its reducing levels represent a stairway to heaven and nearby we enter the sacred tombs of Akhethotep and Ptahotep. Firstly however, we are required to surrender cameras to the armed Tourist Police who maintain a strict vigilance throughout Egypt. At many sites we are to find flash is prohibited lest it assist deterioration of remaining colour of ancient painted treasures. Cameras are returned as we depart.

Standing by the edge of the irrigation line by the Nile where greenery gives way to sand, Memphis is today a village of adobe and thatch. North from it, the entire Nile Delta, only food basin of the country, is irrigated.

Despite the delta is but 5% of Egypt's land area, it is home to 95% of its population!

Farass announces another amazing matter of fact...Westward of Memphis to the Atlantic Ocean are five thousand kilometres. That part of Africa has not a single tree.

He points to his feet.

"The Sahara, biggest desert in the world, begins where my feet now stand."

The maze of palms we stand in, that flourish all over the east, is all dates.

My first taste of dates was in pre-school sandwiches and they remained my love of date sandwiches throughout youth.

Memphis was the original capital of Egypt dating from the 3rd millennium BC until the arrival of Greeks. There is no evidence of its former glory, but it is thought that all ruins disintegrated long ago. All that remains is a gigantic reclining statue of Ramses II and the alabaster Sphinx.

On the way back to Cairo, we call at the village of Horrenaya on the Nile where carpets are traditionally woven by children. We watch for a time as boys ten-or-eleven-years old sit and ply nimble fingers to their task with astonishing speed. We do not buy carpets but the lads are quick to let go their looms and combs long enough to hold out hands for *baksheesh please* for having posed for photographs.

Significant tips are given all.

Back at the ranch, we assemble over English tea in the garden to meet Halina Figon, who heads up Insight Tours in Cairo. She outlines what we are to see in Upper Egypt. She seeks me out and apologises for being 'stood up' at the airport. It seems that, way back in Oz when I made a change in my flight schedule for arrival in Egypt, Insight Australia failed to relay it to head office...so when I failed to turn up on the expected flight, she assumed I must have cancelled. She asked the cost of my taxi fare to the Marriott and unhesitatingly reimburses my E£25.

So, except in Australia, top marks to Insight Tours.

After 4:00pm tea, when I had restocked my E£ and a bundle of Kodachrome reels, we head for the train station and overnight journey to Aswan.

~ * ~

Egypt's Premier Train...

Wow! To give an idea of the difference between France's GTV delivering me some 1,200km Paris to Rome in 17.5 hours, Egypt's Premier line Cairo to Aswan's some 800km is about to have me aboard 21 hours, not including the hour we and a thousand others had to wait beyond agreed departure time to even start. By then it becomes a shambles of getting into our allotted carriages, let alone allotted seats.

And it's no doubt that this happens every day of every year!

Once aboard however, things for us go along more happily. Our group is eleven in number, ten tourists and Farass, while a thousand or more are still on the platform in argument of some sort. By simply smiling, Farass makes it obvious it is no surprise to him. The train is old, dilapidated, decidedly filthy and incredibly crowded, but to our cheers it finally hoots and departs.

Our ten had been filling in time looking out windows at how poor people live. We'd already been told the poor are by far, the greatest part of the population. Houses right up against the rail lines have broken windows patched with cardboard, cracked walls patched with corrugated iron sheets, broken plumbing pipes ending in nothing but space and guttering dangling lifelessly from roofs and walls.

I want to take photos yet feel it unseemly.

We all have noticed how commuter trains and buses have passenger bums projecting from every doorway. How many must get dreadfully injured or worse bypassing cars, buses or trains cannot even be guessed at.

As our train pulls into the platform so late, Farass has us all, luggage in hand, ready for jumping and claiming seats. He knows the exact platform spot where it will be, so has us primed. Despite our seats are booked, settling into them takes considerable argument. I still have my Chivas Regal and several other bottles from Rome to care for, but room partner Cal helps gain our seats. Carriage steward Mahommed threatens those having 'stolen' our seats to move out or he will have them thrown off the train.

He serves dinner on trays, and after it we fight our way to the club car where according to Farass, a party is tradition. Getting there, however, is difficult, for aisles are filled with backpackers. In all non-reserved carriages there is little control. If all seats are taken, backpackers not only sit in aisle-space but sleep in it. Without a seat-class ticket, backpackers are excluded from the 'party,' which all in our troop, once getting there, find wonderful 'fun.' Farass explains that many passengers never even get to bed because the show runs until breakfast.

We reach the party but it is a case of 'how many bodies can fit in a mini-minor.' The crush reminds me of the drag nights at *Die Timp* in Köln. At one stage a waiter, sash about his waist, belly-dances on a table, a glass of beer balancing on his forehead.

Several times the train stops for no apparent reason...Farass informs each time that "The track is under repair."

When I awake early morning, we are hove to again, which annoys Farass because it puts our programme even further behind schedule. I open my blind to see a *Fellaheen* (local farmer) astride his donkey, coming close. 'Astride' is hardly apt in that he sits bareback with a leg tucked beneath him, the other dangling in mid-air. On its other side he uses a stick to prod and tap signals on the flank, sort of 'turn right here' or a 'stop here' message. He draws up to our window, staring ahead at what soon becomes the 'up' train approaching. He is a wizened old man clad in the light blue *gallabaya* (smock) which all peasants wear, his head wound in a dirty white turban. On his feet are rope sandals. Everything about him illustrates an unconsciousness of time or purpose. I take a couple of photographs for my 'slides' album.

At Luxor, where we will spend several days on the return trip by mini-bus, a vast number of passengers exit, yet as many replace them. We shall not arrive in Aswan until late this afternoon or thereabouts...maybe.

While half our group retires to the passenger lounge for coffees, the other half sit with Farass as he answers our several questions about Egyptian life and adjusts our distorted programme. I sip tea while watching out the window, amazed at many of the villages. Nowhere is there colour other than the dirty sand that swirls in the wind and seems to settle on houses, animals, the few trees and the people. Only the brilliant blue of the sky, with not a wisp of cloud offers relief from the relentless desert. Every house is built with mud bricks and has no roof, just sparse space and here and there a few dried palm fronds to offer shade.

"Who needs a roof in a climate where it never rains?" Farass asks. "It last rained in Upper Egypt five years ago, but lasted a minute and a half. No rain entered a house for it evaporated before hitting ground. Prior to that incident it hadn't rained in eight years."

It is incongruous, however, to see TV antennae and electric light poles in villages. They all have power, we are told, TV and refrigerators and a few have washing machines. Water is laid on, if not into every house yet, but in most. Others make do from a central village tap for water pumped up from the Nile. West of the Nile, except for a few odd places, there are no villages in Upper Egypt. Most homes are equipped with a corral or at least a yard for donkeys, goats and buffalo. No house has flooring so most creatures have run of the house.

The pace of life here is indeed slow. Along the river, inside the line of irrigation, is agriculture. A distinct line divides the green of irrigated land from the desert and the green is fed from sluice channels. As it has been for thousands of years, water from the Nile is drawn up by leather bags of a *saqia,* a water-wheel turned by plodding buffalo, a lad with a cane idly keeping them at their constant slow pace. The *shaduf,* a weight-pivoted pump which creaks as it did when the pharaohs sailed by on their barges all that time ago, sluices the water from one channel to the next.

Our Upper Egyptian tour begins on getting to Aswan, end of the train-line and where the Nile broadens into Lake Nasser extending to the Sudanese border 250km south to which there is no road, only dry desert. Here we pick up a mini-bus to visit on the way back to Luxor, many 'left-overs' from Egypt's historical past.

Other than spending a few more days on a private tour of Cairo, I then complete my journey. So for me, the 'big-stuff' now begins.

~ * ~

Upper Egypt...

We arrive in Aswan at 2:30pm instead of 11:00am and the heat hits like a sledgehammer. The air-conditioning aboard the train works for some of the time, certainly enough to ward off the worst of the heat, yet we are unprepared for the stifling conditions of Aswan.

Only three, Ailsa, her mother Marilyn of Calgary, Canada and me, are booked for the extended *Insight Tour* to visit the country's two most spectacular temples approachable only by aircraft or the tediously slow Nassa Lake ferry over the additional 300km. Abu Simbel is Egypt's most southerly historical site, all but on the Sudanese border.

Modern demands for water in both Egypt and Sudan meant the Nile River must be dammed between Egypt's Aswan and Sudan's Wadi Halfa. Such, however, meant Abu Simbel and its 3,000-year-old pair of monumental temples, largest in the country, must be sacrificed. How to save them?

Only by manually lifting them up from their present site and restoring them above what will be the new waterline, a venture declared impossible.

Other than the two temple entrances, they are hand carved into a thick vertical rock wall. The mammoth stone 'bricks' to be raised are each up to 30 tons. Broken up into moveable 'monster-bricks,' they had to be hauled atop the proposed water level and rebuilt... *Cutting every inch without damaging even the slightest of hand-hewn rock!*

They did it 1964 through 1968...the biggest and most spectacular dismantling and reassembling project ever undertaken. I just had to go see it.

The plan for the three of our group making this additional trip is to fly on the afternoon of our arrival, from Aswan to Abu Simbel, take the four hour tour, then take the night flight back to Aswan. The train delays however, makes this timing impossible. Inspections are morning and afternoon. We three must rise at 4:00am to take the very early flight albeit in the dark and undertake the four hour tour, then fly back at mid-day in order to take in the Aswan sites and still get as many hours on the return road in our mini-bus, same day.

We expect to find it exhausting, but even the aged Marilyn insists on joining her daughter and me.

First job after arriving at Aswan is to check in at the 5 Star Aswan Oberoi Hotel on Elephantine Island, secluded in that it can be reached only by ferry. There, it is quiet all around, for the island has no land traffic. The Nile here is much narrower, of course, yet more interesting in that the native *feluccas* with their huge single sail ply southwards on the everpresent northerly breeze or drift north on the ever-flowing current. They are a delight to watch. The island is the site of Pharaoh temples which also had to be raised, the last habitable landfall below the old cataracts. They were as an effective barrier to travel by river as is now the High Dam.

A little lad at the hotel, no more than 7 or 8 years of age, resplendent in his elegant uniform, opens or closes the front door for guests and totes their luggage to their rooms. Cal and I first encounter him as we leave the lift to our room. The lad greets me with *"Ezayak"* and grasps my heavy leather bag to huff and puff, dragging it to my door where with great aplomb takes my door key, opens the door and invites me inside. I tip him 50 piastres (25 cents) and the little eyes widen and glisten before he bows almost to his toes before shuffling in that bent manner, backwards out the door. He straightens up before finally departing to proffer a practised salute. Each time I see him afterwards at his front-door post, he greets me with a bow or salute.

However, our party is under strict instruction to move at the double. We have time to make up if we are to miss nothing of the planned itinerary, to make some visits this afternoon instead of tomorrow. So it is quickly on to the hotel ferry and across to the town where our minibus awaits. We drive quickly north where boatmen shuttle us along the mighty Lake Nasser to the Ptolemaic Temples of Philae on Agilkis Island.

Lake Nasser, a product of the Aswan High Dam completed in 1971 is 500km long and up to 50km wide in places, a huge freshwater expanse.

Our boatmen are the blackest of black people, in fact shining ebony, and their physique is a magnificent specimen of manhood… Nubians, inhabitants of the Nile further south, the land now inundated by the dam. Farass explains they are an extremely proud people sad at losing their home and family burial grounds of countless generations. They fiercely cling to their own language and having so much hate for Egyptians for having destroyed their homeland, many moved further south to Wadi Halfa in Sudan.

The temples of Philae are doubly marvellous, firstly for their antiquity, their history, the larger being dedicated to the God Isis and her son Horus (my 'hero') the falcon god of the skies and the smaller to Hathor. The temples are also marvellous in having been so laboriously moved stone by amazing stone from the valley floor before the water began to rise, deep water now covering their original site. Agilkis Island in fact was reshaped to truly reflect the original island of Philae.

We nearly expire in the heat, the elderly of tour-mates having a hard time of it yet never complaining. Old Marilyn continues to ask stupid questions and Farass continues to handle them with admirable patience...

"Is this old or did someone just build it to look old?" she asks of a refreshment kiosk on the edge of the site.

But my large hiccup? The film in my camera seizes and will wind neither forwards nor backwards...a major necessity in my even being here in the middle of a desert!

The hotel recommends a particular shop in town..."But it closes in fifteen minutes."

I race to the wharf and frantically watch the ferry almost having to tack from the strong northerly breeze, ply ever so bloody slowly across the Nile towards me. In the fading light, *felluccas* and *sambuk* (small fishing boats) would make ideal photographs. *How bloody sad!*

By the time I reach the far bank and run to the shop, every soul in the street stares at this stupid white man running. It is open but the miserable cameras available are of no use to me.

Because I fly out before dawn tomorrow to see the most magnificent of all Egyptian temples, a highlight of my trip, I am desperate!

I choose the best they have.

"What? You don't take Diners Club?"

They take only Egyptian pounds in cash.

"No, there are no facilities to change any sort of card or cheque open at this hour."

The hotel will change my Traveller's Cheque but this shop closes in 30 minutes.

The only thing working for me in the moment is the gleam in his eyes when realising he is making a good sale. I tell him the only way I can pay is for him to keep his door open while I change a cheque across river at the hotel. Yes, he will wait until I get back.

Can I trust him to repair my camera overnight without exposing the photographs already taken? I bloody have to trust him because I have three whole days in Luxor and need my better camera for that.

"If you can fix my camera overnight and print out for me every photo that is on that first half, I will not only pay for that service, even though I pay for this new camera now, I will give it back to you for your shelf stock. But it must be every photograph on my spool and I will know if any is missing."

After ensuring he understands, I return to the ferry which had waited for me. During the trip back, for which I tip the driver for making so many special trips, I go straight to the lounge. Cal and I had asked Farass to be our guest for drinks in the lounge before dinner as we want to pump him with more questions. For the occasion he forsakes the western garb he had been wearing and has already arrived in a formal *gallabaya* though has dispensed with the traditional turban. And he is happy to drink beer.

"I find no enjoyment in the wine you people enjoy, but I do like beer."

Does that make him a 'maligned' Muslim?

We learn much about Egypt's fears over maintenance…"With the dam now giving us additional power as well as additional water to increase gardens, the lack of seasonal floods gives 'down river' farmers a lack of silt to wash salt away. Rising salt tables crumble the stonework of ancient temples."

He is very worried about the future.

On our present tour he leans close and lowers his voice…"That Marilyn woman needs watching. She has this habit of wandering off on her own and getting lost. If you do not get that flight back here tomorrow night, Ric, the entire group will have to have another night here and we miss out on much of the history Luxor has for us."

On the morrow he reminds me, "I have given your name to the English language guide up there and he will meet your flight. But please keep your eyes on Marilyn. Whatever you do tomorrow, Ric, ensure you three are on that evening flight back here!"

~ * ~

Abu Simbel...

Our wake-up call at 4 for a flight leaving at 4.30 means we miss breakfast. Farass has coffee with us and slips packets of bread and cheese into our hands. He gives me the three plane tickets for both flights.

He stares into Marilyn's eighty-year-old face. "If you wander off anywhere on your own up there, my dear, there is every likelihood you will be whisked off to some slave market to serve as a white concubine, never to be seen again."

He winks to Ailsa and me and wishes us a happy Abu Simbel visit.

This would be my first experience of flying with Egypt Air and I am anxious to see how it performs. It is yet to fly me Luxor-Cairo, then Cairo-Bangkok.

The plane is late, of course. Ailsa and I sit, both with eyes glued on Marilyn.

There are no seat allocations, so when told to board it is every man for himself, but there is a wide choice. We have no luggage, so I first ensure Marilyn is at a window and Ailsa on the aisle. The flight is short and gives a wonderful sweep over the temples...an absolutely dramatic sight!

As daylight breaks further, we board nominated buses and are warned to ensure on return to reboard the same bus. All are numbered. By the time we reach the temples, Marilyn complains of her balance reeling. The heat is proving too much for the old Canadian woman. By the time we had walked half the several hundred metres, she is convinced she can go no further..."I must have shade in which to sit and wait for you."

The only shade is back at the bus stop. Ailsa opts to return, sit her in the bus with the driver, then catch me up. I cross my fingers.

She finds me okay but with the alarming news that the bus is locked and there is no sign of the driver. She had sat Marilyn under a shady tree and told her not to move.

We cross fingers.

The temples are indeed mind boggling. When the military decided to rid the kingdom of the child King Tutankhamun and killed him, three kings later, RamsesII of the 19th Dynasty, 3,200 years since, proved the greatest of builders. He here built a temple dedicated to himself and alongside, another for wife Nefertari. Neither was 'built' other than their spectacular entrances were literally carved by hand into the rock cliff walls. Words are inadequate to describe its inside. A particular point not advised by Farass is that a camera-flash inside the temple means confiscation of camera.

What hurts more is that the bastard camera-shop man must know this yet used my ignorance to drag additional £sd from me. I'm almost hoping I can find fault in his saving the first half reel of film...maybe I will.

Back to travel, however, I am utterly dismayed how way back then, all these great chambers were, without machinery, carved with such brilliance. Apart from sophisticated entrance doorways on the outside, every chamber had been carved with not only high ceilings, but including lavish rock furniture, lavishly dressed human figures, their jewellery and pet animals...entirely complete atmospheres, all without modern tools, then painted, much of the paint still colourful.

Back to the present...Before the valleys were flooded, the original temples were, with machinery for sawing through solid rock and modern hand-held electric tools to ensure perfection in exacting details, severed into massive blocks to be hauled atop... an incredible feat when the façade of each temple is 33m high, guarded by four statues of Ramses II each 20m high. Inside are twelve chambers extending 200m into the mountain and 30m in width. In the main chamber eight more mammoth statues of Ramses soar into the heights of the ceiling.

Outside, but 30km from the Sudanese border, Ailsa and I and many others nearly die of sunstroke. All hasten for the shade of our bus to happily find Marilyn dutifully waiting. Ailsa and I are anxious to arrive on time, yet reckon all others hope the cool air in the plane would prefer a longer flight.

When the bus drops us at the wharf for the hotel ferry, the driver informs us we must hurry. Farass had told him it was urgent we get away in our minibus to Luxor.

I whisper that I need my camera and if he waits I will give him a bottle of beer. He waits.

Yes, he had fixed my camera and saved all that was on the reel, so I return his new camera and sort of half ran back to the wharf. At the hotel, all others are waiting with the impatient Farass, our luggage already having been packed and left with him. We three wanted something to eat and because the plane had been late, so we miss lunch as well as breakfast. Farass understands but needs to leave NOW!

He promises to stop at a take-away food store 'somewhere' down the road. He does, and two of our three Abu Simbel team anyway, reckoned Farass had done a good job in ensuring we missed none of the Abu Simbel wonders, despite how late had been the overnight train. As our mini-bus made the best of a badly damaged road, Cal produces his mouthorgan and we have some community singing.

~ * ~

Kom Ombo, Idfu & Isna...

On a broad sweep of river 50km north from Aswan is Kom Ombo, a Ptolemaic temple dedicated to both the Crocodile God Sobek and the God of the Morning Sun, Haroeris. Many extremely intricate carvings are particularly well preserved there.

A further 60km north is Idfu, site of the temple Horus (my hero again), God of the Skies. It began building in 237BC and was not completed until 57BC. It remains one of the best-preserved temples in Egypt...my 'hero' seems a perfect 'God.'

Before leaving, I will try to find a model of him for my china-cabinet.

The sun beats unmercifully as we scamper from one shady patch to the next. All agree we dare miss nothing. All those who had earlier denied hats buy wide brim ones and make improvised fans from brochures. Marilyn, beyond walking in the heat, waits in the bus. We all by now have learned to carry plenty of bottled drinking water.

Along the road is ample evidence of the thin-green-agricultural-line along the river, beyond which the desert stretches to both lateral horizons. Here the *fellaheen* can literally stand with a foot in each of lush plantation and burning desert!

When others complain of hunger, our unscheduled stop for food is at Isna, the only place Farass can stop for food westerners can eat. "I was once told by an Englishman that the food Egyptians prefer is little short of goat's droppings garnished with blowflies."

He explains as we approach Isna that the only available meat may be sheep's lamb when available, camel or goat, all of which are considered delicacies. Few farmers have chicken. The average *fellaheen* family eats only with a salad of green peppers stuffed with rice, oranges, tangerines and bananas of various types.

At our café, the host has only local language so everything is translated by Farass. "Here," he explains as darkness settles in, "we have a choice of goat's liver sandwich or Mars Bars." The ladies groan, rub their bellies and most opt for Mars Bars.

While my goat's liver cooks, mine-host sets down a hookah, the traditional water-pipe smoker for Farass who sits by me, and a plate of sweetmeats to share. Marilyn's eyes pop at just the sight of food and dives into the sweetmeats, little grey balls with a marshmallow texture. Farass moves closer to me so she can fit on the other side of him and the three of us together empty the plate.

"What was that?" I ask him of the sweetmeat dish.

"Goat's eyes, Ric."

When my sandwich arrives, it is very dry bread which doesn't appeal, yet the goat liver is tasty. I make no comment on the goat's eyes, but Marilyn vomits.

We arrive at Luxor as the sun sets, light enough to see the river is indeed busy, many wharfs and many ships, two being tourist liners. The city's industrial and residential areas across the river look large.

Farass sighs… "At last we are back on schedule."

My Life, My Travels

~ * ~

*Luxor **aka** El Uqsur...*

Farass anxiously sees us installed in Hotel Isis and welcome sights await us. From our balconies are views of the broad expanse of the Nile. Between us and the river is the most inviting of swimming pools by lots of lounge seats under colourful umbrellas. It is a quick change and into the water for several of us and as the daylight finally exhausts itself, I realise how long has been my day, and how much of it on busy feet. I pass up invitations to join others having dinner in the town and opt for a poolside grill. Cal goes with them but despite it being even after sunset, the day is stinking hot and I want to spend more time in the pool, and then to eat afterward.

After a comfortable dinner with a couple of beers, I happily lie back on a garden lounge beside the exotic Nile and fall sound asleep.

When awoken by Cal and helped up to our room, I am quickly again, in sleep.

~ * ~

Day 6 dawns and a full programme awaits. At breakfast we note that Farass has spirited our minibus to the west bank of the Nile, so after eating we cross to it by ferry and drive to Deir El Bahri and the Mortuary Temple of Queen Hatshepsut. She ruled as Pharaoh for 20 years from about 1490BC and is generally referred to as queen despite insisting she was both sexes. Like the Abu Simbel temples, this is carved into the side of a mountain, the other side of which is the Valley of Kings. Into this side, however, at the end of a long and obviously decorated causeway are built three pillared terraces with colonnades leading into great halls and chambers, the wall reliefs depicting the queen's life and times. It lends particular emphasis on marine ventures, clearly illustrating the craft crews and even their cargoes of gold and jewels, incense trees and even how the obelisks were brought from Aswan to Thebes.

Despite these particular hieroglyphs being worn, much detail remains evident. Ahead of the massive barge with three rows of deck to support great weight, thirty-two craft tow it, men in the leading boats with poles testing river depth. Estimates of the laden barge put the weight as high as 5,000 tonnes. The hieroglyphs also depict details of sea battles, the men's uniforms, the process of battle, the arms etcetera, considerably more graphic than could any manner of ancient writing have illustrated.

In the Valley of the Kings we are briefed on several tombs considered the most worthy visits and are left to 'cruise' the exhibits for some hours. More than sixty tombs have to date been discovered in this valley, which dates to the 2nd millennium BC and some are open for inspection, flash photography again disallowed. Many tombs are vast complexes of halls and corridors, walls and ceilings decorated with religious ritual and etchings of the pharaoh's life and possessions. In Tutankhamun's tomb in particular, paintings on walls of the burial chamber remain in good condition. Sites of tombs were ever intended as sacred…where he could lie in peace while his spirit lives into the hereafter on the fruits of the wealth buried with him. Most of the known tombs have, over the centuries, been plundered.

Biggest and most colourful of the tombs I visit is of Ramses VI, yet the most interesting is of Horomheb, not a pharaoh but a general who murdered Tutankhamun to take his throne. They really buried this fellow…down, down, down we creep, ever conscious that we must climb back up…

"Why doesn't someone put an elevator in here," comments a lady from Louisiana.

On departing the Valley, walking back to search among the throng for our bus, we are besieged by an army of souvenir hawkers, those I generally wave away and try to ignore. I limit my number of souvenirs yet I had made up my mind that one I really want is an alabaster statue of Horus, heavy to lug, but my 'essence' of Egypt.

It invites disaster to even hint interest, for an absolute mob clusters about you with their hand-hewn pieces, never accepting 'No' for an answer. One has just what I want and he is chanting "One hundred pounds, sahib, one hundred pounds."

I keep waving him away.

"Fifty pounds, sahib, fifty pounds."

I keep waving him away.

"My children will starve, sahib, but twenty-five pounds, twenty-five pounds."

Farass had told us that these hawkers, their wives and children make their products for which the material costs nothing. "So their only cost," he explains, "is the time making them. Every penny in a sale is better business than getting nothing."

"Done," I tell him and every other worrisome creature gives up, to harass others.

Back in the bus I show my Horus to Farass who tells me it is a well-made piece for which he would have been happy to pay more.

Wow, but is that what he tells every client? I don't care because I simply love it. Right now in 2020, I have sat Horus right here on my desk, watching what I write!

Because we had to pass it, Farass stops at the mortuary temple of Ramesus III whose great deeds included repulsion of invading Libyans in 12th century BC.

We stop again at the Colossi of Memnon, two enormous statues of Amenhotep III, 3,400 years old (14 centuries before Cleopatra) which once guarded the entrance to his now vanished mortuary temple, but stands lonely in an open field. Each tower measures 18m above the plain, their shoulders a massive 6m, fingers each 1m long. All is carved from a single block of granite.

The Temple of Luxor stands in the centre of the modern city, created by Amenophis III in 1500 BC (XVIIIth Dynasty) and extended to Ramses II. At the entrance to the court of Ramses stands his colossal statue of 1,000 tonnes. The Temple of Luxor is sometimes referred to as the temple of columns, 214 in all, intricately carved and many with headstones still in place, original colour preserved in the dry Upper Egypt atmosphere. The massive obelisk standing tall on its pedestal is twin to that stolen by France in 1830 and now stands in Paris's Place de la Concorde...the site of the famous guillotine.

Farass points out the Islamic mosque built over the courtyard of Ramses II in the 14th century and used for prayer ever since. "I worshipped here this very morning."

He points too, to the stains on the walls of the temple, worrying signs of the rising water table and salt erosion.

At a tourist market we are let loose to browse. Who do we lose? Yes, poor Ailsa takes her eyes off her mother and off goes Marilyn. A half hour later, a new blow to Farass' timetable, she is found in another group's bus, her arms laden with papyrus paintings and a stone God, thinking that bus was bound for Calgary.

After a long day, it is home to the ranch for a swim and dinner in the hotel.

Day 7 is our last temple and our farewell to Upper Egypt.

The Grand Temple of Karnak, dedicated to Amen-Ra and originally named *Ipet-esut* meaning Most Esteemed of Places, is the largest religious monument in the world, its circumference exceeding 4km (the imperial students claim its area is 137 square acres). Karnak was built by Amenophis III and extended by Thothmes III who added riches gleaned from his 17 invasions of Asia. Far eastern plants bloom in the formal gardens and instead of the common reed, exotic wildfowl flutter amongst tropical flowers. Two sacred lakes are still in evidence, although today are fouled by rising salt. Huge obelisks grace the temple, red granite of Aswan 200km upriver, the biggest of them 30 incredible metres high and weighing 323 incredible tonnes.

Oh, imagine the problems of getting them all this way downriver?

On our flight back to Cairo, I think long and hard about the Egypt I have seen, and somehow it is difficult to avoid feeling jaded at the sheer age and size of its monuments. Any one of them standing alone could earn itself the title of 'a wonder of the ancient world.' Indeed, what I have seen is wealth of such history…incredible monument after incredible monument to boggle my mind. The sheer extent seems too much to properly absorb. I am thankful for my microtape recorder that retains so much to write about and to relive year after year.

Nothing can strip from me the awe-inspiring magnificence of Egypt's history and I have seen but a fraction of it. Admittedly much money comes from international aid, for Egypt is a poor country, but the dedication in preserving present sites must be admired. Thousands upon thousands of Tourist and Antiquities Police are employed to

My Life, My Travels

maintain vigilance against those who would deface or desecrate the monuments for souvenirs. Miscreants are treated none too gently... find themselves quickly and roughly, in gaol.

Let me warn those who seek to save the cost of tour agents, to travel to Egypt independently...

"You are foolish!" You will find yourselves misguided and robbed every turn you make. And when packing, be sure to pack the right attitude. Throughout the Islamic world you will be pestered by hawkers in a situation you cannot master.

~ * ~

My solo look at Cairo...

Our tour finishes with breakfast at the Marriott, but I have two further nights booked as a single to visit a few sites missed when with young Amr Ali el-Haq Da'oud.

Farass had left us as soon as we had been reinstalled in the Marriott last night to pick up his car and drive to his farm in The Delta. Halina Figon, general manager of Insight Tours waited to 'sign off' on behalf of responsibility for her tourists as from tomorrow's breakfast, and also to sit with me for a matter of minutes. We had a confidential agreement that I would report my impressions on her company's tour.

In my own experience as a GM, feedback on company performance is ever welcome.

"I have three comments to report, Helina. Firstly, thank you for obtaining my extra nights in the hotel here at your company discount rate; secondly that I give you top marks on planning your tours. The only problem raised by most was the lack of at least a little western style food available on the mini-bus journey, but that is the only complaint I heard. You are fortunate in having Farass, who works his butt off to overcome seemingly helpless problems. None of our ten failed generosity in what we put in the leather purse I passed around. You have a wonderful asset in that man."

Cal and I, both tired, dine lightly in the garden restaurant and have an early night. Robed waiters buzz between tables and date-palms, the very atmosphere a consciousness of ensuring travellers are content. I choose *Niefa* (marinated grilled goat ribs) with

Tamia (bean-cakes fried in oil), rice and salad. *Kissra* is the thin unleavened bread for sopping up juices but only by the right hand. The left hand is for personal hygiene. Egyptian coffee is always a delight.

Having farewelled the rest of our group, I plot my day…I shall tread across the Nile via the Kubri-6 October and grope my way to the renowned Groppi's Café and dally there before generally getting a measure of the city's people treading street after street of cinemas and shops. After such a strenuous eight days, I will take it easy today.

The Shari El Qasr El Nil is a busy boulevard in this largest city in Africa, dating back to 640AD, thronged with an enigmatic mix of old and new everything, smart young women in chic gear brushing sleeves with turbaned men strolling hand in hand, their covered wives three paces behind. All is hubbub and honk as noisy traffic sprays choking fumes that the crowd seems not to notice and people weave in and out as motorbikes laden with parcels mount footpaths in order to beat the traffic snarls. Here and there a donkey cart stands stubbornly in the centre of the melee slowly unloading stores, unheedful of the chaos it causes.

Groppi's Café stands on the busy Midan Tala'at Harb where traffic policemen face futile odds. For an hour sitting over coffee and baklava, I feel as if in a kaleidoscope funnel, odd shapes swirling by…Here a sheik steps down from his limousine, wives and children falling in behind, there a beggar spreads his mat in a gutter to grovel alms. Beside him a street vendor hawks Kofta and Kebabs. At kerb tables, businessmen parley their contracts over hookahs.

The frantically busy Shari Tala'at Harball, the way to the Midan O'rabi where stand the Grand Hotel and Royal Palace, teems with people, cafés, fast-food stalls, retail stores, movie theatres and forever honking traffic. Holding hands permanently on the horn is undoubtedly an art of which every driver is proud, be he in his car, taxi, bus or transport vehicle. The cacophony of pitch and tone is an ever-present intrusion in one's ears.

I leave the hubbub, not consciously, for I have no idea what lies ahead or around any corner. I know only that my sense of direction tells me left is towards the river and The Marriott. Not that I am anxious to return, despite somewhat footsore as the temperature continues to climb, but I know that by the time I get there I will be ready for rest.

By mid-afternoon my stomach is howling for lunch. I find a vendor with magnificent peaches and nectarines. I buy one each for 20 cents and suffer enormous guilt as I must run the gauntlet of dirty people and children begging for something to eat.

If I buy something for any one, I will be stampeded by thousands.

Close to the hotel I find a 20cm x 25cm black man painting on a cork sheet background in a glass frame with metal corners, a magnificent impression of Rameses II. I had seen them in Luxor but worried about getting anything glass-bound home without breakage. But on this second sight I weaken and it is cheaper here than it had been in Luxor. I buy it and today it proudly stands in my home alongside Horus.

Next morning it is a smorgasbord breakfast and I have but two objectives: the Khan El Kalil Markets, a 'must' on any Cairo tour calendar, not that I want to buy anything more, yet these markets are legendary. And I discover why...

Had I believed the kaleidoscope of humanity passed me at Groppi's Café yesterday, I am sure this is where they were bound. Every rascal, honest trader, gullible buyer and astute buyer, is here with a seemingly unending product range. It is a warren of lanes and alleys covering an area of several city blocks, surely the largest bazaar in the world, where I could easily spend days searching, discovering, learning and trying to find my way out.

Hopefully in a future time, I will allow a full day here rather than a half.

After a salad luncheon, I taxi to The Citadel, the great fortress built in 1176 by the renowned sultan Saladin of Crusade Wars fame. Within its precincts is the alabaster faced Mosque of Mohammed Ali who ruled Egypt for the Ottoman Turks at the turn of the 1800 century. He is renowned for inviting all the *Mamluk* princes, early traditional enemies, to a banquet. As they in their magnificent finery ride into the courtyard, the portcullis crashes down and waiting marksmen kill every one.

The Citadel is another monument which must be left to guide books to do justice, for simply the study of its centuries of history is almost a lifetime of dedication.

The Citadel stands oblivious to all else, simply gazing down on Cairo City.

I can only report on The Cairo Marriott, the biggest hotel in the entire Middle East earns its 5 Star reputation, expensive but one with more client-comfort attention than any in the world I know. In 2020 I am still of that mind.

~ * ~

My last words on Egypt…

I find it more difficult to leave than arrive…yes, even than having my luggage snatched out my hands without anyone policing such an outrageous practice.

I've two big hints for those travelling in the Egypt I find in 1990…

*Ensure on entering that you declare personal items like camera, lap-tops etcetera or you will have difficulty getting them out when departing without paying export tax.

*It is illegal to take Egyptian money out of the country; you must take it to the exchange window **before** having your passport stamped ie: **before** going to the duty-free store.

Now for the typical Egyptian crunch! With the exchange window stationed **before** getting to the duty-free store, you will find that that store does not accept either credit cards or foreign cash. You must have Egyptian pounds.

!?!?!?

Believe it or not?

I simply hope one day soon, someone realises that futile situation.

Eleven

Bangkok, Thailand...

Cairo to Bangkok is an eight and a half hour hop and after four hops with Egypt Air, I have little to applaud. My departure is a half-hour behind schedule and in the 8-1/2 hour flight we sight the crew twice. First is to hurry down each aisle 'tossing' a mediocre meal in each lap. Second is to hurry past collecting dinner trays. For the rest they simply, having landed, hibernate somewhere until opening the doors. There had been no checking for safety belts on take-off nor for landing. In fact, on landing, several male passengers were sitting on aisle-armrests as we hit the ground; one fool falls to the floor. The plane has no 'service-please' buttons and if one wants a drink it is a case of "Go to the kitchen and ask." The only drink available is water in plastic bottles. They do offer straws.

By the time I am through customs it is 1:00am. At the hotel booking desk I ask for a B Class hotel in or near Patpong as my tourist handbook of the day recommends (thank both Buddha and God that tourist reference books have improved since 1990), so I take the airport bus that fortunately is able to drop me and my by now extremely heavy piece of luggage and two bottles of wine I had bought at the Bangkok Duty Free store and yes, I am at last able to buy on my credit card.

They put me into the Bangkok Palace at $us40 per night which they assure me is an easy walk to Patpong. It is 2km. A tuk-tuk (pronounced took-took), a three wheeled motorbike with roof and a seat that with a crush, holds three small people. Unless agreeing a price prior to boarding, you will be robbed. Realising you don't know how far is your goal, they take you in a circuitous route and charge you by time. Always ask at your hotel desk the fair price of a tuk-tuk to your goal, for on leaving the door of any hotel you will face a score of babbling faces. You tell them how much you will pay and you can safely choose from those remaining.

All I had been told about Thailand is by one of our group in Egypt. Other than that, street fumes are as bad as Cairo's and that the Patpong night market is worth visiting for clothing and excellent painted artwork. I can quickly add that strolling city streets in the evening, one has brochure after brochure pushed under your nose.

I decide to give it a few days because I'd also been told to try Thai Air.

For one half-day tour I rent a limo so I can tour with closed windows with a lady guide named Oddy, to show me major temples. Buddhism comprises 95% of Thailand's 60 million and their temples are praised. Right alongside the Grand Palace of a country claiming to be the only one in the world never to have been under foreign rule, is Wat (Thai for 'Temple') Phra Chetuphon which houses the gigantic Golden Reclining Buddha, 46m long and 15m high. At 10 baht ($2 in 1990) it is a very cheap entrance. Oddy then drives me to a jewellery factory and joins me to watch the seemingly magical fingers of both men and women, mostly young, doing the finger-work. She mysteriously disappears and a salesman takes over, bowing and smiling and asking which diamond ring or brooch I will buy for my cherished one at home.

I find Oddy having her nails painted, slap a $au10 note in her lap and take a tuk-tuk to my hotel, annoyed with myself for having falling into a stupid trap...I'd done no homework on Thailand before giving a 'stranger' a free hand to fleece me.

I spend the rest of the day walking and nearly suffocate with traffic fumes, yet am enthralled. Putting the bad vibes aside, I realise there is much in Thailand to see and no doubt enjoy. I go to the Thomas Cook office and they give me a booklet explaining how this 'two-class society' (indicating the middle class is yet emerging) struggles to join the 'tourist' market.

I have been in only its major city, which claims eighty percent of the country's secondary industry, that the rest is farmland, mostly rice. The population has two major classes, exceedingly rich and exceedingly poor. The middle class is still emerging and education is in dire need of westernising. So have I been judging my first few days with the wrong attitude?

Six years later I am to, only because I know it is cheap, use Bangkok for a two-year assignment to write two particular books. I let out my home to holiday makers. Alone with both kids in different states in their own married lives, I discover there is so much to learn of this Thailand. Those two years have become twenty-four and the two books so far, twenty-seven.

I'm still here and at 90, still, it seems, writing, yet I doubt further travelling.

Another significant experience is flying Thai Air. On this 3-month tour, I have flown eleven flights with seven different airlines. Thai Air and Swiss Air have both been as efficient and courteous on the ground as in the air...all others have been better in one and poorer in the other or poor in both. Since then I have remained wherever possible, with Thai Air.

I thoroughly enjoy my first adventure intending to both study some of my family history and seeking information worth assisting other travelling adventurers.

It's been a pretty lopsided result, yet a wonderful one.

BOOK THREE

South America

March – May 1992

Columbia
Peru
Bolivia
Paraguay
Argentina
Chile
Easter Island *(Rapa Nui)*

Plus a few words on Tahiti

Twelve

And that inverted Bowl we call the Sky,
Whereunder crawling coopt we live and die,
Lift not they hands to IT for help—for It
Rolls impotently on as Thou or I.
      —*Rubáiyát of Omar Khayyám #LII*

  In February 1992 I suffer a nasty travel setback, quickly followed by a wonderfully positive one.
  A pain in the gut to a 63-year-old guy who hasn't been in hospital since a kid with something simple, and since been thankful for never having a sick day off work, suddenly becomes a threat to my programmed life. After three days in an IC coma and a fourth for what they call 'good luck,' I have ten days in ward-care. I'd had half my gut removed with cancer of the bowel and they tell me I must start changing many ways of life. When out of my coma, first thing I am conscious of is having been fitted with a colostomy bag. They tell me it is highly likely I must wear it for the rest of my life.

"We cannot know until we see how your body reacts to bowel evacuation. I'll need to measure you weekly, then monthly. By mid-year we should have things clear."

What they had failed to take into account is my determination!

"Sorry Doc, but I fly to South America next month."

He nearly explodes…"Simply not possible, I need to…"

I switch off, putting hands over ears. After a little more exchange, I say, "Doc, I understand all that, but I have been offered the greatest opportunity of my life and I have already grasped it. It's an unfinished assignment."

I can save a lot of preamble here if only to give you, dear reader, the result…

Bloody hell, I already have so many visas stamped in my passport, so three weeks later, wearing no colostomy bag but packing lots of medication and seventeen pages of the surgeon's explanation of my operation, including diagrams, that should I get any pain I should immediately go to that city's biggest hospital and ask them to read it.

On my flight and every one since, I've ensured having an aisle seat near a toilet and I've never worn the colostomy bag. In my mind, it is pretty obvious that the docs have done a bloody good job for I've never had a pain since.

How did I win this contract? I'll tell it briefly…

Australia's only national newspaper early in 1992, *The Australian*, emailed me asking if they could interview me in Sydney. They had come across my article on Brisbane's World Exposition. "We like its approach and hope you might be prepared to write in that style, an article on the 1992 Easter Parade in Peru's Cuzco."

Bloody hell, what a challenge! There is only one answer!

Next day I am on a plane to Sydney and come away with a contract to conclude it any time before the end of 1992.

I spend however long in South America as I choose and they will pay the cost of either flying to Cuzco, or flying home from there. I choose that too, but must let them know which, within a week.

I dive into researching both and roughing out a three-month budget. A condition is that where there is a choice, I must fly Qantas.

It doesn't fly to South America. To approach from the north, closest is via Los Angeles and from the south, Tahiti.

Wow, if I go one way and come back the other, it covers many countries. I can go either way so long as I am in Cuzco for Easter and home by December.

I have four good reasons for choosing 'via Los Angeles.'

* I have friends met on previous journeys with whom I can stay in Santa Ana while recording notes on Los Angeles.

* The only country in South America that I want to visit that doesn't have an embassy in Australia is the gun-running Paraguay, but can obtain a visa in Huntington Beach CA.

* Thirdly, Easter Island is an absolute must in my history programme and is in the Tahiti neighbourhood and Air Chile flies Santiago, Easter Island, Tahiti.

* Flights via California are the more expensive.

I reply to *The Australian* offer, my preference to go via LA and could they please post me the contract. I quickly sign and return it and begin applying for visas from all countries concerned. All but one gives me a sixty-day period and it is in the midst of my plotted tour so no problem. My USA visa is 30 days and all South American countries 60. The French Polynesian permit for Tahiti is twelve months and I require but a few days.

Qantas flies from Melbourne–Auckland–Fiji–Honolulu-LAX. Only worthwhile incident worth telling is during a meal-time. My US neighbour remarks on how his education put such emphasis on avoiding wasted time and effort, "Yet have those masters ever watched our penchant in eating with knives and forks?"

Having cleared customs in LA, I rent a car and drive to Santa Ana.

Oh, wouldn't it have been wonderful news to tell them if I could only wind the clock forward twenty-seven years to December 2019?...A Qantas Jumbo makes a world record for a passenger aircraft non-stop Sydney to New York, longest air hop in the world, while I must suffer three set-downs just to CA.

My Santa Ana friends are celebrating their new car, the first

Lexus brand in their country. They take me sightseeing, insisting on pointing out the exact house I must visit in Huntington Beach.

They laugh at my latest book purchase...*How to Speak Spanish in Ten Days.*

I had realised that in 99% of cases when one needs help in another country, people will, if you have tried getting your message across in their language, go out of their way to help. At Huntington Beach I am asked by an extremely large lady why I have so many South American visas already in my passport.

She is happy when I explain, giving her approval with a mighty rubber stamp thump.

With now every legal requirement achieved, I drive to Los Angeles for three days of sight-seeing and note-taking and on the third, surrender the car at LAX.

~ * ~

Bogota...

Flying Colombia's airline Avianca is a fortunate move. It gives excellent service both on the ground and in the air. After midnight, not too long after taking off from our only stop Mexico City, amusing things happen. Passengers begin running about like bees in a hive. Women rush to and fro to toilets with littlies and in every aisle space mothers strip children of travelling clothes to don them in their Sunday best. Every head is brushed, combed and sprayed. The lady sitting across the aisle, noticing my interest, tells me, "Tomorrow is Mother's Day. The children are obviously being met by grandparents."

On arrival at 6:45am I have no problem with customs. Hand luggage is fed through a photographing machine testing for drugs, and the money exchange window is closed, which has me at the mercy of taxi drivers. The fare is $us10 and I have only 20s. He gives me 5,000 pesos change and I am to later learn it should have been 6,000.

I have a four-night booking at the 4 Star El Presidente Hotel, $us34.70 per night including an excellent breakfast. A comfortable hotel, yet one wonders when both on the footpath outside and immediately inside the front doors are guards, rifles in one arm opening and closing the door with the other.

On the wall behind the 'welcome' desk is a large written message in Spanish and English..."*On the streets, beware bag-snatchers.*"

It is a clean and comfortable room and after unpacking I decide after an enjoyable breakfast, with my wallet in a zipped-up pocket on what I call my 'fisherman's vest,' a sleeveless vest with pockets small enough for coinage, another large enough for a book. I wear it when flying so my hands are free. I don't carry a camera, for this survey is but to vet my surroundings. It becomes an 'incident.'

At the door, the 'inside' guard points to my zipped pocket and gives me a thumbs-up.

Huh, here armed guards are opening and closing the front door when in Egypt's Aswan, it is an eight-year-old kid bowing and saluting!

Less than fifty metres at the street corner of *Carrera 7*, at a red light, I am approached by a lady addressing me in Spanish.

"*Yo no entiendo Española, señora.*"

I had learned to have that down pat. She nods to a plain clothed man. Flashing an official looking credential card, he speaks in broken English, questions like, "Where are you going? How much money do you have on you?"

I show him my passport and journalist card. He notes that I had arrived only this morning, then wants to see my traveller's cheques. I tell him they are in my hotel's security safe. He notes my passport number and writes something against it and gives me a phone number. "If anyone tries to sell you drugs, please phone this number."

I ask him to point out a bank for changing traveller cheques and he has the woman walk me around the corner "This bank, sir."

It is Sunday so she leaves me to go my way. I feel quite intimidated, yet know this is a country with incredible drug problems....

And bag-snatchers in streets!

The streets are crowded and I cannot but note that everyone seems happy enough and most are well dressed. I am easily seen a visitor for everyone has a naturally tanned skin and I have lost my summer tan. I note, however, that this is yet another large city (fourteen million) where drivers take little notice of traffic lights. Even when crossing on a green light, one must take care. Motor traffic is thick, as are pedestrians. On every corner, even those with traffic lights, police are on duty, taking no notice of traffic infringements but direct all interest on pedestrians. All are heavily armed with snub-nosed machine guns or repeater rifles and have a metre-long wooden baton swinging warningly from their hip.

Footpaths are dangerous. Even in city centre along every block I walk, big holes have been made to repair cables and never recovered. Everyone must watch for foot safety on footpaths as for road safety on roads. Like my hotel having armed guards at its doorway, armed police are at doorways of every building. Every ATM booth is like Britain's old telephone booths, yet here the door can be locked from the inside while you put your cash in safe places on your body, before returning to the street.

Bogota is many things, but is certainly not a city for the fainthearted. On three of my four nights, I am awakened by gunfire, running and shouting and I read that every day, 15 stripped bodies are found in dumper bins, gutters or small hotel beds. Traffic pollution is extreme, almost suffocating. There is no such thing as 'clean petrol' or 'clean exhausts' in this city of seven million motor vehicles. Despite being practically 'on' the equator where one expects it to be hot and steamy, it is decidedly mild. At 2,500m altitude, now at 10:00am in autumn, I need a long-sleeved shirt, skivvy and jacket.

It is a dramatically interesting city. *Museo Nationale* tells the history of the country and is so well presented I am sorry at not having my camera. The building is an old-time gaol delightfully restored, retaining much of the gaol atmosphere. The order and organisation is in stark contrast to the disorder outside.

On the edge of the adjacent park, I am besieged by hawkers. Dressed as if home or in LA for instance, here I am obviously a visitor, so likely have more money on me than locals. In grey trousers and my 'fisherman's vest, I am accosted by all and sundry trying to sell me drugs or emeralds (for which both are world famous) or diamonds. One insists in stumbling English, "Velly special cigarette, velly special"…no doubt full of cocaine or heroin. If I buy an emerald from everyone offering, I would need another large suitcase.

For as many blocks as I can see, *Carrera* 7 is lined with troops armed with hand batons and hip-pistols. Kerb barriers are being erected all down the avenue.

Some dignitary due?

I go and get my camera, buttoning up my jacket over it and return to see a huge crowd assembling. I hear band music ahead so keep following the crowd.

At *Parque Santander* there is much colour and spectacle. TV crews assemble in front of the Santander Statue, a guard of honour in traditional uniform of last century. There is colour galore to photograph as the parade comes past. Amid fanfare, what I guess is El Presidenté himself arrives and I note that on every building opposite, in opened windows and on every balcony, even some rooftops, scores of armed troops survey the scene.

Using my sharp-elbows, I gain the rail erected to maintain the mob, near where a young soldier with a badge labelling him 'Gonzales' patrols the 'business side' of the barrier. He invites me, camera and all, over the barrier, to stand by him.

"Front seat at the theatre without even having to ask?"

I've chanced on some anniversary in Colombia's history. Soon, El Presidenté exits from his armoured vehicle to walk straight past me to a stage that had been set up. On his short walk, so many armed guards surround him that neither I nor all the people behind me can see even the cap of his uniform, yet the cheering is deafening.

I look up and every one of the guards atop buildings opposite have rifles aimed around the crowd that El Presidenté passes until arriving on the stage. Only once there can those in the crowd see him, closely surrounded by more guards.

We are, for the next hour, treated to a wonderful parade down *Carrera 7* of division after division of startlingly uniformed soldiers ten abreast, all in various colours and with rifles of their historical time.

Thanks to Gonzales, I take some wonderful photographs and at the finale when I look to again see El Presidenté, he has been whisked off from behind the stage into whatever hands had awaited him. I look for the guards atop the buildings and all are gone.

But what a magnificent parade! And how lucky am I to have chanced upon it.

Behind the stage in *Carrera 6* is *Museo del Oro* (Museum of Gold), the most magnificent of features and where photographing is not allowed.

In this city, I find it not surprising.

I stroll further down *Carrera 7* and try photographing the presidential palace but soldiers run at me in force. I recognise 'No No,' one of the few Spanish words same as English. Photographing the palace is not allowed.

It is in a part of an ancient area with centuries old buildings that no attempt has been made to maintain or restore.

Next day I take the cable car (1,600 pesos, $1.33) into the heights where I look down and see the city so tiny that I cannot pick out even the park where I enjoyed the parade. The mountainside proffers nostalgia, for it has many clumps of eucalypt trees. It takes me so high that breathing is difficult, especially climbing steps on reaching the very top. In the *El Señorde Montsarrat* chapel gardens, it is moving to watch the people where a model of *Christo* lies bleeding. In their hundreds, tearful souls force their way to touch the casket, lifting up children to kiss its glass walls, to then draw away, wiping at tears.

A touching scene.

It becomes a waste of time having taken today's delightful photographs, however, for having descended from the heights to return to the *Museo Nationale* to photograph the gaol restoration, I am set upon. It is a delightful day and I can easily breathe again at city level where I can see the Museum in the not too far a distance. It is parkland in between. Yes, I had read all the advice saying not to walk alone in Bogota and this tree-lined avenue around the park is so close that I take a chance.

Can you imagine how one feels when I see four louts coming at me, clipping open Swiss knives? The closer they come, the more certain I am that these are my last seconds of life.

Just before reaching me, from behind comes an arm around my throat at the same time as a knee kick is jabbed into the back of my knees. Down I go, five on top of me, four with open knives. Fortunately, they use them only to slash my camera free of its leather strap. My fear is such that I can almost feel the blades jabbing into me.

I am not further harmed but in that same moment I hear the screech of braked tyres and a man shouting. I look up to see him armed with a curbed Arab type sabre, jump from his car to give chase, but all are gone. At the same time too, a screech of tyres from a police motorbike coming from the opposite direction stops abruptly, yet the policeman makes no attempt to make chase; he comes straight to me. The car driver introduces himself as Chavez R. Moises and tells both the policeman and me that he keeps the sabre alongside him when driving so he can in such a situation, at least frighten off attackers before they do more harm. The policeman pats him on a shoulder, looks me over and points to a slash mark in a trouser leg, but no blood marks. He then leaves without asking a name and Chavez and his wife drive me to my hotel, see me safely handed over to the outdoor guard and refuses the thank you bank note I rake from my wallet. The door guard asks him to follow us to the desk.

He and the hotel manager inform me that it will be useless asking the police for a statement to claim insurance once home. The hotel instead writes a notice that Chavez R. Moises signs as witness to the robbery, signing it over his rubber stamp of *Anti Delincuene Fuerza (Anti-crime Force)*. I am a little more than 'in shock' and am taken into the bar for a drink the manager insists is 'on the house.'

In big red letters I write on my conscience, 'Practise what you bloody preach, Ric'!

Such is the mood of Bogota.

Annoyed with myself for having lost so many wonderful photographs, the next day I shop around but cannot find a suitable camera. At the airport, for I fly to Cartagena, they have nothing either. At the information desk I am told the Airport Cambio is closed but it has exchange machines. Slide a US note through and if torn or even creased, it rejects it. A good condition note goes through OK and pays out in note form, local equivalent.

Hmm, rejecting slightly used US notes when their own pesos are the most dilapidated filthy things one can imagine?

My Bogota summary:

Plus Side? Great beer, best coffee in the world (honestly! In fact I later read that coffee is one the country's two largest exports, the other being emeralds.). Everything I see is very cheap and people hospitable.

Minus side? Dangerous. The presence of police and military everywhere is intimidating. Outdoors, much is dirty, even sluggish with dreadful pollution. Public transport is unspeakable, very cheap but by the sight of it, dirty.

~ * ~

Cartagena, highly recommended holiday city...

My Lonely Planet guide recommends Hotel Bella Vista on the road from airport to the city and I am booked there, a copy of the booking in my pocket.

In the Bangkok Airport waiting room, I chat with a Colombian lady who grew up in Cartagena, now married to a Canadian in Toronto. She is home on a family visit.

We meet again at the taxi rank. "Where are you staying?" Adela asks.

"I am booked into Hotel Bella Vista.

She frowns deeply.

"You know it, Adela? And don't like it?"

"It is miles from the city on a lonely beach. As a hotel it has a bad name. Let us share a taxi, for to my hotel we pass the Bella Vista. I shall ask the driver to pause there."

Yet Lonely Planet recommends it?

We chatter about her happy early life in Cartagena.

"You will be amazed at the difference between it and Bogota. It is clean, tidy and safe to be alone in most places."

'Most places'?

As the taxi turns a bend, there before us is the vast bright blue Atlantic Ocean and as the bend straightens, "And there," she points to the left, "is Hotel Bella Vista." She leans forward to touch the driver's shoulder. He stops and turns off the motor.

A broad but lonely building painted a dirty white sits a long way back from the almost black sandy beach. The only people in view are children playing with a football, not on the beach but in front of the hotel.

There is no other building in sight. Everywhere around it seems lonely…certainly not the travel scene I seek.

"Do you want to see where I always stay? Single rooms at 20,000 pesos ($us30) with a good breakfast, a three-story hotel with excellent lounges, right on a beach and a bus to the city at its doors?"

I tap the driver on the shoulder. *"Conduce por favor."*

~ * ~

Meeting Adela proves that chatting with local people if finding the opportunity, can pay positive results.

Hotel Flamingo on Avenida San Martin at BocaGrande, beachside of the Cartagena city, 20,000pesos ($us30) with breakfast is a great value. BocaGrande is a poor imitation of Surfers Paradise (my neighbouring suburb on the Gold Coast) with lots of high-rise apartment buildings on its Caribbean beach, yet the high-risers are mostly not only empty but derelict. The beach sand is black. I am told that lots of even the new condominiums will never be lived in; they are far too expensive. They are built with foreign aid money providing essential employment, yet once either the work goes over budget or when the building is finished, the project is abandoned and another started!

No, this is no joke. I am to later find the same situation in both Bolivia and Paraguay.

Hotel Flamingo is excellent value, clean, reasonably modern, young and helpful staff right on the main drag as well as beachfront. However, if you are staying anywhere in Colombia, check your valuables into your hotel's security desk. All rooms have barred windows but mine had been wrenched out at some stage. Like most vandalised things in the country I am to find, it has not been repaired. On the first floor is a breezy lounge overlooking the street markets and right alongside is a busy alfresco shop. Facing the beach out back is a huge garden with thatched gazebos and plenty of shady trees. To get onto the beach is simple if the garden guard is on his post (most of the time). He unlocks the huge gate-lock in the two-metre-high barbed wire fence to where hotel chairs are arranged on the beach under shady umbrellas. His name is Paco, a most obliging fellow who leaves loaded pistols tucked under two or three of the guest-garden gazebos' thatched roof edges. He remembers which one (they change daily) to use as his 'office,' the only paperwork being the daily newspaper. He speaks excellent English.

On the morrow, anxious to cash a traveller cheque and buy a new camera, I take a bus to the city. It is packed full of local people and I really do feel the 'odd man out.' Because city streets are so narrow, the bus terminal is outside the city wall and it is a surprisingly long pedestrian and busy tunnel to get there. The streets are also busy and I am sent from bank to bank for no one knows which city bank is today's turn to change travel-cheques.

And this is the nation's major tourist city!

I am to find in both Colombia and Peru that it's difficult to change a travel-cheque, a popular international need to save one having to have large amounts of notes in bags or pockets. 5 Star hotels are the exception, but not even my 4 Star Flamingo does it. It is bloody hot and I am turned away from four banks. Disgusted, covered in sweat from the blazing sun, I get a bus home and oh, how unkind can one be treated with shame? Especially shame of a tourist earning a living from observing things?

My bus pulls up directly across the street from my hotel and as I step on to the pavement, what is right in front of me? A bloody bank with exchange rates in its front window and next door a store selling cameras and everything else a tourist may require?

I hold a hand over my face in case anyone from the hotel recognises me, slip into the bank, change my cheque and next door buy a quite satisfactory camera and stock up with more film. Sticking my chin up and out in all bravery, I cross to the hotel.

There, I turn to look back to see how I could not have noticed the two before, to see that next door to the camera shop is a restaurant. I return to read the door-menu and find it attractive. For tonight's dinner, I tuck it into one of the gaps that my brain is supposed to have.

Along with other hotel guests, I see Adela lunching at the café next door to the hotel so join them, comforted in that if seen catching this morning's bus I do not have to tell any lies, just withhold some truths.

I practise as I sit, my answer if asked how I spent my morning. Adela asks…

"Oh, just took the bus to the city, mightily impressed by the tunnel under the wall, walked around many of the city streets until foot-sore, ogling at the beautiful garden boxes on every house's windows, bought a new camera just across the street here and am now ready to ease my feet and enjoy something to eat."

She is content with that, happy with me so satisfied at so many of her suggestions. She now recommends a half day tour at the Castille San Fellipe and parts of the Old Town and its history, visit the Conventa de Santa Cruz de la Popa, highest point in the city with its massive and fabulous 22-carat gold altar no more than 50m from the wretched poor living in cardboard boxes, and a full day excursion to Islas de la Rosario including lunch on Isla Media de la Naranja where one can swim in the most attractive little beach. "That island is a dream," she adds.

I ask her to come to the desk with me after lunch to help me make the bookings.

"Me too," said a single and a twosome.

We did so for the morrow and next day. I settle my lunch with short strolls with them in the afternoon.

Around the block behind the buildings opposite is what we guess are homes of typical local families, but oh how wrong can one be! They are medium sized houses with gardens, a barbershop, a grocery store, clean looking children on swings and a few real young'uns with model cars, pedalling along footpaths. We later learn that is the extent of the town's few 'rich people.'

Back across the road and down the side of our hotel to the beach, expecting to see people surfing, is another surprise. Out from under the trees comes a strong wind and very few people are about. We turn to face a large poster, a warning to stay amongst crowds. We agree that all are part of what Nancy calls a 'mishmash of styles.' Nancy and husband George from England's Cornwall, recent retirees like me are both some ten years older.

Most locals I find are handsome, both men and women, for few local women can afford make-up and smart clothing and mostly had as hard a physical working life as men. The country obviously has but two standards: the very rich and the very poor. All have a tinge of Indian gold about their complexion, very black hair and high cheekbones.

Dinar Dino's has starched tablecloths and napkins but a long way from silver service. A litre of beer, a satisfactory coque-au-vin, coconut tart, coffee and cognac cost 2,000 pesos ($15). We pay separate charges and find that outside, this block and a bit more has a night-market atmosphere. Footpaths are covered with tables of hawker-goods flogging everything from t-shirts to toothbrushes that seem to have 'fallen from the backs of trucks.' *"No Gracias"* is a phrase quickly learned and repeatedly practised.

Discos are disappointing and mixed crowds are mostly young with shallow pockets.

In bed I watch TV despite no English, to learn that today a bomb exploded in Cartagena city killing three and injuring a score. In Bogota there is talk of a new constitution to stop the rot that pervades throughout the country, the still burgeoning drug trade and the violent crime rate. Inflation is 'happily' down to 22.4%!

Next morning the bank across the road lists 637 pesos to the USA dollar and next door, the Cambio lists 600! Yes, fact!

We take off on our half day tour and when our bus leaves the front of the hotel, a guard with hand on a pistol in a hip-holster, takes up duty on the step inside the bus door which he locks. When we see a huge statue of a virgin on a rock in the middle of the huge harbour, I get a number of giggles when I call out the suggestion that she is likely out there because she can't feel safe anywhere else.

At the Conventa de Santa Cruz de la Popa, highest point in the city with its massive and altar that is worth 'multi millions' of pesos. On our side of the bus we can see only a massive stone wall doorway with a rotating iron frame as its door. Through closed and locked windows on the other side of the bus, the wretched poor live naked in cardboard boxes. The 'trough' in which they stand doubles as a putrid sewer but they stand in it, pleading hands out, palms up, for any sort of gift.

We are in an air-conditioned bus and are warned that when the door is opened exactly an arm's length from the rotating iron door-frame, armed guards from inside will quickly usher us one by one, through it. On no account are we to dodge past our guards to give gifts to the people on the other side of the bus.

There is a sign: **"Guards are not allowed to endanger themselves from murderous villagers. You are responsible for yourself. You have been warned."**

We must quickly file through the rotating iron grill to where it is 'quite safe.'

The Castille is in fact not a castle but a 62 gun fort, an incredible piece of architecture of the sixteenth century. It was designed to as well ward off shipping from entering the harbour to attack the town. Should invaders get ashore, the Castille's catacombs are two metres of tunnels with great holes in the floor that invaders, in the dark looking for the gold stored there awaiting shipment to Spain, would fall down into darkness. Waiting below were defenders with sabres and pikes.

Of course, Cartagena has ever been Spain's storeroom for all the gold stolen from the South Americans, those who Spaniards also converted to Christianity. British and French ships invariably waited outside the harbour to attack Spaniards leaving.

Naval battles therefore, meant death to the weakest Christians.

I take photographs galore of the gold within the church on the peak and the cannon defence, aimed to sink the enemy waiting 'out there.'

Once back through the rotating gate, I am not allowed to use my camera on naked natives living in cardboard boxes, their sewer the creek underfoot, until an announced approval, by which time of course, we are well away from its stench.

Ah! Only 50 metres above their heads are those millions of dollars' worth of gold in the temple.

Today's Spaniards still fear attempts displaced natives must resort to, to at least eat.

How much pride should Australians feel in allowing its natives find food and water?

~ * ~

8th April 1992...

15,000 pesos ($31.40) for a day's excursion to *Islas del la Rosario*.

We are a dozen passengers on a motorboat, Nancy and George, the negress Dulce from Isla San Andres and a handsome spunky young Jamaican trying his best all day to mate her, two Columbians and I speak English. The other five are from Bulgaria and have none and we have two guides.

We are but a half-kilometre inside the harbour entrance when a naval boat comes alongside, all its crew in uniform and armed with regulation machine guns and who have no sense of humour.

"All keep facing away from them," whispers our tour guide,

"they will want to see your passports." He already has them, along with a list of our hotels.

Dulce whispers, "Say nothing unless asked. Any one of us could be in trouble."

It takes about twenty minutes for each of the naval officers to go through our passports before handing all back to our guide. Not a word has been exchanged, nor are there any as they turn on their motor and drive away.

We are all given back our passports and without another word our two guides start the motor and we clear the heads into the Atlantic Ocean. On each headland is an ancient fort, the closest of which several of us photograph.

Islas del la Rosario, the resort island where we lunch, is owned by the tour company and is very short on water. They offer a small ration of drinks and flush by bucket, the little island's only toilet, with sea water. It has coral reefs for diving, beautiful white sand on their little beach and a little coral lagoon, clear and pollution free for swimming...

Oh, after all the squalor of the cities, what an idyllic little island.

Lunch is plentiful and they have a couple of rooms if anyone wants to stay for a day or more. We call at another island with huge *tortugas* (turtles) galore and a marine museum of sorts, but after equivalents in Noumea and La Roselle, I won't compare.

So, everyone satisfied with our most enjoyable day, we start for home.

Waves begin turning into quite a heavy 'chop' and here arc fourteen people facing a very small notice declaring in Spanish according to Winston: *Registered to carry eleven people.* It is quite noticeable that the driver has stepped up our speed. They explain that after sundown, entry to the harbour is closed, so we bump and bounce unmercifully and all foreheads are heavily creased. All but one are told to don a safety-ring. It is not stated, but it is clear that thirteen is what the big cupboard inside the bow, holds.

The driver says he is moving further out to sea where we will not be tossed about by the changing tide. Many among us, particularly women, are looking frightfully scared. I feel like joining them. We are now a long way from shore in this small boat, alone at the whim of the Atlantic Ocean. I am more than familiar with the massive breakers the Pacific Ocean hurls down on Broadbeach in winds like this, but say nowt.

Maybe in order to take our minds off our situation, Abilio, holding Dulce in a tight embrace of protection begins telling us that but two weeks ago six or seven bombs blew up in Bogota, that it is so unsafe to walk around there now that even university students will not walk alone. He says Lima, my next port of call, is worse. He says my plan to cross Bolivia by train is nothing short of lunacy.

Once the tide begins changing, our launch indeed finds it less choppy and we make almost frightening haste to get through the heads into the harbour. On every face, smiles replace the frightening stares. The harbour is delightfully smooth and our soaking 'safety-rings' are returned to their cupboard in the bow.

We watch a most beautiful sunset.

The other restaurant across the road from our hotel is a considerably higher standard than its neighbour. Several of us dine at La Olla de Cartagena (*Olla* means 'cooking pan or stew-pot'), surely Cartagena's most elegant eatery, expensive by local standards but within our agreed 'splurge' range. I put blinkers on my ecological conscience and order *tortuga* in coconut milk. Ah, magnificent. Likely I will never again let myself eat turtle so I savour this first and last taste sensation. Dessert and two coffees (and I again insist Colombian coffee surpasses even Greek), all for 7,300pesos ($12). It might be a dangerous country, but cheap.

Over breakfast in the garden, I watch the house boys take tents and beach-lounges from the yard on to the beach. Only on Fiji's have I seen workmen move so leisurely or carry so little on each trip.

I have Winston, the lad shunned by Dulce last night so had to again sleep in his own bed, join me to go see the city 'fort' that has been with its city wall and slave market-place. It is admirable work, every area around the huge forecourt of prisons, army barracks and torture chambers, everything today painted in garish colours, here gold, there a light blue, elsewhere orange or scarlet.

Cartagena has some magnificent buildings, not large but quaintly rustic. Footpaths are as broken as in Bogota. A museum worth visiting is *Entrada al Palacio de la Inquisicion,* which in its original building is well restored, along with its torture chambers.

In all Columbian museums, everyone is able to take photographs.

Sitting alone in a garden gazebo to update my notes, the Hotel Flamingo security guard Parco, rushes over to me...

"You go Lima tomorrow, Senor Ric?"

He thrusts a newspaper in front of me.

"Read me what it says, Paco."

He half reads, half tells in his own words...

"Country in turmoil. Prime Minister suspends Parliament. State of emergency. He make himself Prime Minister and shoot anyone not happy. Lima streets like war. Army tanks and troops on every corner to stop bombs and murder!"

"I am even more determined to go, Paco. I am a journalist, a man paid to tell what he knows, things people in general don't get Tomorrow I am due for a very early start so plan a light dinner... French Sandwich at the alfresco café, then it's upstairs to pack. I am abed by 9:00pm.

Each day to date there have been power blackouts at some time or other and my luck takes a twist for the worse when up at 4:00am for shower and shave.

Ever tried taking a cold shower in the dark?

Having dressed in nowt but a towel and with only my cigarette lighter showing the way, I grope my way to the front desk. I need a torch from the night guard.

He is sound asleep under a hurricane lamp and as I wake him, he makes a startled grab for his side-arm before realising an all but naked man is more likely a guest than intruder. He has no English so with some difficulty I explain I need a torch to shave.

He grudgingly obliges.

Ever tried shaving with one hand because torch batteries are so low it has to be held right up to its target?

I'm just so glad I packed last night. I am to hear when later in Asuncion, that Bogota, to conserve power, turns it off for all domestic and retail use, all afternoon on weekdays!

This is early April so God help them when winter arrives.

Before unlocking the front door, the guard puts on his night-porter cap and goes to check that my room hasn't been robbed of anything. Downstairs again, he holds up a lamp so I can see him smile. I ask him to open the door.

"When taxi come," he stumbles out, which I reckon exhausts all his English.

Only when the taxi arrives does he unlock all three deadlocks.

God help us all if ever a fire breaks out!

Only when I am in the cab with my luggage does the driver lock us in, gives me a thumbs up and we take off.

As we reach the airport, daylight begins hinting.

~ * ~

Cartagena summary:

Plus side: Safer than Bogota yet need for caution; great food and service, a scenic delight, public transport efficient enough, all very clean and cheap.

Minus side: Stay amongst tourist crowds.

I sadly erase many of the credits I've paid *Avianca Airline*. My plane is a jumbo direct from Spain en-route to Bogota, stopping in Cartagena to set down tourist travellers and honeymooners. I am met atop the mobile staircase by a sleepy-eyed stewardess…

"Sit where you can find a seat." I find an 'empty' one piled with clothing and the woman beside it feigning sleep as I move it all into the aisle. When she complains I deliberately forget any Spanish I have and answer in English that I have been given leave to take any seat. The man beside her waves a hand as much as to say, "Don't argue."

It is a ninety-minute flight so I too try sleeping. On landing we are given breakfast coupons for the airport dining room and my stomach is pleading. I have but an hour before my flight to Lima and I've yet to queue for quitting Colombia. Before eating I need to see my luggage placed when getting ticketed for Lima. I change my Colombian cash for $us. By the time I pay international departure tax and queue forty minutes (yes, forty minutes) to get through passport control (Colombian officialdom is just too intricate to believe possible) all the time under the alert gaze of machine-gun toting police I hear "final boarding warning" for my flight to Lima. So, I cannot eat.

    On the broad scene, I've enjoyed the little I've seen of Colombia yet regret having so many risks. I would like to return and see more of it and Cartegena illustrates it is trying hard to please.

Am I now to discover what 'dangerous Lima' has to offer?

Thirteen

Peru...

Oh what a time to visit a country in political turmoil!
In my working life I never ran from responsibility and will not back out on one now.

As my plane approaches the terminal a huge banner reads: *Welcome to Peru.*

I am to be met by a Condor Travel rep. taken to the hotel I chose from Lonely Planet, leaving me free for two days to see a museum and major Lima sites. Then I fly to Iquitos for a few days to experience Lima's jungle life, then to Cuzco for my assignment. Condor Travel sees to my every move.

Who wrote the line...Famous last words?

Eduardo is my Lima nursemaid, a tall guy, forty, dark complexion, anxious to "get out of this airport as quickly as possible."

Yes, the heavily armed uniformed military outnumbers travellers.

Or are they police? Either way, each is heavily armed.

"I need to exchange money," I tell Eduardo.

"Sorry, you can do that at hotels here. This airport could suddenly erupt in gun-play. Wait until you see our streets. We could have a civil war on our hands at any moment."

Into a modern car already with driver, we are soon in the streets and at every corner tanks with armed soldiers atop have fire-arms at the ready. Everywhere!

"I am unhappy at your choice of hotels, Mr. Richardson. You've been here before?"

"This is my first time in Peru, sir. I chose it from Lonely Planet. Please call me Ric."

"Thank you, I am Eduardo. They have certainly been misinformed. It is Z class."

He is right; it is 'the pits.' It is in a factory area, my tiny room furnished with a single bed and a chair with a broken leg. Pegs in a wall are for clothes. There is no window but a door to a small balcony which can be easily reached from factory windows and the door has a burst lock.

Not a store in sight and I am here for three nights? I cannot stay where it serves no food and there will be no restaurant in this area.

I have two other problems…The hotel does not change cheques and Eduardo, my only security in Lima, has already left. Being Friday, he has likely gone home and does not come to fetch me until 5:00am Monday. I must find a bank.

I am told one is up this street and turn left at the second corner.

I run that gauntlet of tanks and personnel/gun carriers and soldiers everywhere, all with rifles at the 'ready to fire' position.

At the bank I am directed to the traveller-cheque window. It is 3:15 and banks close at 4:00. I queue and at 3:30 they cannot change cheques. Having been warned to change all Colombian cash before leaving, I have no change in any currency to even make a phone call. They point to another desk where I am told in broken English, "Because of the political plight, money is virtually frozen.

Go to our Head Office, two blocks that way then two blocks to the right."

Running the street gauntlets, I arrive on the stroke of 4:00pm and every window has a long queue.

People wanting to withdraw their all before its value collapses?

They point to window number 5.

"*A que ora apuerto?*"

"*Cinco Señor*". So they close at 5:00. I queue up and at 5 o'clock a bell rings and people galore in the queues throw up their hands in disgust. I ask if there is anywhere at this time that I can change a cheque and they tell me at my hotel or come back to the bank tomorrow morning at nine o'clock.

Eduardo's brochure is in a pocket. The map shows Condor Travel four blocks away. Assuming it will close at five gives me little hope but I run 'til exhausted and three times get pulled up by soldiers for questioning; a running man is obviously worthy of being questioned. I run again to find Condor has moved.

Bloody hell! I don't believe this! Is it really happening?

An old man sits on a step smoking a pipe. Of course, he has no English.

"*Donde estan? Escribalo favour!*"

He marks my map...5 blocks away. I look hesitatingly at my gold watch and cannot but help noticing his eyes gleam at it also. I pull down my shirt cuff and run.

I hate Condor Tours with a great hate!

And why doesn't some clever bastard invent a telephone you can have in a pocket?

Without a penny in mine, I hail a taxi...

"Hotel Claridge *por favour, Calle Cailloma*."

En-route I get him to understand he must wait outside while I get my luggage. He is then to take me to any three- or four-star hotel. I realise I leave myself wide open to his honesty but I've no option. I cross fingers about his choice of hotel but with my passport in their hands, they should lend me enough to pay him.

At the Claridge I collect my bag and inform the desk clerk I do not stay. He throws his hands wide and asks for some payment so I take out a traveller cheque and my Diners Club card and tell him to take his pick. He shrugs his shoulders and waves me off.

The taxi informs me that Miraflores, the tourist area on a beach "Is the only safe place for foreigners just now."

He drops me at El Condado Hotel. It claims itself 4 Star but charges 6 Star prices. I have to accept and the taxi driver wants "$us5 in US cash please." I give him five and he gives me a hearty handshake.

The desk clerk cashes a traveller cheque but has only $us notes in cash.

He signals the doorman who comes to the desk, takes my $us200 dollars out to the street to return with a huge sack over his shoulder, assuring me it is 200,000,000 Intes.

I tip him a million ($us1) that makes me feel great!

I am to learn that most exchange in Peru is done not at banks but with money-exchangers on the street, but only on a cash for cash basis. Peru had recently introduced new currency; the *Nuevo Sol* (new sun) equals a million of the old *Inti* and is equal to $us1. For how long it can retain that value is anybody's guess. Both currencies, however, are still in circulation although few have pockets big enough to hold Intis enough to "buy an egg" I am told.

When my budget is $us30, El Condado gives me a delightful corner room with steam bath and TV with several English language channels for $us115 a night, plus breakfast.

Shit, and that taxi driver no doubt backed up to this hotel for a handy 'thank you, do it again' type spotting fee. And I'm bloody hungry. I haven't eaten since that coffee on the plane and cannot imagine what this hotel asks for a meal. And I'm here for three nights.

I ask the switchboard to find the new Condor Travel telephone number.

"Go to the bar and have a drink, Ric." I tell myself. "It will be expensive but you've just become a multi-millionaire."

It is expensive all right, a gin and tonic followed by coffee cost $us17.20.

Yes, but I guess that black-tie guy strumming the grand piano isn't cheap to hire.

I daren't feel it safe to wander streets alone, searching somewhere cheaper to eat so settle for the hotel's 'coffee shop.' I ease my desperate half stomach's dilemma with a Chicken Maryland and coffee for $us24 but prefer it being called 24 million Intis. And the coffee is dreadful, a strong base poured from a bottle, topped with hot water...not a patch on Colombian coffee and several times the price.

I find the hours before able to phone Condor Tours a burden. I'll be gentle, simply leave a message for Eduardo to not call for me at the Claridge come Monday, but El Condado which I am finding even more luxurious than London's Inn on the Park.

From TV tonight I gather the self-made Prime Minister Fujimoro clearly has the people behind him as well as the army... great strength! His objective is to quash the current graft and corruption in high places and hasn't been getting positive action from his ministers, so wants to start with a clean sheet. He has sacked them all. The working class is behind him as well as the poor and even some of the wealthy. He is really acting from a position of strength.

Saturday blesses me further in finding myself speaking English with Debbie at Condor Tours who assures me Eduardo will be told to pick me up here at 5:00am Monday.

I am sure Lima has more Volkswagons than Berlin. Taxis here are 'volksies' as are so many cars with company names. And it's likely all government clerks drive them because they are cheap. There are even 'stretch' models with two or three doorway entrances along each side.

The *Lima Guera* visits every morning nine months of every year about 1000am, blocking out the sun and sky for the rest of the day. True, Lima has no sunshine for nine months of the year, which foreigners find depressing. The everyday climate is as if under heavy cloud, dark, hot, humid and polluted because traffic fumes cannot escape. The 'dark' months are March to January.

I find the hotel charged me ten percent to cash my cheque, so I get only $180 for every $200 cheque which makes them pretty expensive ways of avoiding huge inflation. Next time, I will know!

When I find a Saturday bank that changes cheques, it takes me an hour and a half for one simple transaction. I queue, wait for the clerk to assess my validity, fill in his paperwork then refer me to the next window queue. Three times until the final window doesn't pay in any Peruvian currency, but $us. I then must go out on the street and barter with money merchants, his clerks laden with sacks of even *Nuevo Sol*.

Cafés are a dime a dozen along the streets and being Saturday, every one is full. To have coffee I share a small table with an elderly fellow with a string bag full of bread and greengroceries, all loose, no wrappings.

A noticeable absence of product in Peru is Coca-Cola for they have their Inca-Cola in exact replica bottles. Its sickly chartreuse colour has as sickly a taste. Another significant absence in packaging is the normal size bottled drink. The few available are sold on the basis that you bring an empty bottle to replace it. In the supermarket I shop for my lunch and reasonably priced dinners, actually very cheap, but drinks without bottle exchange are thrice the normal price.

In the little supermarket near my hotel, I buy cooked chicken pieces, a ball-shaped loaf of bread, cheese, potato chips and beer, plus yoghurt for what I call 'a song.'

I take quite a liking for Peru's *Causen* beer and it has bottles without a surcharge.

On telly tonight I have a laugh. It is a *Skippy* episode that I watched when a kid, here dubbed in Spanish.

Sundays in Lima, streets are as deserted as yesterday they teemed with people. Not a time to go outdoors. I can even hear surf, for I am so used to living right 'on' it in Broadbeach. I try where I had coffee yesterday, but it seems like a ghost town. When

I see the beach only five teenagers are kicking a soccer ball around and laughing.

I play safe and return to the hotel before they see me. Forced to spend my last day in a Lima hotel room watching dreary TV channels when my schedule has me in museums, cathedrals and other busy pastimes, is simply annoying. Yet one can't stop political wars breaking out.

I am waiting when Eduardo and driver call exactly on time, to drive me to the airport and see that I get my ticket okay. He asks what I did over the weekend and when I tell him I queued in bank after bank for five hours changing a traveller-cheque, they roar laughing, only to have to offer apologies.

"Are you going to write that in your articles about Peru?"

"I am obliged to write how I find any country I visit. However, in this case I must include that I came at an unfortunate time. Yet I still have much to see in Peru. Amazonia must be exciting and then Easter in Cuzco."

"Both, Ric, are worlds quite different from what Lima offers at the moment."

We drive through San Isidro, the 'Mayfair' of Lima, home for its rich and famous. All fences are not only behind high concrete walls with heavily locked gates but on top have rolls of razor-wire set in broken glass. Some houses have miniature watch-towers behind the wall, with armed gatekeepers. Many gates and walls, I am told, are electrified.

And many a resident behind these walls are likely ministers sacked with even the law now after their hides.

Beyond San Isidro is squalor-land until reaching the airport.

Fawcett Airline is the most no-frills airline imaginable. I am booked with them for three flights. Their airline lounge in the Lima airport is very much Hotel Claridge style, filthy, smelly with garbage, broken seats, chalk and blackboard notices and our flight is not called over an intercom announcement, but a woman shouting that our plane "is that one," pointing through windows we can hardly see through.

Inside the plane is as tatty as the terminal 'lounge.' Two seats in my bank of three are faulty, their backs even tied with wire to stop them flopping down. I am later told that the alternate airline flying to Iquitos in the Amazon wilds named 'Air Peru,' is popularly called 'Air Perhaps.'

Geographically, however, flying out of Lima is like flying out of Zürich…no matter which side one looks from you see magnificently scenic mountains. Here however, we are all of a sudden above the *guera* and have the majesty of the sun shining on snow which tops mountain tips all year around. The dampened spirits that Lima airport instils in one is of a sudden lift…lifted to mighty heights in the mighty Andes.

Once over the mighty crest of the mighty range is a different world. The mountains are suddenly left behind and the valley floor captures the entire scenery, an endless sea of jungle green broken only by of a red river…yes red…no more *guera,* smog, pollution, litter left by teeming millions, when below us there is no sign of man. Suddenly nature has taken back its unspoiled world. In every direction the jungle just disappears into a horizon, the red ribbons twisting and turning in haphazard patterns.

Such is my first sight of the world's mightiest jungle and tributaries of the world's mightiest river. A land with red soil.

I feel like forgiving all the shameful things I have found in South America.

~ * ~

Iquitos and the Amazon…

What with the ruggedness of the Andes and foreverness of jungle with but vestiges of a village here or there, each surrounded by impenetrable, roadless landscapes, it isn't surprising that 'lost' tribes are still being discovered. Iquitos stands on the edge of the Amazon, nervously clinging to its patch of cleared ground, seeming to dare the jungle to creep back, pushing it into the river.

A Jungle Lodge car meets me and drives through abject squalor to the Jungle Lodge's office in the town. We travel the most broken 'made' road ever in that it is more pot-holes than bitumen. Yet who needs a road maintained when there is nowhere to go but the airport? There just 'ain't nothing else' but roadless jungle! So, there are few cars but hundreds of three-wheeled motorbikes like the tuk-tuks of Asian cities, noisy, smoke belching vehicles cheap to run. The town is a jumble of unbelievable slums with but here or there a smart house, the latter always well-fortified with barbed wire and big dogs.

I've a half hour to spare before leaving the Camp Office, so walk up the main street to where I can overlook the river, the banks of which are also filth and squalor. It would be a long walk down to the river but even from here I can see that the surface of the shallows around riverboats is awash with garbage and oil slicks. One only smart building with a glorious garden, paint still clinging to walls, roof painted rather than rusty and the nation's flag fluttering proudly is so conspicuous that I want to photograph it. Again, I have gun-toting soldiers come running, waving and shouting. I find it is Peru's inland naval headquarters and photos are not allowed.

The few cars are as ancient and rusted as houses, but then, outside a town with streets you count on two hands, cars are but a superfluous commodity. Taxis are tuk-tuks and the motorbikes that outnumber cars several to one, seat two or three. Pick-ups are three-wheeled bikes with a tray in front, sometimes with cartons piled so high the driver has to stop every few metres to stand and see what is in front.

Despite the only Peruvian town in the Amazon basin, Iquitos is not one you want to come if you want reasonable hotels, restaurants or tours unless, like me, simply curious to see a different type of community. However, though, there is no political drama here.

Have they yet got the news that has turned Lima into such a dangerous place?

To locals, today is like yesterday and every day in the past of their lives.

Up the river I am taken in a thatch-covered launch, amazed at how quickly the stench, litter and everything about me is suddenly fresh, green, the aroma of air clean and simply the natural teasing smells of nature. The Jungle Lodge launch is a one-man crew with all side-seats and a canvas roof. We motor upriver for an hour and I discover the 'hotel' where I booked, hardly worthy of the name 'lodge.' It is indeed primitive, well past the heyday it had no doubt once enjoyed.

I am greeted by a sole young fellow, Amando, who tells me he will be my guide during my stay and I am to find he is also manager and chef with two young lads in their teens as staff. He is a likeable fellow, anxious to tell me about his beautiful wife and little daughter and new son who live in the town. He gets home 'every other week or so' but his wife often visits him here overnight.

Before even showing me to my room, he takes me for a short jungle walk. It is steamy and mosquitos are obviously short of thin-skinned flesh for they send quick messages to others that a thin-skinned white bloke has arrived. The size of eagles, they attack me in great numbers. Local people, dark skinned Indian, are of attractive facial appearance, high cheekbones and jet black hair. Approaching the village, naked children scamper off and Amando tells me they have run to tell their parents we come. By the time we arrive, three men in grass skirts are waiting with blowgun and darts. Bare-breasted women hover in the background with handfuls of beads and necklaces for me to buy, and naked children stand, fingers in mouths, watching. I am given lessons in shooting darts from the blowgun, my target a palm frond stuck in the ground at ten paces. Much to the delight of the children, one time in ten, I hit it.

Amando tells me to bow to the women, but that on the morrow I will have better opportunity of choice to buy handmade souvenirs. He suggests I give them 500,000 Inti ($0.50) and he tells them it is to buy something for the children. They seem pleased.

My room is one of a half-dozen off a veranda which is an arm of several verandas stretching out as if a fan from the 'guest lounge' which is a bamboo floored gazebo style room without walls. All have thatched roofs. At the far end of each veranda is a 'bathroom' and 'toilet.' The bathroom is a shower. If you want one, you let Amando know and he sends a lad in a row-boat fifty metres downriver where there is a rusty tank and a battery fed pump that feeds water from river to bathroom. There being no electricity, there is no hot water. I will let my readers guess what I think of the toilet, just explain that it is something emptied once a day somewhere in the jungle. It has paper toilet rolls.

My room is big enough to put my bag on a stool, hang clothes on hand-hewn bamboo shirt-hangers on rusted hooks on bamboo walls. My room is of a 'single' denomination so the bed is 'single,' raised off the floor nearly up to my knees with a foam rubber mattress on a bamboo frame with a clean pair of linen sheets to sleep within...quite comfortable, actually. A clean and obviously near new mosquito net covers all. I daren't like to think what the pillow is made of, but I use a pair of trousers. I have a bamboo chair and the floor is strips of bamboo lashed with rope made from banana leaves. Walls are the same, as is the ceiling from which hangs a hurricane lamp.

Ah, that answers the box of damp matches sitting on the pillow.

In the gaps between the bamboo slats of floorboards and wallboards, are sheets of fine wire gauze, stretched tight to ward off snakes.

Fortunately, they look fairly strong and not yet rusty with holes.

An aged small mirror hangs on one wall. The window on another is just the wire gauze but no glass. I've no idea what the roof is made of and I doubt bamboo comes in corrugated sheets.

Sticky and sweaty, despite it is not yet lunchtime, I ask Amando if I can have a shower. Despite I travel with my own, they provide soap and clean towel.

It takes only about a half hour for a young lad to stroll to the jetty at riverside and row downriver some fifty metres in a canoe to the rusty metal shed where the pump begins its whirring, and I have my river-water shower. When Amando sees me emerge, towel about waist, he waves to the lad who disappears again. I assume he paddles his canoe back to the bamboo jetty for I've returned to my room to dress in shorts, and Tee-shirt.

Lunch is a meat of some description and rice. I can buy either beer or Inca-Cola at room temperature or have free water from any of the huge ceramic water catchment jars under each veranda's roof.

From a bamboo shelf on the bamboo wall of the 'lounge' I take a book to read, one obviously, for there are some score or more in English, left over during the many years Jungle Lodge has been in business, by visitors pleased to relieve their luggage of that extra weight.

Suddenly there is excitement! The sounds of a launch break the jungle silence, the same as that which brought me here this morning. I guess there has been another plane. Possibly Peru Perhaps has arrived from the city?

Yes, a single gent who introduces himself Jack O'Connell of Reston, Virginia, USA. "I am happy to meet you, Jack. You are indeed welcome."

Amando doesn't quickly take him off to the native home to learn about blowguns but straight to his room on a different veranda from mine and it doesn't take him long to file away his things to join me in a beer.

"You find it a bit of a let-down, Ric?"

"No, Jack, I'm quite impressed."

Was that almost a dash of surprise flash across his forehead?

"Er, I...Do you know where there is a toilet that works?"

"Oh, you must have been given a cheap room."

"I thought it was all one class but my room is the shits. You have a better one?"

I lean across and punch his shoulder.

"I arrived only this morning and know exactly how your brain is spinning. I'm in the 'D' shaft in this fan of rooms and I watched them take you to the 'C' shaft. I haven't yet tried my toilet. Amando is Complaints Manager here. Go see him. He is somewhere behind the only other door in this whole jungle. At least it's the door he came through when I had lunch. Maybe he is also chef?"

"I have to go piss," and he stands up.

"The only other staff I've seen is a kid who pisses off the 'A' veranda."

Jack begins to get the message and grins, then heaves himself out of his chair and goes off through the door Amanda had used off the 'front' room on arrival.

Jack comes back through the same door, Amanda behind him, making for the 'C' shaft toilet. Jack unzips his pants and pisses off the veranda in front of his room, giving me a thumbs-up while at it.

Jack then has a shower, same procedure as mine. We then have more beers over a dinner same as I had for lunch except the meat is chicken, subsidized by a sizeable wedge of bread, still warm to the touch. A jug of instant coffee is served with sachets of sugar and powdered milk. All the staff, four in number, disappear once dinner is served, never to be seen again until morning.

Interested in what the social life of a four-man lodge in the wilderness might be, we ask of Amando at breakfast, best meal of the day I report in my notes, mountains of fresh fruit, guavas, melons, bananas and a various delight unknown, where they had gone.

They had played soccer at an Indian village and stayed late, getting very drunk.

The river on which Jungle Lodge stands is the Momon, tributary to the Amazon and it is everything to the jungle people, all of whom are Indians. It is their roadway, lifeblood of their farms, their bath and its swampy banks, their sewer. A few villagers walk into our camp from the jungle this morning, laden with produce for the market in town, hoping the launch would be in. They didn't mind a bit…just knew Amando would put them aboard whenever the launch next comes.

After breakfast Jack and I are taken on a large canoe just a short way upriver to where two eddies meet. We just sit as if stranded and never had I heard (or not heard) anything so quiet. There is just the rustle in the leaves of the overhanging jungle. We reach up from time to time to guide away trailing vines. What we think is forest either side, we realise as the canoe then glides through undergrowth, is really swamp as if the jungle is growing on water, a floating forest…

and the magnificent, eerie silence? I take a photo and the sound of the shutter is like a rifle crack.

The troubles of Bogota and Lima could be, in fact are, a million miles away.

We hear just the twittering of birds and the occasional call of a monkey which keeps out of sight. Clusters of wild orchids and other exotic flowers of unfamiliar description grow way up in the canopies. Butterflies are as big as soup bowls.

We are told not to trail hands or legs over the side, for this is alligator country.

Amando eases the canoe into a bank and we walk to a village to meet some locals to see how they live. Naked children and all but naked adults, their house built on shaky bamboo stilts, grow their own food and make trinkets from berries and fish scales dyed with berry juices.

They show us how they make the strings and twines from bark and from grass. Dogs, pigs and chickens have the run of the village and share the people's floorless houses like pets. Amando speaks the Indian dialects and I buy a fish-scale necklace for my sister.

During the afternoon we read novels.

At sundown the two young lads take us upriver in the same canoe and we drift down, each keeping quiet and listening to the night sounds of the jungle. In the otherwise eerie silence, we hear various night birds or animals and a lad whispers its name.

One is again spellbound at the remoteness of it all.

On return, dinner is on the table, again basic yet the best of the little available, after which the boys break out their hand-made instruments for an impromptu concert, all in Spanish, of course, Bassillio on guitar, Rafael on castanets and Amando on the *Caho*, a sound-box in which is a taut guitar string played with fingers as if on a harp.

Jack and I shout the boys beers and they are as happy as we feel.

On the morrow we go down the red Momon into the brown Nanay river, then into the yellow Amazon. We stop off at Barrio Florida, a village at the confluence of the Nanay and Amazon where people live in unbelievable squalor. One has the feeling that if it weren't for Amando and Bassillio, who keep us firmly in a tight little group, they'd in a trice put a knife in our backs.

I whisper to Jack, "I cannot say so, but I want to take photos of the filth and litter in which these people live, but should I do, I fear the consequences."

Jack doesn't speak but gives me deliberate nods.

We share relief when Bassillio suggests we make for the far side of the Amazon for our return journey, that the current in the now one-kilometre wide Amazon makes our battle against the down-river drift easier. During the crossing, I tell our two hosts how much I see the Amazon means as much to these people, as does the Nile to Egyptians.

I'm also of the opinion they'd never heard of either.

Dinner is the same as last night except the chicken has become fish. We have another join us for the meal, Paco, who is the biggest, noisiest yet friendliest Macaw in the world. His screeching is ear-splitting but he takes his turn sitting on Jack's shoulder, then mine.

We ask for more coffee but are met with a shrug. The kitchen fire is gone out and there can be no more coffee until breakfast. We are forced to buy beer.

Amando's young wife and littlies have arrived to spend the night and she would indeed be one of the prettiest girls I have seen in all my life...no make-up, yet vibrantly beautiful. I of course congratulate Amando and express my envy. His smile illustrates his pride. After dinner, Jack and I play chess and he is much stronger than me.

Breakfast is early because my flight from the town is at seven o'clock. There is no water for shower at that hour, so I cadge enough from the kitchen for a shave and to douse my hair. I am looking forward to sharing the trip with Amando's wife and littlies. Jack has yet another day to serve but comes for the ride, to return with whatever time the ferry comes to fetch him. He and I check out the melons we had so enjoyed at the Lodge and Jack buys some more.

He cuts half from the pile on the barrow to check it is the same, to take back to supplement the scanty meals. I could call it funny to watch, but poor Jack is horrified...he opens his mouth wide, to in fun illustrate just how wide he can make it, when a rat scampers over the barrow's edge to run across the cut slices ready for sale. Jack's mouth snaps shut like a clamshell, the half melon flying into the air as his arms jerk in fright, to fall with a splattering 'splodge' on the ground where several mangy dogs fight over it.

I cannot but burst into laughter.

After farewells I leave him then, for the airport and to enjoy the sights of the return journey as I had the other day...the 'red' jungle and the sheer magnitude of the awe-inspiring Andes goes on and on, twisting and tumbling almost inhospitably jagged, to the very horizon.

I am again enthralled.

~ * ~

Lima again...

We need to approach the airport from the ocean so once over the Alps find the 'surf' uninvitingly placid, but the general views beautiful indeed. The water however becomes quickly grey in colour, then quite brown. I can see now what why the guide books claim that even the locals will not swim in the Pacific Ocean off the Peruvian coast. The 'brown' is Lima's sewerage.

This time landing in the Jorge Chavez International Airport, I note that all around the airport is high barbed-wire fencing patrolled by the military...an ominous sight.

Eduardo is dutifully waiting and this time we drive directly down the beachfront to Miraflores along the Costa Verde. All is being rebuilt; all we see is scars of earthworks.

They spend money doing up the tourist strip, yet like the Colombians, leave the peasants to live in squalor.

"I have taken the liberty, Ric, of booking you into the Jose Antonio Hotel on Avenida 28-de-July. Still in Miraflores, it has a more sensible price and I have many visitors telling me it is comfortable and clean."

"A million thanks, Eduardo."

Once settled in, I go bank-hopping again and must be improving my technique in changing traveller cheques, for this time it takes me only one hour and five minutes to be happily served. Temperature today is at 28c low and 31c high which is norm for me, although humidity is 96%, a nasty sweat-building height. With the *guera* hovering over us, there is no sun to reduce the moisture in the air.

Tomorrow is a 5:00am pick-up, so I restrict my exertions and find sufficient 'crowd' in the streets to where a museum is open... smaller than anything in the city, but with at least some new information for me. I am relatively lucky. Walking back to the hotel there are even more people abroad, so all is well. Certainly, I look forward to Cuzco and Machu Pichu for they are Peru's biggest tourist attractions where I can wander at will.

Oops, or is that another 'famous last words' oversight?

I realise hiccups are all around me, just waiting to bounce.

I watch the TV until 9:00pm, shower and while dressing for dinner I hear gunfire, running and shouting in the street. From my window, however, I see nowt.

I am first to arrive in the dining room, but not a soul mentions those sounds of gunfire. As others arrive, most have North American accents and all realise the strain on locals of the rarity of what has just happened here...an entire parliament closed and one man seeming to have the people behind him turning it into a monocracy...it is whispered what a familiar situation befell Germany under Hitler....?

Again, I had an early night, none of us even considering going out, but I feel great when sliding under my plate on departing the table, a million inti!

Over our 4:00am breakfast for the Cuzco flight, I recognise an Oz accent in a woman and daughter. I catch her eye and ask, "Where are you from? Whereabouts in Melbourne? Whereabouts in Glen Iris? What number in Aintree Road?

Bloody hell, her family home is 63 Aintree Road, exactly opposite in the back lane of where Maggie and I had lived in 62 Maitland Street, Glen Iris. She admitted to often stealing our red apples that in season hung over our back-lane fence. How close can such coincidence occur over a breakfast table so far from Melbourne's Glen Iris?

Train travel into the Peruvian mountains had been temporarily suspended due to recent attacks by The Shining Path, a communistic anti-government terror group, so we all had no option but to fly to Cuzco. What I had failed to consider was how unprepared I was for the weather 'up there.'

At the airport I am confronted because every other passenger bound for Cuzco had slung over their arms, anoraks, scarves, gloves and fluffy-coifs. I am in shorts and T-shirt and my luggage has already been whisked away.

I'll just have to be quick getting quickly from the plane on arrival, and snatching my bag before Condor Travel luggage is put on our bus.

All the 'brave' elements in my strength already have me starting to shiver.

~ * ~

Lima Plus side: Can't think of much. I've simply had no option of seeing anything of style of life, interesting sights, in fact anything to be able to give fair marks to Lima. Taxis are cheap, but like taxis everywhere, if there is no meter, you will be robbed.

Lima Minus side: Beware Inca-Cola. The *guera* makes life depressing during all but the hottest summer months. Tour company transfers are essential. I warn against thinking you can save money by travelling independently. Even without the political crisis, there is danger in being alone or even in uncrowded areas if in a pair. Flights to jungle areas are the poorest standard I've ever fallen foul of. Trains cannot get over the mountains in Peru, only one unique one over the top ridge from Cuzco into Bolivia. But you need be brave to use it. I am to risk it... Not dangerous but bitterly cold all year around.

I urge you not to consider lone train travel anywhere. I had no chance to try city travel in Lima but from what I could see, its standards are poor. I've already in my notes under the *Lonely Planet Travel Guide,* noted remarked how poorly I consider their

South American reporters. I even feel they could be suable over recommending Hotel Claridge... but since 1992 they may have improved or gone bust.

~ * ~

Cuzco...

In a highly better aircraft, the crew is as offhand. We again fly seemingly straight up into the air until atop the Andes then for the rest of our one-hour flight it is more magnificent mountain scenery. We don't drop far to land, for Cuzco is 'way up there.'

Once off the plane, I shiver until seeing my bag amongst the pile for Condor visitors, its two white 'flags' against the black-pack beckoning me. I run for it, asking the driver to wait while I snatch something warm. It takes only minutes to find my Sloppy-Joe (Aussie expression for a warm, long-sleeved Tee-shirt) and neck-muffler. He grins and points to his own head, but I shake mine. I never wear headgear.

The big bus pulls up to San Augustin Hotel and we are met in the lounge with our first cup of Coca Tea and are asked not to follow our luggage upstairs until we had consumed three cups. Coca Tea in the Andes, even in April, is essential. We are shown where it is in bottomless taps on a power water heater and told to help ourselves several times a day.

"Otherwise you will find your balance senses giving up on you," we are warned.

I giggle to myself...*All my life I had told myself that I never get sick, but since my recent belly-bust in the hospital I remain over-conscious of how long between toilet trips I take, subject to when having eaten.*

Bloody hell, I sure was in trouble when running all those blocks searching for Condor Travel when first in Lima!

Mirabel, the local Condor guide, tells me Eduardo had phoned her to be sure to see me get well looked after. But happily, I quite love the Coca Tea flavour.

I book an afternoon English tour of the little town. I am free tomorrow (Good Friday), then Saturday we go to Machu-Pichu, arguably one of the most exotic of travel visits. Sunday I am booked for the colourful markets in Pisac. I have the whole of tomorrow to street-walk to sense the pulse of Cuzco, seat of and centre of the Inca civilization, and preparations for the Good Friday 5:00pm Easter Parade.

Maribel gives us all a map of the city and deliberately emphasises the area shaded in red...near half the city. "It is the Red City. If you tread a toe over the red line into it, you will be murdered."

Can you imagine the shock that this rebounds in everyone's belly?

"It is fraught with danger to every one of you, and me. In it, the people are absolutely possessed with religion, one you and I don't belong to, which to them means you should not be allowed to live. You will observe your danger when on Saturday we go to Machu-Pichu. We go by train and the station is inside that Red City. You will be locked into your buses with armed guards and bus windows are sealed."

My God, I'm sure everyone is spellbound. None is uttering a sound.

"I will remind you of it before you leave. It is a long day so has a very early start, a take-away breakfast at 5:00am and the bus for the station leaves at 5:15 sharp. Otherwise," she tells us with a grin, "you can safely enjoy your visit to Cuzco."

I am awake bright and early, enjoy three cups of Coca-Tea and at breakfast she beckons me to her table. She points to a spare chair beside her.

"I believe you write travel articles for an airline. Which one?"

I grin. "I write travel articles on any place, for a London agent who collects travel articles, all for sale to airline magazines...any airline, any route I choose. On this occasion I am on a personal assignment...an Australian newspaper is paying me to write an article on Cuzco's Easter Parade."

"Oh, I am fascinated. Have you established from where you will watch the parade?"

"I want to be on a level with the parade, where I can take photographs close up. I want to see the faces of those marching...the people to me are more important than the statues they help bear."

"I know the parade back to front. I've watched it every year of my life. Can I keep behind you, alert you to what is about to follow, give you some sign that might help?"

I pat her hand. "Yes, indeed."

After a good breakfast, I take to the streets to be accosted by an eleven or twelve year old lad with a tray of dreadful ceramic models of children and unrecognizable animals. His little tray of wares hangs by a braided loop around his neck.

"You man Nortamericano, eh?"

"No, Australianaro."

"Ah. Capital Canberra, and kangaroos and kookoobooroos."

As he half runs backwards ahead of me I correct him on the pronunciation. As a salesman all my early life, or forever really, in business, I don't have the heart to send him off. He's tried hard and probably knows some few details like that, for every country in the world. I ask the price.

"3 sol." He picks up a piece of shabby handiwork.

I pay him 2 sol and keep walking.

He keeps hastening beside me, his grimy little face aghast...

I tell him, "1 sol for Canberra, 1 sol for Kangaroo, but you got Kookaburra wrong."

I put the useless piece back on his tray and quicken my pace.

Top marks for enterprise, I reckon.

I notice every car parked at the kerb has no windscreen wiper. When enquiring I learn they will be in the car's glove-box. If left attached at the windscreen, they'll be stolen.

At a little shop I buy a small bottle of drinking water for $us2.62 when Inca-Cola is $us1.00.

Maybe because the bottle is expensive?

Posting a card from Colombia costs 30 cents. From here, $1.00. *Tourist city prices!*

I am amazed to find the cathedral closed.

And the museum.

And Library of Historical Records.

Bloody Hell...and this is Good Friday where there are no doubt scores of statues, portraits, Christian carvings and such, all significant to Christ's death?

I read the big placard outside the cathedral that I had been particularly anxious to see inside, on its history. Built by the Spaniards, begun as early as 1559 and is reported the city's greatest repository of colonial art.

And it is closed for the entire three days of Easter...the only time I can be here!

The church alongside the cathedral is *Iglesia El Triunfo*, oldest in Cuzco dating from 1536. Unfortunately, also the *Convent of Santa Catalina* is closed, also the *Convent* of *Santa Domingo* built on the foundation walls of the ancient *Temple of the Sun* called Qoricancha or Golden Cloister.

And this is a 'must' on brochures...the best existing example of Inca masonry.

And the *Archaelogical Museum* also highly recommended, is closed.

I feel bloody shattered. I've walked the kilometre around this parade ground and every damn religious interest is closed for Easter? At home, along with Christmas, it is the acme of religious services.

I am desperately lost!

When my brain feels easier to read, I have it urging me to explore more than this huge central square. I have been informed that the parade begins at 5:00pm, at this time of year here, still with plenty of daylight left for photographs. Here above the *guera* we have glorious sunshine at 5:00pm.

At 4 o'clock decorations on upstairs balconies begin being strung, and kerbside, ropes are being strung at hip level all around the square. The sun shines beautifully and already near every window around the square illustrates just how many people will attend. Every balcony already has people bearing chairs and stools from inside.

I'm already excited. I'll be closer than any of those people.

Already I have a jacket pin giving me right to be inside barriers yet am under instruction not to find my way amongst the marching group. Brass bands are warming and lighter ones are already playing what seem to be hymns with a very slow marching beat. Photographers are setting up cameras on balconies, many also with a jacket pin.

At 5:00pm crowds amass around the square, not just two or three deep, but a score, many having trouble with children ignoring barrier ropes but running wild.

At 5:30 I am beginning to worry about the sun getting already low.

By 6 o'clock I feel shitty. In the dark, distance for the flares in my camera have a limit and it is now reaching the stage where I want to be right up in front of the marchers, sometimes on the roadway and sometimes kerbside…if possible.

But this is South America, Ric. Running late is natural. Several people with cameras, however, are illustrating annoyance.

But do they hear my thoughts?

Suddenly a blast of trumpets has everyone cheering and the gates from the cathedral open and out march the parade leaders, some score of brass instruments, trumpets, bugles, kettle-drums and huge drums, their deep, slow thumps, the timing beat to all other instruments, very, very slow with several seconds between each. That timing thump persists for the entire march…each is a step, then pause. It will take an entire hour to circle *Plaza De Armas del Cuzco* when otherwise, 5 minutes.

And suddenly electric lights that brightly illuminate the entire square, switch on.

I suddenly realise as the halting steps of every man in the parade desperately struggles to keep to his feet under the weight of iron and marble statues, undoubtedly near every one of the massive monuments from the cathedral, churches and museums of the entire city. An army of poor wretches already sweating and they've moved but a metre.

No wonder, with all these massive symbols having to be moved out of their rightful places, that all were closed to visitors!

I spend half the march shuffling backwards on my haunches either in the very front of the procession or on each side of it, the outside being gradually thinning as eager crowds get pushed from behind, closer and closer to the poor sweating men bearing the 'impossible' weights of their burdens.

Their shuffling, painful steps never vary from the slow time-beat of the drummers.

Every woman is in tears.

Are many of the tears not necessarily for the love of the tortured Christ, or are they for the pain their menfolk must be experiencing?

And the slow *beat, pause, beat, pause, beat pause*…continues incessantly.

I will have it drumming in my ears for days!

Onlookers chant, weep and bless themselves without pause. Some prostrate themself themselves on the cobbles in the path of the procession, police having to move them with baton strikes and even whips, yet some seem to deliberately suffer the pain. The vestments and raiments worn by priests in the entourage are magnificent, many being replicas of 16th and 17th century robes.

For one who is, after all the wars I have seen, even from afar, non-religious yet conscious of being protestant rather than catholic, understanding little of the ritual, I am somehow in deep sympathy for these fellows illustrating such reverence.

Am I somehow feeling cleansed of guilt at being non-religious?

Once the tail of the march passes through the gates, to continue to the cathedral walls however, the silence is maintained.

By arrangement with friends, I queue for dinner at the Roma Restaurant built on a street corner of the square, in itself part of the original *Inca Pachacutec's Palace* which after the conquest became the house of conquistador Francisco Pizarro.

"How many times did you have to stop to renew your Kodachrome Slide film?"

"I reckon God had his time absorbed in giving strength to all those burden-bearers."

I tried to time my dinner menu back through the ages and ate *cuy* (roasted guinea-pig pronounced cooee), a delicacy of Inca times, washing it down with pisco.

~ * ~

Machu Pichu...

Come tomorrow, the hotel blots its copybook in serving our take-away breakfast for the *big* day of visiting *Machu Pichu* the world-famous City in the Sky. It is supposed to be served at 5:00am as our bus to the rail station *must* leave at 5:15 or we miss the train.

Take-away food isn't brought to the table until 5:13 and as the bus driver begins pumping its horn, the lucky ones with hats scoop hatfuls of apples and run for the door.

It is chaos. I grab a sandwich and run after them and we learn later that three people did not make the bus. They could only sit and curse all day over missing the greatest event of their expensive holiday.

As the bus crosses the red line, the *'red mob'* is waiting and begins banging tin dishes at windows, smashing hammers into the bus, even breaking windows but the bus-driver puts down his foot and speeds up so quickly that surely some *'reds'* must have fallen under. Scores of them line our route for the several blocks we must drive before passing through the 'neutral' railway station gates.

I will break whatever interest my readers may have, for it is essential anybody wanting to avoid this 'red people' 'event' I must explain that that dreadful experience is no longer valid. I depart this 1992 tale for the moment to simply report that the 2020 internet map shows that the rail line today leaves from the inner city, thus avoiding the dangerous 'red experience' I suffered in 1992...

We all are happy once on the train under armed guards, to find we are soon climbing higher in the mountains. I've occasionally experienced rail-line-switchbacks on steep mountainsides, but here the immediate rise is so steep that there are several switchback stretches in succession. For one agile enough to extend half his body out a window, it is a photographer's delight! The higher we go, the more woollies we don. Before long the city below looks like a Lilliputian village.

The sheer grandeur of the scenery reminds me in many ways of Yosemite National Park, except by many times closer to the clouds. In the few valleys between peaks, all Aussies remark on the 'gum-tree' forests of the only trees to grow at such a height. A few among us even keep windows open to savour the eucalypt aroma.

The three hours climb up the mountains is not for the faint hearted...many times one wonders why we simply fail to slide over the steep sides.

Arriving where the train can climb no higher, we still have to stretch backwards to see the Machu Pichu city still 'way up there'! We climb from there by bus.

Our road is another series of switchbacks and I have a window seat right over a back wheel...or does that wheel hang over the emptiness at every second corner? In the eight kilometres to reach Machu Pichu, there are sixteen such hairpin bends. To those with eyes closed and holding breaths, it seems more!

The 'city' of Machu Pichu is in fact where four hundred people grew corn and sweet potatoes and built a sophisticated system of irrigation. If the surroundings were a theatre we would call it 'up there in the gods.'

It is essential that you follow a trained guide who in your language details the significance of what you see. He or she in their microphone can tell you the 'why' of what you are seeing, and the how, else the venture is purposeless. The guides have developed marvellous abilities of conveying what archaeologists have discovered and are still assessing how people who left no written language, lived, but have to hurry to tell all that we now know. I miss much of the commentary, for in order to breathe at this altitude one must keep resting, to then catch up with the guide who is on a time limit. The limit is to ensure catching the day's departing train. Lots of underground passages beneath many a building added to Inca's accommodation space for with only rockwork as building material they needed 'understairs' whilst today we have 'upstairs.' So we are ever hurrying to keep up with our guide.

Every inch of Machu Pichu is exciting. There can be no disappointment when everything those people did, seems magic. It is sad the tour has to be so rushed but if you travel in a pair, ensure when one has to sit and rest then catch up, your partner gives special attention to what you miss, to tell you later. One tends to feel like skipping lunch or missing so many tales of 'back then.' What I had not realised is that if booked many months ahead, there is limited facility to stay overnight. One must be prepared to best the bus journey again each day for the accommodation is down by the train station as every spare little piece of ground up top had been put to good use by the Incas. There are always many little bits and pieces missed and hours cannot be increased when the train trip from Cuzco and back is six hours. It is indeed a long day to try to absorb it all.

During the train journey we discover the history of potato. A guide tells us South America has today, five thousand varieties, two thousand of which are still transmitted to markets all over the world. On our trip home, a wide range is on a platform for passengers to buy.

Arriving in the city it is dark and we again run the *'red attack'* on our bus.

My feet are so tired I have dinner in the hotel so I can get to bed A.S.A.P. Meals in Cuzco are always enjoyable. The only decent wine is Chilean, but so expensive I stay with *Cusquena*.

~ * ~

P'isaq (local spelling for what we call Pisac)...

In Pisac it is Sunday Market and I am surprised to find that thirty kilometres from Cuzco the little lad selling poor quality little 'icons' greets me with "Hey, Señor Australiana, I remember Kookaburra."

He tries selling me another little model or to get another dollar or two from me but I pat his shoulder and shoo him off. There are many stalls, each a blanket on the ground. Women spread handiwork and hold up a card with prices. There is a distinct large square shawl that every baby's mother uses as a sling or to carry items instead of a basket. They also wear them as woollen shawls in lieu of coats. They are so popular and so unique a design that I picture it, corner atop, draped on my living-room wall. She asks 12sol ($12) but I beat her down to $8 if I take her photo which costs another $1.

It is a bargain and in 2020 it hangs on my bedroom wall, still corner-point high.

We bus down the Urubamba Valley, lunch in a hotel's garden lounge with wild llama wandering from table to table for handouts, then on to Ollantaytambo, a very steep site, and I am finding breathing difficult. The air is so 'thin' that when our guide simply races to the top, I am struggling to drag myself slowly after him.

It is well that I persevere when others don't, for we are shown a natural eerie type 'fortress' made of the natural rockwork when the Spaniards lost their only defeat in conquering the country.

I reckon I know what defeated the Spaniards…they couldn't climb bloody higher!

Back in Cuzco I shan't say I am pleased, for at so many sites I would have loved to stay longer, but my entire body so misses its usual seaside, sub-tropical air.

Cuzco Summary…

Plus side: Both the town and various ruins are simply magic stuff. They do try hard to overcome these faults, yet are behind world superiority in dotting every 'i'. Time will overcome many of these problems.

Minus side: If not in a tourist group you will miss 90% of what you came to see. A brochure or booklet in each hotel room would be an asset. At San Augustin, one of the top tourist hotels, they get you up early because of the distance to sites, yet so early in the day with such cold air, we have no hot water to shower or shave.

The breakfast fiasco for early up days was unforgivable.

~ * ~
Puno and The Floating Islands...

We are told that all our train tickets are for carriage F, right behind the two engines needed to pull the six carriages for the highest train journey in the world.

Typical of organisation in Peru, every passenger tending to mark off in our minds that we need car #F does a countdown as we walk along the platform from Carriage A. The order of carriages is ABCEDF.

Only in cars E and F (First Class) are armed police ensuring safety for Tour Group passengers against theft. If taking this unique journey, try to get window seats on the left hand from which the scenery is unforgettable. The train climbs until reaching highest any train can safely go, for we are above the tree line, even beyond the Aussie Eucalypt Gum-tree which enjoys the title of highest green life in the world's highest ranges.

I am now into an area with not a tree between me and the horizon. When finding ourselves level with the range's highest peaks, the train starts to slip and slide on moist rails. We are held up more than an hour while they spread sand on the rails ahead. Several of us get out to 'stretch legs,' but I cannot take the freezing temperature and am quickly back aboard. Next 'site' is Puno on the northern tip of Lake Titicaca but this train does not get that far.

It is the highest rail journey in the world and takes six hours to cover our 350 km. On the crest, there is facility for the day's 'up' train and the 'down' train to pass and the down train is waiting. The few locals in the area, most of who have never travelled as far as Cuzco or Puno, are allowed to mount the train but must remain on the platform atop the few steps, hoping you or I might approach them to see their handiwork made from the yellow grass, the only plant they have. It supports the few head of cattle and pigs. Occasionally there is a family with a horse for commuting. They have llamas which yield wool to spin. There is hardly a motor of any kind on the plateaux, for the people have next to no money but hordes of children! The death rate is also high. Houses are adobes with roofs of thatch and earth as floors. Most houses are but one or two rooms and all is subsistence farming at its most basic. The train is their only link with civilisation but few can afford to use it.

All dress in colourful traditional garb, the brightness of the costumes a stark contrast to the drab landscape. I'm told most are born and buried on the *altiplano*, never having left it to see a city.

When the train reaches Juliaca, it stays one hour while changing engines to climb to Puno. Again, we are advantaged, for having booked through a tour company they have a bus waiting to take only us that last 30km. Those who bought their own tickets must wait that other hour in the freezing cold. Even so we don't get in until after dark and it is even more bitterly cold. There are but two hotels. I stay in Hotel Scillistani, right in the little town. We are told the other is a luxury hotel a long way out on an island where they "Have you captive and everything is expensive!"

Scillistani is basic but comfortable, reasonably priced and the food is good. I shiver and wear a skivvy, sloppy-joe, anorak, gloves and what I buy just a few doors away, a woollen beni to both wear both awake and asleep! An appeal to the concierge scores me a tiny radiator which warms the room somewhat while I am at dinner. No hot water for shower at this time of day. They have hot water only during mornings.

Tomorrow we visit the famous 'Floating Islands.' The local Indians are *Aymaras* and have a different language from the *Quechuas* in Cuzco.

Had I thought peasants on the *altiplano* eked a living from subsistence farming, Uros people have even fewer opportunities. Everything (yes, everything) comes from reeds growing in the lake. Most inhabitants have never travelled more than a few kilometres from home and survive practically without money. They cope with the constant cold because they have no option.

Water in the lake is constantly 6c degrees. The very islands are reeds-en-masse floating on the lake. As the bottoms rot, more are simply added atop. That top is their floor. Their metre-high walls are reed. The thatch on every house is reed. The fuel for their cooking fire is reed. Canoes, their only means of transport, are reeds. They use no furniture, but sit and sleep on reeds. Even the small gardens in which they grow small potatoes are of reed compost laid on reeds. Chickens and pigs have free range of the little islands, including houses.

The entire township has not a grain of soil, just reeds afloat on chilly water.

Each photograph taken costs $1. It is their only income.

We visit the one-room schoolhouse to which a teacher comes from Puno daily.

Our guide is another Eduardo. He tells me it is so cold in Puno that he and his family, which cannot afford heating in their apartment, sleep all together under six blankets.

After two days of this area, my lips are cracked and sore and my eyes smarting from the icy wind. This is their autumn.

With great difficulty I go back to the big lady whom I had photographed at her cooking position, again sitting of course, and with lots of giggling and finger language we agree on $us5.00 if I photograph her building a fire to warm stones that, helped by the sun, warm the small fish laid on them to make meal. She lets me taste one bite of her dinner of fish with a tiny potato, their only 'hot' (read 'warm') food.

She grinds the seed from the ears of the reed into a sort of flour for baking a sticky-finger bread.

I didn't get to ask how that is done, for she has clamped her mouth which I guess means my five dollars' worth has expired. I nevertheless pay her $us6.

Back in Puno I walk the town in ten minutes seeking its bank, hoping it can change a traveller cheque. Murphy takes a hand when I am informed it doesn't have $us but only Nuevo Sol. I don't want that because I leave the country tomorrow.

"Seeing I will be in Bolivia tomorrow, do you have Bolivian currency?"

The four staff of the town's bank roar with laughter. They suggest I take the Nuevo Sol into the street and change it with the money vendors (those with the sacks on their shoulders) for $us.

I probably get stung, but it all seems to tie up near-enough in my brain-box.

The next morning we leave Puno in a minibus, skirt the shore of Lake Titicaca, stopping for an hour in the little town of Juli. It is market day and, in the square, ladies squat on rugs selling all sorts of wares. Men dress in Sunday best (drab suits brought out on special occasions for the last twenty years, I reckon) and march to a tin-pot band in support of Fujimoro, the Presidenté who has appointed himself dictator in attempt to stamp out graft and corruption.

Approaching the Bolivian border at Yunguyo, we sight the highest peak on the Andes, 6,550 meters (more than twice Aussie's Kosiusko). On the Peruvian side of the border, I try to quit my remaining Sol and Inti for $us, without success. Peruvian people just don't trust Peruvian money.

I must take it out with me, yet they demand it is paid in $us. Those of us without a $us in our pocket have to borrow one until over the border. Without it, we cannot get a release stamp in our passports.

50 metres further on, over the Bolivian border, they are not only happy to change $us for Boliviano, but happily cash the traveller cheque. They even accept my small balance of Peruvian Sol and Inti.

I hadn't realised that the Boliviano is so weak that any other currency is profit.

Summing up Peru...

Peru has much to do if it wants to attract tourism. It has a magical history, scenery in tremendous variety and attractions galore, from the steamy jungles of the Amazon to the awe of Machu Pichu and Floating Islands on Lake Titicaca, highest lake in the world. In servicing the tourist, they rate far below world standards. If one is prepared to accept inconvenience, the shortcomings add to the uniqueness and character of the way of life, yet for those who want to enjoy their travel in comfort, the lack of electricity in major centres is a problem and hotel plumbing is reminiscent of the Greek islands.

Thankfully, the frustrating farce of money-changing is temporary.

Fourteen

Bolivia...
    Bolivia time is one hour behind its northern neighbours and visitors do not need a visa...they will accept anyone with any sort of money. Their latest good news is that they have reduced inflation to 43%.
    Just across the border is the town of Copacabana where Condor Travel hands us over to Bolivia's Crillon Tours. We lunch at a little restaurant and take a quick tour of the church which dominates the tiny town...built in 1678 it is the centre of a big festival every year. The wealthy church is resplendent indeed with a solid silver altar with gold statuettes, a marked contrast to the poverty of the people who persist in giving the church needful pennies. We are told as we bus to LaPaz, the world's highest capital, that despite family poverty, the birth rate of children is the highest in South America.
    "If they've no money, what else can a man do with his time?" asks a male member of our group.
    I am continually reminded that the Catholic Church is the most revered of any pastime on this continent. This little town of

Copacabana's 2,000 people becomes three times a year, 5,000. From all over Bolivia people pilgrimage to it, to trek up the mountains overlooking Lake Titicaca. Compared with Peru, the town is clean and the Hotel Patria on the town square looks inviting to hungry tourists.

After a ridiculously cheap but magnificent lunch, we board Crillon Tour's hydrofoil and speed south to Island in the Sun, believed by locals to be where the Inca civilisation began. Inca lore claims the sun was born there and is even today 'sacred.' The air is thin and I choose not to climb to the top for a view. I stay to photograph children with their pet llamas for a dollar each. In passable English they tell me that three commandments are taught every child…Don't be lazy, Don't steal, Don't tell lies.

We arrive on the eastern shore at Huarina's small but smart museum of Bolivian history. We are each, according to our personal language, given a tape and earplug as a commentary guide and are let loose among exhibits covering peasant farmer lifestyles. In another bus, all downhill, I am happy to sight the first trees in the last three days, yes, eucalypts. Around yet another bend, we pull to the right and are told to look out over the side and 'down there' is LaPaz, like the mini-city of Holland's *Maduradam* except LaPaz is real, simply seeming miniature. No wonder, I later realise that only small aeroplanes can land in LaPaz. The capital's major airport is down in jungle country.

As we drive downhill for the rest of our journey, a prominent snow-covered mountain is pointed out…"That is *Illampu,* Bolivia's tallest."

Our guide Doris gives us a rundown of recent Bolivian history, the loss of the two wars they've fought, one resulting in surrendering much of their Chaco district to Paraguay and another, loss of their only access to the Pacific Ocean to Chile. Because the wars sapped the country of so many men, these are now a significant minority. In its 164 years of independence, Bolivia has had 189 governments. The people have become used to coups, military takeovers and unstable government. It is South America's poorest country and in 1984 the inflation rate had been an incredible 24,000%!

With it now 'only' 43%, people must still live frugally. Salaries are paid twice daily, when leaving for lunch then when finished for the day. That way they can spend it before it has lost even more of its value.

"Your population?" someone asked.

"We don't know. There has not been a census since 1936 but the estimate is 1 1/2 million in LaPaz and there is no estimate for the rest of the country."

We pass the city airport, highest in the world at 4,100 metres and it has the world's longest runway at 5.1km. Even so, in the thin air, only small plane can use it. Santa Cruz, 800 kilometres away, is where worldly people commute.

Arrival in LaPaz is a shock. We twist and twine on our road, side-views only of rock until we turn a bend and of a sudden, here is the city. We can from here look up to the snow-capped mountains surrounding it...a spectacular scene.

Crillon Tours drop me at Hotel Rosario, booked from home and finishing any pre-booking in South America. From here on, I am on my own day by day. My plan is to fly to Santa Cruz on the jungle floor then train east into Brazil's Mato Grosso, then south through Paraguay to the world's biggest waterfall, Iguazu, the 2.7km wall of water, into Argentina. What I have to discover here, however, is just how dangerous is the rail journey from Bolivia to Brazil. I've had several warnings about it.

Tour guides in LaPaz indeed improve on what my *Lonely Planet* provides. Rosario has everything a traveller needs, even a tourist office. Restoration is still in hand; house lounge, dining room and bar are complete and three floors above are so far all tourist accommodation. On the top floor, my room is so new that my bed is being made up for the first time. There is yet no lift and I must trudge up the three flights of stairs and in the thin air, this is tiring. I must stop and rest halfway. My single room is yet the only complete one on the floor and is delightful. Fortunately, they have someone carry my bag up. Oh, how nice it is to have a spanking new room, brightly painted, modern bathroom with plumbing that works and a toilet that flushes. In South America so far, these are available in only 5-star hotels. So far anyway, Rosario is priced at 4-star. Next to my room but yet unfinished is a glass-roofed solarium with *jacuzzi*.

I lock all my gear in my room to walk down the hill to the town before the banks close, to change cash. It is a delightfully clean city with people aplenty as are cafés, yet I still shiver. I change money, conscious that I keep enough to pay my food bill and shopping without having to change yet another traveller-cheque.

Tomorrow I will make up a parcel of souvenirs and the extra-warm clothing I have had to buy, for after leaving this altitude I shall need none of it. Postage from here will be cheaper than further south.

It is a slow climb back to the hotel but then find the dining room and food is good and cheap. Several Australians are here and I already feel good about Bolivia in general. That night I sleep soundly.

Tourist company Turisbus has a desk at the hotel and after breakfast I sign up for an afternoon tour of the city, then for tomorrow a full day tour of the *Tehuanaco* ruins, Bolivia's biggest. Strange system, they book only pairs for the half-day tour of the city. If the bus company has another single, I get it for the listed price and if alone, I pay double! Luck is again with me for there is another single and I'm to be picked up at 2:00pm.

In the meantime, I walk downtown to send off postcards and post off slide films for processing and the now redundant clothing. It certainly is nice to walk around in this highest capital city in the world feeling safe, yet with some difficulty in breathing in what they call the 'thin atmosphere.' It is so hilly that I have to take it slowly, an old city yet with several modern buildings, mostly empty.

As I had found in Cartagena, it is unlikely these buildings will be tenanted as no company can afford the rents. If they don't build them, they will lose foreign aid from 'the rich powers' and the number of unemployed would worsen. Bolivia has few motor-cars, men dress very drab and most women wear traditional garb. Those in bowler hat and pleated skirt are married. The unmarried wear no hats and wear un-pleated skirts.

Beats laying out money you don't have for wedding-rings, I guess.

I lunch in the tiniest of cafés with no idea what is the strange tasting paste in the freshly made bread as lunch. Back in the hotel, with the 2 o'clock bus not arrived at 2:35 the tourist lass phones the bus company. The other of my 'pair' had cancelled, so I don't get my city tour. I've simply been 'stood-up' without notice.

I've a wasted afternoon for I cannot face more walking the steep city hills. I dig out my novel but cannot concentrate.

I'm here to bloody 'see' the place and note interesting places!

I lay the book on my bed, put my woolly sweater back on and take off down the hill.

I will make my own bloody 'city tour.'

The tour lass is at her desk as I pass, so stick my head in the door to ask her opinion about my plan to train through the jungle to Brazil. Looking startled, she freezes.

She points across her desk to the empty chair.

As I sit, she swallows whatever had been in her mouth.

"Train from Santa Cruz to Corumba alone? Only a misguided fool would try that, Mr. Ric. To board that train alone is suicide! Nine out of ten in the Santa Cruz ticket office will refuse to sell you a ticket, and the tenth will be in the pay of the 'passengers' who will rob you of your clothes and luggage, then throw you from a window as food for the wild-life."

I swallow extreme disappointment. Corumba on Brazil's side of the Bolivian border is but spitting distance from Paraguay, a country renowned for gun-running. And the Matto Grosso Pantanal is reputed as a land of 'lost tribes,' a land I would love to visit.

There is no road through that part of the world nor any flight, just the lonely train.

I am sensible enough to be led by people who know this part of the world, so have no option but to fly to Ascuncion, then make my way to Guazu Falls from there.

"When can I do this?"

"Tuesdays with Paraguay Air, $us380 or Fridays with Lloyd Bolivian Air, $us211."

"Why the big difference in price?"

It seems Bolivia hits the opposition with taxes so its own airline gets the patronage.

"Your system imposes a $us169 penalty on me if I stay to spend my tourist dollars in Bolivia, but I can save this by leaving tomorrow to spend them in Paraguay?"

She shrugs shoulders and I tell her I think it Irish rationale.

With planning like that, no wonder Bolivia lost its two wars.

So I don't get to see the *Tehuanaco* ruins, and the hotel refunds the two further nights I had prepaid. Nor do I see more of Bolivia so I go for a final walk, not down to the city again but on the current level in the opposite direction.

I soon reach a pretty little square with sidewalk cafes, even further amused at the dress of simply everyone. Up a very steep hill and on a narrow-cobbled street is a marketplace of tents. The entire street is a shopping bazaar.

It would seem that LaPaz has no department stores as we know them. All retailers seem to be mum-and-dad type businesses, even for furniture or clothing and in markets is how people shop twice daily. I take several photos of people lugging new furniture on their backs and hope for their sake that they live somewhere downhill rather than uphill.

Filled with disappointment, I turn for home for Coca Tea which I've been taking frequently, and to pack and eat a hotel dinner.

Come morning at the checkout desk, I ask how much I should expect to pay for a taxi to the airport and another guy checking out suggests we share. He is a Brazilian from Rio and also flying to Asuncion. We wait together, fly side by side and consequently share lots of conversation. Edgard Neto and I are to correspond for years to come.

News for travellers reading this is that I find Lloyd Bolivia Airline most efficient. We land at only Cochabamba on mountain edge before dropping to Santa Cruz, Bolivia's major airport at jungle level and from where I'd planned to entrain to Corumba.

In the descent from the *altiplano,* we fly through some of the thickest cloud I've ever experienced and on touching down in Santa Cruz, the rain falls in torrents, typical jungle weather. The consolation is that I can at last again breathe in comfort. I had expected a hick town but its airport is one of the most modern I've encountered since leaving home, even the new one in Athens. We are here for an hour, but having cleared through customs in LaPaz, we are not allowed to leave the transit lounge.

Despite sad at reneging more out of Bolivia and seeing the Pantanal countryside, I am excited that I shall see more of Paraguay than planned.

As we take off, it's a noticeable change from the *altiplano* for it is again all green cultivation as far as the eye can see, green jungle in red soil. We fly through an incredible storm to rock and bump our way for the next hour.

Bolivia summary...

I can unfortunately have little to say...Plus Side: Crillion Tours is efficient and professional, an excellent introduction to the country from its north. It is cheap and with excellent beer. Its people are gentle and helpful.

Minus side: That a positive attitude engendered by one tour operator can turn negative for the other, by an unknown change of mind.

A tip for travellers: LaPaz is the highest capital in the world and the rare thin air makes life uncomfortable. Some can become physically distressed by even slight exertion. Plan your trip so you arrive overland rather than by air, to give your system an opportunity to better acclimatise. Bring altitude sickness tablets and drink plenty of Coca Tea.

~ * ~

Asuncion, Paraguay...

All is green and wet as we fly in. It has stopped raining, but all is soggy red soil.

"I am sure the rain stopped for us to walk from the aeroplane's stairs to the bus," Edgard explains.

Once indoors, what am I to find in this country's habits? Like Bogota? Lima? LaPaz? or something entirely different?

First impression of the airport is that it is neatly clean, neither new nor old and seemingly organised, no armed soldiers or signs of panic, just soft music in the background. Unsurprisingly, it rejects Bolivian currency which I had carefully cleared in favour of tax-free wine on departing. And I have no problem at all in exchanging my traveller cheque for *guarani,* local Indian language for 'money.' For my $us200 cheque I receive 240,000 *guarani.*

Again, I share a taxi because we pass Edgard's regular hotel en route to my booked one.

On arriving I see that it claims itself one of Paraguay's best hotels, modern and comfortable yet is in need of renovation.

I had forgotten to ask Edgard what I should expect to pay for the taxi that did not have a price meter and the driver asks for 30,000g which sounds exorbitant. As in such instances, I wait for the hotel doorman to open my door, to ask what I should pay.

He audibly informs me that "10,000*guarani* would be very generous."

I let him open my door as the scowling driver drags my luggage from the boot.

I tip the doorman. The hotel is somewhat expensive compared with what I had been paying, but feel ready for some pampering.

Hotel Guarani occupies an entire city block and has a huge pool, gymnasium, steam-room, shopping arcade and as I sit in the lounge with an excellent beer, note that it is where Asuncion people come to be seen and where the beautiful people drink and dine...

real 5 Star ambience. I check out the pool and gym to see if massage is included anywhere and yes, and no appointment is needed. I am immediately into a steam-room to sweat up then enter the massage room, towel about my waist as usual, to find the masseur is a huge woman with arms like bullock thighs. Before I can turn to see if there is another room notice, she whisks the towel from me and lifts me onto the massage bed...

At least she's not going to cause me getting an erection.

And happily, she's turned me face down.

It certainly is taking so long, and with such heavy pressure, well worth the $9 and a 10% tip that she's surely not going to turn me...

Suddenly I feel a great arm slide under my belly and the other under my thighs and tumble me over.

The front massage is quick and she takes considerable care not to touch me *there*.

I happily pay her $10 and live to see another day.

Yes, it was indeed an excellent massage!

Across the wide hall are the bar on the left and the dining room on the right and beyond each are glass-wall doors into a garden that surrounds the entire hotel except for the entrance. I shout myself a beer. It arrives on a tray, an opened large bottle of their most palatable *Baviara* along with nuts to nibble and a fancy-folded serviette for 3000g ($2.15).

Dare I have another? I still suffer from the disarming effects of my strange massage fears, yet time overcomes them.

I don't have another but stroll into the garden and wander, discovering that the hotel takes up the entire block. Traffic flows around every side. The swimming pool is huge! And dinner? Cheap at half the price! For 3,000g($15) I have duck with all trimmings followed by peaches, pears, figs, dates, coffee and a half bottle of reasonable wine.

Maybe I should come and live here?

One thing to like about Asuncion is that it seems more like home than any South American country so far. How sad they don't have a decent surf beach! Even driving from the airport, houses with front lawns and front fences…trees throughout the *'residencia'*…all looked just like home.

Come morning I take a stroll across the hotel's street, one of the four surrounding a housing block-sized square. Even the people here look more like westerners, not dark-skinned with cheekbones, the features of Indians. And they dress more like us.

Paraguay is unique in that it is the only country on the continent to have achieved independence from Spain without a war. One thing it shares with Bolivia, however, is its shortage of men. Chatting with honeymooners in the hotel lounge over drinks, she asks how many men to each woman does Australia have? Both are amazed at my "fifty-fifty."

"Paraguay has never known equality. We have two women to each man."

He explains that whilst Paraguay is the only South American country to win independence without a war with Spain, it has had wars with every neighbour, losing every one. The number of men killed has ever been a problem.

"One time," he adds, "we foolishly took on the combined might of Brazil, Argentina and Uruguay and came off a dreadfully poor loser. The country has seldom been free of military and oppressive dictators…"

His bride puts a finger to his lips and looks about to see if others might have heard.

I don't spoil their honeymoon by asking if I can sit with them for dinner.

Waking up Saturday morning it's nice to breathe normally. I go walkabout and many streets are given over to markets. Lots of people are about and goods are set out not on tables but on mats on the ground like in the Peruvian uplands. Goods are similar to those of western street markets. In the main street LaPalma and for several block after block, are strolling musicians, street theatre, marching girls and sidewalk artists. In the square opposite the hotel are chess games and fortune-tellers. It seems all Asuncion turns out to be part of festivities.

The city is right on the western border of the little country, standing at the confluence of the Paraguay and Confuso rivers and from my 7th floor room, tall for Paraguay, I see on the far western horizon, the river that is the border with Argentina.

At the hotel desk, day tours list set prices for pairs and I'll have no part of that, rather spend the day amusing myself among the happy crowd at a parade. Marching girls from neighbouring countries, each with their proud national flags...all a reminder of the military parade I'd witnessed in Bogota. Streets surrounding the square are given over to the march which is indeed colourful. There is little doubt that Latin people love pomp, and when it comes the turn of the Paraguayan team to strut its stuff, the crowd grows wild. There is no doubt South American countries have unenviable histories of military disasters and political oppression, but that everyone is wildly patriotic.

After a late but smaller dinner, I cross a side street to a bar to discover that Carousel is more than a bar. I am met by a 'domo' in black tie and ushered to a bar where four scantily clad but beautiful damsels descend on me. One throws an arm about my neck and plants a kiss on my cheek, another in my shocked moment, in just in a lacy black G-string, hoists herself on my knee and begins prattling away in Spanish.

Shit, realise I...I've landed myself in a bloody brothel. This is the last sort of problem I need.

I struggle afoot, apologise to the doorman and scamper back to the safety of the hotel.

I've decided to make Asuncion a lazy time, a chance to recharge batteries while in a decent pub. Tomorrow I fling myself over a lounge by the pool. It is a particularly hot day and as humid as only a jungle country can be, and it's a good large pool. A Miami Florida lady is draped on a sun-sofa nearby and tells me I am being sensible, for all the expensive tours she had taken, 'turned out flops.' "There was little to see anyway, so I enjoy myself better here with a good book. There is a good bookstore downtown."

After my small dinner last night and faced with those beautiful girls that just weren't my type, I'd rather return to my habitual taste of satisfaction, a decent dinner and find a tour-book with hints on what I should do tomorrow.

I begin with a huge steak for dinner, so tender that I again choose to eat with two forks, my dessert a *crepe* cooked at table and a half bottle of Chile wine for $au23...an evening that hints of disappointment that Maggie is not with me.

The tourist office in Asuncion city is not where Lonely Planet has it marked. I note to inform them when home, that it is now on Park Boulevard.

A Monday visit to the bus terminal via taxi is a longer way than I should have taken a bus. And this other side of town shows me a different Asuncion. It has no separate bungalows like those I saw coming from the airport. Here people live much like in countries to the north and everything is stained red from the soil because grass doesn't seem to grow here. In this part of Asuncion, I certainly would not like to walk alone.

The bus station is huge! Fare to Ciudad del Este, a city on the eastern border with Brazil called Puerto Stroessner (until the last revolution when Stroessner is disgraced and all his statues torn down) for only 10,000g ($us7) to travel the length of the country.

Very cheap!

But then I see the buses...all are in need of some sort of restoration. The trip takes an entire day, stopping for lunch at a dingy town (I am to find all small towns somewhat dingy) called Colonel Oviedo. I had spotted from the taxi, quite close to the bus station, a car rental service so take a bus travelling back that way. That uncomfortable trip convinces me to drive, even if several times the price.

And I can stop if I see something interesting. Yet being alone, am I in more danger should I have trouble? But this ain't Mato Grosso.

I look for all the reasons I should choose to drive. What did Omar Khayyám say?... "*...and Wilderness is Happiness enow*"?

"Can I have a test drive?"

"Yes. I shall accompany you."

I am happy and he is happy.

"Our eastern office is not in Paraguay but Brazil. The city of Ciudad del Este is in both. The border divides that city."

I show him my passport with the visa for Brazil and my Australian driving license.

"You probably don't need either, but just as well you have them."

The price is thrice the bus fee but I trust my driving more than the bus, which takes an entire day because it stops all along the way. I will arrive earlier so can 'look around.'

On the morrow I taxi to the car yard and buy a map. Again of course, I am driving on the wrong side the road, but there is no centre line or side line and even when crossing a road on foot I'd got used to looking first to my left rather than right. And there are not too many great holes in the bitumen. As I cruise past a signpost pointing left to Colonel Oviedo, it reminds me that it is where the bus stops for lunch, yet I am here by 10:36am.

So yes, I'll be at my goal hours ahead of the bus.

Most country houses seem small when I expected to see large 'hasciendas' with farms of livestock wealth. Such are few. And when I get to Ciudad del Este on Brazil's border, I find it a city of absolute squalor! Its main street is store after store of modern electric domestic appliances and little else, all busy, no doubt fighting each other over pricing, for lots of vehicles with Argentine and Brazilian number plates are laden with purchases at obviously cheaper prices than at 'home.' The goods are the only clean things in the entire city. Mangy dogs either alive or smattered on roadways abound, and rubbish of all sorts blows about the streets from the strong yet no doubt welcome, wind.

I wind up my car windows against the stench.

No, I wouldn't like to live here, but there is much everywhere to interest visitors.

On my map it is but a half km to the car-rental yard on the Brazilian side of the border and my brain whirls with interest in why the boot of my car is locked, yet not with the same key as I have for driving.

Am I smuggling merchandise across a border for this company?

Fortunately however, I am never questioned and still wonder if I had been the 'patsy' running guns or drugs in my car's boot.

A lad from the car yard drives me to the bus stop where I leave for Argentina after my hurried visit (an hour) in Brazil.

I am very happy that I don't have longer in this part of both Paraguay and Brazil.

Argentina's Puerto Iguazu, I'm told, is but an hour away by bus.

My Paraguay summary:

Plus side: Ascuncion City culture is more familiar to Australia than northern neighbours, and it's cheap. If considering retiring to a South American country, from what I've seen, stick to cities. I certainly recommend Hotel Guarani. By 2020 I'm sure it will have a different masseur. Standard of its major highways is reasonable and car rental is cheap. Minus side: Avoid Ciudad del Este or to whatever it is renamed…many South American cities are named after successful military generals, yet torn down when he is disgraced, which is often…so many cities or highways keep changing names.

Beware taxi-drivers.

~ * ~

Iguazu Falls and Argentina…

Argentina is one hour behind Paraguay and Bolivia. Its 'Australe' is no longer the name of their currency which has been divided by 10,000 to make '1 peso' which (for the moment) is \$us1. In 1992, inflation is running at some 24%, far better than the 3,000% they suffered only three years ago.

Puerto Iguazu township to Hotel Internacional at the Falls is a 20 kilometre bus ride. It is the only accommodation, a 5 Star hotel with 6 Star prices. In 1992 the only other accommodation is 20km back in the town. Internacional has two room prices…with a view to the Falls, $us142 per night; the other side, $114...both extremely expensive by South American standards.

The ten-minute walk to the Falls via a large underground tunnel, is subject to not only deafening sound but that you are being sprayed by water in the very air you breathe. From either, you cannot escape.

Suddenly, however, there they are, right on the actual Iguazu Falls...

WHAT-A-SIGHT!

You can shout at the top of your voice to the partner at your side but cannot be heard. There is so much water whirling around in the air that within seconds, every garment you wear is drenched. It is also shattering to the ears.

The width of falling water is 2.7km! Unless paying $us200 for ten minutes in a helicopter, no one can see the fall all at once for it is in an S-shape.

I wear a jungle rain-cape with hood and am drenched from spray before even emerging from the tunnel. To suddenly see this in front of you, you are already being deafened by the roaring sound. Its very intensity is frightening.

I am one of the few brave enough to walk to the very end of the timber 'jetty' that juts out on angular struts from the rock cliff on 'our' side, to look down the 80 metres (250ft) to where the water falls into the tumbling river. It is frightening.

I would like to stay three nights so I have the opportunity to see the falls from both the Argentinian aspect and Brazilian, but that would mean an extra day...I instead spend $200 for the ten minutes over all in the helicopter...worth every cent!

The notes and coins of the new money are released, yet the old peso in both are also in circulation that makes one very confused. In Peru it had been difficult enough for twin currencies for my ageing brain, arranged by the million, but here it is 'by the ten thousand' and if wanting to avoid an expensive mistake, I need pencil and paper.

In 1992 there are no such things as Facebook so it costs me $us10 to receive 100,000 australes (10 pesos) so I can send postcards home.

Local beer is Santa Fe but is not a patch on beers in Colombia, Peru, Bolivia or Paraguay.

It rains the entire two days and nights I spend here, but that does not spoil a thing for the very air we breathe is damp, inside or out.

I still cannot see how one can see the falling water from the Brazilian side, but from the Argentine side one sees the actual contact.

I again find it difficult to bear in mind the 'late' dinner hour in this part of the world. Even in 5 Star hotels, most restaurants don't open until 8:00pm. If you arrive at 8:30 you eat alone. Most arrive between 9:00 or 10:00 and even 11:00. First night here I eat in the main dining-room and, much to the delight of the head waiter, order steak-tartare. With great flourish he mixes it at my table. I had been told by many that Argentina is the beef capital of the world and I need to test it. My penchant anywhere is 'bloody blue' as Aussies call the rarest, but 'tartare' is the ultimate. It is simply not cooked.

On my second night I eat in the less expensive 'Family' dining room.

If not part of a guided tour, leaving the hotel is either difficult or expensive. The only bus service does not enter the hotel's huge grounds but in the 'dry' area some hundred metres walk away, one trundles your own luggage to the bus. The alternative is taxi for all the 20km. I am in luck that the rain has stopped, for I walk the 100m to the bus-stop.

At 7.45 the sun is shining brightly and I am accompanied by not only the roar of the Falls but the persistent screeching of scores of vibrantly coloured macaws, all the way.

It is a 6-hour bus drive over pot-holed roads to Posadas, where I will stay a day or two. From there on, I have no forward bookings for either accommodation or travel, so can take things on chance. I have a list of the sites I want to see and Posadas is the closest town to the Santa Ana and San Ignacio, sites I'd seen in the movie *The Mission*.

My Life, My Travels

~ * ~

Posadas, Argentina's Missiones province...

Being early for a seat, I am invited by the driver to take the front seat right behind him. "You can see more of our country from there and will not have people passing in front of you."

The 300km to Posadas is a comfortable ride, for the road is in good condition. $16.35 for the 6-1/2 hour trip is reasonable. I am amused that the driver has on his dashboard, a thermos of *Yerba Marte,* a caffeine 'stimulant' marketed everywhere in the country. Argentinians carry it with them and sip it all day long and I guess likely into the night. On several occasions, he pulls in front of a store and his conductor leaps out, returning with the driver's thermos topped with boiling water.

Hotel Posadas is $50 *con desayuno* (with breakfast) for bedroom with bath. On the next street is a delightful restaurant La Querencia, two meat courses, a bottle of wine, a cognac with coffee for $22.90. Argentina is certainly a more expensive country than in the north, but I've been expecting it and budgeted accordingly. When La Querencia's manager, with a smile, asks what my 'talking to yourself into that machine' is about, I tell him I write articles for travel magazines for airlines. He fetches from his desk a 10cm *Yerba Marte* cup, a metal cup with a thick wooden insert enclosed. It is printed:

*'CHURRASQUERIA * GALETERIA, La querencia, BOLIVAR 322.POSADAS Tel. 34955.37117'.*

"I hope you might mention my restaurant in your reports," he requests.

I still wonder how it is manufactured with its thick wooden inner lining and a solid metal outer lining when the vertical shape varies. With its metal 'straw," it too sits in my china cabinet.

Another example of how chatting with locals can end up being helpful, is at Hotel Posadas. On asking the desk clerk about help to visit the *Missionies,* I end up with hiring not only a car with driver but a high-school teacher in the English language, all at a cost well within my budget. The teacher is his daughter, the driver his brother, both free on Saturdays. The day will cost me $us140 and the BMW is modern.

Tina is a sweet lass, Nico wanders through the exhibits with us, contributing his historical knowledge on how Spanish invaders and the Indians with their own beliefs. It is truly a telling exercise. So many of the temple ruins and what could over the centuries be restored of ancient Indian settlements tell the dreadful difficulties of the early years. Locals insist that somewhere there must still be hidden many millions of gold handicraft by early Indians who had no written language. They give me a great day of information and the story of each architectural ruin.

Sunday is a quiet day in Posadas and having been afoot most of yesterday, I spend the morning reading. Come afternoon in a supermarket I buy a large can of *Yerba Mate*, hoping it will prove as non-narcotic by Australian customs as is Fiji's *Kava*. And I am to have no problem with that.

My hotel has no dining room other than for breakfast and here, restaurants close on Sundays. I find however, a very busy pizzeria. Although I find pizza fattening and avoid it, at a 10:00pm dinner I front a large pizza and two beers all for $10.90. The policy insists no food be left; leftovers are to be taken in a 'doggy bag.' That helps me; it can be tomorrow's lunch.

Posadas is on the southern side of the Paraná River and on the northern shore is Paraguay's *Encarnacion* so each accepts the other's currency. On Monday I quit my remaining *guaranis*. This availability had also been learned from chatting with locals.

I settle up at the hotel and take a taxi to the bus station. For Buenos Aires I have to book a seat. It is a long haul, but rather than fly I prefer to see the countryside, much of which is along the border of Uruguay. It is now noon but I cannot get a seat until 9:00pm. so have a long wait and an overnight trip means seeing no countryside. It is 1,060 km, the fare is $us41 and the bus arrives at 7:00am tomorrow morning.

At 6:30pm, a bus comes in and I ask if it has a spare single seat and yes, I am lucky also that it is a window seat. On a longer route than the later bus, it also arrives at 7:00am. Only two hours out, we are halted by machine-gun toting police. They announce that all luggage locked up below is to be inspected and everything we have with us in the bus will be individually searched. Seven other buses are also under inspection. We are told this is a regular occurrence because of the continent's considerable drug trafficking.

A special 'drug traffic' department of the Argentine Police Force makes random raids. All luggage is opened. If locked and nobody comes forward with a key, locks are broken. All is done by torchlight. A couple with a baby has even their pile of nappies inspected piece by piece and the mother has to lift the baby out of the hand-crib while it is searched. The bus carries several cartons of consigned freight and random ones are slit open with bayonets. I, of course, have several souvenir pieces in my pack but nothing concerns them. They leave all exposed so we must repack our own. We then rejoin our bus and police inspect every piece of luggage aboard. It takes another two hours before getting under way. Each is 'felt all over' by an officer of the same gender and no one is detained as we get back on the road.

After two lengthy meal-breaks at 24-hour diners with food of good standard, and with limited leg-room I sleep fitfully. I recommend anybody taking overnight trips in train, bus or boat, have a pair of eye-shades in purse or pocket.

~ * ~

Buenos Aires...

Having stopped at a Uruguay border customs office for brief passenger exchanges and despite the time for drug inspection, we arrive in Buenos Aires' northern bus terminal at 7:00am. Except for considerable litter along the roadside, I see enough to illustrate things are more like home than any spot north. With luggage retrieved, I ask a taxi driver to take me to Florida House Hotel (my Lonely Planet guide) and he tells me "It is now closed, sir."

Can I trust this guy?

I ask to be taken to a similar downtown hotel and he delivers me to Hotel Concorde on Calle 26 Mayo, $us50 per night including a full breakfast. It looks comfortable enough yet not central enough for safe walking at night. So once installed and with a city map I go walkabout and choose The Regis on Ave. Lavalle in Esmerelda at only $us33 *con desayono,* central to all parts of this city of 14 million. It is a great location for walking out at night, for it is a major road and directly opposite a metro station.

On TV I see lots of public awareness ads on the dangers of cholera which has broken out throughout South America. They warn people to be careful about disposal of rubbish and personal hygiene, yet by my standard of living, the litter here is dreadful. People think nowt of chucking food scraps from car windows and buses. Even this morning, driving through the approaches of Buenos Aires, the amount of litter along the freeway is shameful. On that very subject I am to find come evening, rubbish collection in plastic bags left kerbside are ripped open by scavenging dogs, cats and beggars such that garbage is strewn along many city gutters and footpaths. People here simply wade through it, seemingly unaware of how unsightly and unhealthy it is.

On Monday I find Lan Chile, neighbouring Chile's airline and bring forward my bookings to Santiago and Easter Island. I am in mixed minds here, for I otherwise like the atmosphere in life better than neighbouring countries north, but am feeling physically tired and in a different aspect, look forward to making my way home...a disastrous situation for one also seeking different ways of life in different parts of the world! I give myself two more days here.

The Plaza San Martin end of the city is *très chic*! It is where 5 Star hotels abound...also a Cartiers, a Pierre Cardin and a Harrods, its building the same unique style as in London's Knightsbridge. To walk the first three or four blocks of this end of Avenida Florida one passes the cream of boutiques and stores carrying the smart names of the retail world. Big department stores are on the broad Avenida Cordoba. Florida and Lavalle are pedestrian malls, both thronged with people day and night for block after block and they house restaurants, cinemas, bookshops, cafès and nightclubs.

My Hotel Regis is in the heart of it all.

I enjoy Buenos Aires so much that my planned two days become five. It is not a cheap city but one can eat well at reasonable prices. Hotel Regis, like many I've discovered throughout the continent, serves breakfast but has no other restaurant facility. One eats lunch and dinner 'out.' On my block is a choice of eateries with meals at $12 to $15. One can always buy bread, cheese and a bottle of beer (wine is expensive there) for the odd 'eat-in' meal which I do often in order to watch news on TV.

On Avenida Florida, I buy an Agatha Christie and a Wilbur Smith novel and on the front window of the bookshop a large crowd is gathered, everyone pushing to get a look at the window's display. The entire wide window is given over to memorials of the *Malvenus* (Falkland) Islands war between Argentina and Great Britain. The short history of the islands, since the time of England and Spanish wars is that since the 1700s the Falklands have been taken over in turn by Britain, France and Argentina, each over centuries claiming right of ownership. In early 1982, Argentina attacked the islands in an endeavour to kick the British out.

Ten years ago today (2 May 1982), the British sank Argentina's sole battleship *General Belgrano* with the loss of hundreds of lives. A new book is being released on its loss, written and told through Argentine eyes. The display is back-dropped by the country's flag and funeral decorations with photographs not only of those killed but of the many British 'atrocities' in the short war. The mood of the crowd is indeed volatile. Many are in tears. I keep my mouth shut in case my English voice is recognised. I hide my English language novels under my jacket...if taken for English in this moment, I could be lynched.

On the bright side, I buy for lunch: bread, cheese and beer, and take them into a park where hundreds are spread on lawns, likely office and shop staff on their lunch-hours which in Argentina are 1:00pm to 3:00pm. This atmosphere is indeed more like home.

I then find my way to what had been the royal palace and chance on an exhibition of the Changing of the Guard, very much like that in London and conducted in true military splendour...all in traditional uniforms with broad epaulettes, swords and muskets. The entire city seems one of plazas, monuments and flags. Much is laid out like the spokes of a wheel, broad avenues reaching out from various plazas...a carefully planned city. Major boulevards are wide and choked with tooting traffic. One stretch of Avenida 9 de Julio, incorporating the roundabout and landmark obelisk where Evita Peron staged her massive rallies, an eight-way intersection, there are no less than fifteen lanes of active traffic. Add to these a further twelve lanes that are entrances and exits of an underground parking station and you have some indication of the boulevard's breadth.

Like Paris, there is an underground metropolis of railways.

How one's mind works when eating dinner alone, the trivia with which it sometimes occupies itself, can be amusing. Next door to my 'pub' is the restaurant La Casona Nonno which I highly recommend. It is large and 'touristy' although locals use it for the camaraderie among many, including the staff. Apart from watching people, my mind wonders if there might be some significance in the coincidence of room numbers I have had in various hotels during my journey. There has been a 707, 202, 909, 303 and now for a second time, a 404 (and to Chile's Santiago I am to be in a 909) and many of my flights, Boeing 707s.

After dinner I stroll Avenida Lavalle between Pelligrini and Florida, up and down as many are doing. It is reminiscent of the promenading at dusk in Mediterranean villages, people simply happy to stroll about chatting with friends or strangers. It is quite a lively scene at any hour of day or night. On my last day I do more than on most...choose different parts of the city to stroll, different parks of which there are many, to sit and read or simply watch what so attracts others. Or I visit museums and churches. What is extremely important is that I can enjoy both the loneliness of 'self', or meet and chat with those living an entirely different sort of life.

Most of today I explore the monuments in the big park bordered by Lavalle and Talcahuano where people living in high density housing come to read, relax or sunbake...old people, students, even musicians who bring their instruments with them to sit in the sun and rehearse.

My last night in Argentina I live it up at La Estancia on Lavalle nr Pelligrini where they grill beef, pork and lamb whilst still on their respective bodies, in the huge window spaces off the sidewalks, over enormous fires...what they call 'traditional gaucho' style...a huge indoor barbecue with, for those either passing the doors or already inside and seated, the most teasing of aromas.

The Buenos Aires airport is a long way out, 47km with freeway conditions all the way. A taxi-bus leaves from alongside Hotel Colon on Pelligrini, just a block from the Regis, so is convenient. It leaves every half hour and costs only $1.50.

Having lunch in the airport restaurant, I'm lucky to chance on Claudio Pedro, an economist and most interesting guy, on his way to Europe. In talking of Argentina's history, he remarks that it was the same British expedition of 1806/7 to wrest South Africa from the Dutch and attempted to take Argentina from the Spanish, but were not successful. In 1810 the locals did it alone.

Buenos Aires summary...

Plus side: By comparison with all its northern neighbours, it is safe. Or at least where I stayed, within crowds...a western style city with a western style culture. Lots to see and do, a rewarding city for strolling around sophisticated smart shops and world-class hotels. Magnificent plazas and boulevards, museums, gardens and fountains and lots of traffic with sensible drivers.

Minus side: Wine is expensive. Shares with Peru the distinction of being one of the more expensive countries on the continent, though still cheap by the standards in which I've grown up. Litter and garbage pollution are a serious problem.

~ * ~

Santiago, Chile...

Chile is a tall, skinny country with, on Friday 8 May 1992, 340 pesos to the $us.

Airline Lan Chile provides excellent service and comfort.

Flying into Santiago is reminiscent of landing in Cuzco. It nestles at the foot of snow-capped mountains that remain part of its skyline as far north and south as one can see.

An efficient tourist desk at the airport has a list of hotels with prices and staff to help.

Hotel Gran Palace @ $us39 with breakfast appeals, but she fails to tell me that a taxi from the airport will cost me eighteen times the price of an airport bus. Or should it be an oversight of mine when doing homework on Chile? But then, the bus depot is six blocks away from the hotel, while the taxi brings me and luggage to the door.

The hotel is comfortable, but unusually is but the top few floors of an extremely tall building. On the pedestrian mall of *Huefanos*, it is quite central and at night I walk to the *Plaza de Armas* where crowds always gather. Enclosing the square are the cathedral, museums and post office. One side is given over to a souvenir bazaar, but the park, unlike most other cities, is the centre of activity and is absolutely packed with people.

First morning is always walkabout to get my sense of bearings and feel the pulse of the place and I make for Amex to change the last of my traveller cheques. With accommodation already paid in advance, and my flights already paid to Easter Island, and in that prior to 9/11 one need not affirm positive dates on prepaid air tickets around the world, means expenses are entirely on present cash and my A class Diners Club credit card limit. It will comfortably cover me to Tahiti and home, so during the rest of my journey I am not going to find myself hungry.

I head for *Sierra de Santa Lucia,* an unusual park on city edge also recommended as something to 'go see.' Originally a pile of rock sticking up from the plain which in early days had been turned into a fort to protect the town, remnants of both fort and chapel survive. It is well worth a visit, but despite a scenic elevator part of the way, quite a climb to the top. It is close to the university and students use the park for quiet study. Great views of the Andes treat my eyes and I feel happy that people about me seem content about safety. I feel however, it is not the sort of place to visit alone at night.

Every town in South America seems to have its *Plaza des Armas*, always the centre of town and focal point for activities. *Armas* literally means 'assembly' and nowhere have I seen better service of any city's Place of Assembly than in Chile's Santiago. The gardens are immaculately maintained, extending a welcoming feel. Night and day it is packed with perambulating residents. Fountains and seating benches are plentiful and kiosks, pavement artists, sidewalk cafès and political sprukers, photographers, strolling players, jugglers and inevitable shoe-cleaners abound throughout the city. Surrounding buildings are usually floodlit at night. Friday night at least, there are street theatre, clowns and comedians and contented crowds. The carnival atmosphere in Santiago extends along streets off the plaza, streets which are pedestrian malls during days, at night become street markets. It seems half the population converges on the area. Sidewalk cafès and restaurants do roaring trades and activities carry on until midnight.

Chile's people eat even later than in Paraguay and Argentina, absolutely not before 10:00pm. In the city heart, every other street is a mall and every block, for all are regular squares, has its cross or star-shaped arcade or gallery in its centre, such that for block after block there are off-street thoroughfares attracting shoppers into multilevel galleries. What is unusual in this South American city are wide footpaths so that even on streets with vehicular traffic, pedestrians are not continually forced off kerbs into traffic.

Also unique is that most people seem well dressed. People give the impression of having money in their pockets and enjoy a reasonable standard of living. Odd beggars, mainly children ask for handouts, yet even these are better dressed than elsewhere.

The most obvious thing about the city is that it is clean. Conspicuous by their absence is garbage in gutters and doorways. One can walk about without nostrils being assailed, and sitting in sidewalk cafès people don't drop confection wrappers and cigarette butts, they seek out the rubbish box they know will be nearby.

It is pleasant to walk without tripping on broken pavements. In near every way Chile seems a more sophisticated country than its neighbours.

In a café packed with office workers, I have the biggest lunch in weeks, a whole half chicken with a pile of French fries and two beers for 2,640pesos ($7.75).

Everywhere north of here I'd been told that Chile's wines are the best in South America and I add my voice to that. On arriving at the expensive City Hotel coming up lunchtime, (in Chile, 1:00pm through 3:00pm), I poke my nose into the dining-room to suss it out. It is packed so I decide to come early one night and test it for dinner. Tonight at 9:00 and it is yet empty but yes they will serve me and I order a mid-priced half-bottle of dry red. I am served a *Santa Emiilliana Cabernet Sauvignon* 1987, little tannin and as full bodied as Aussie's good reds, a pleasant wine at a surprising 900 pesos($2.65), astoundingly cheap!

At 10:45 two couples arrive. I had finished an enjoyable dinner and gone outside to *Plaza de Armas* to find it thronged. In one spot a pair of comedians has its large audience in fits of laughter but at the speed of the language I am baffled. In other groups, pavement artists, clowns and jugglers throughout the huge park have large laughing audiences. All is a very happy atmosphere.

Next day I visit *La Place de la Consitution* with the elegant *El Presidente's Palace de Moneda*. The cathedral dates from 1541 and inside is most ornate. Then to the museum on Estardo 21 de Mayo which tells the history of the city. The museum had initially been the *Casa Colorada* which must have been a magnificent home. It is an excellent museum.

Musio de Santiago is another historic building on the plaza telling the history of the entire country and only 400pesos is a meagre entry fee.

On my last day in South America, I feel considerably more heavy-hearted than leaving any other capital city or country (except maybe Cartagena). Here the people are outgoing and friendly and there is a satisfied feel in their hearts that seems to be lacking elsewhere.

Is that there is no graffiti in Santiago a sign they have earned an enjoyable lifestyle?

For my last dinner I try their fillet steak with French fries and onions, a couple of fried eggs atop, with a mixed fruit pudding with custard and ice-cream and wine and coffee all for 6,000pesos($17.60).

On a beautiful morning, I feel quite fresh and choose to walk the six blocks to the airport bus station, trundling my luggage on a good footpath. I pay 500pesos($1.50) to the airport. Coming from Buenos Aires, Lan Chile Airlines impressed me, so I look forward to my passage to Easter Island (Or in native language, *Rapa Nui*).

Santiago summary...

Plus side: Most things compared with the rest of the continent are 'Plus Side,' even public transport. Everywhere I go they cater well for westerners. Money goes further for its value than elsewhere. I would like to return and see more of Chile.

Minus side: Nowt.

Fifteen

Rapa Nui – aka Isla de Pascua – aka Easter Island...
    A Chilean responsibility (according to Chile) yet an invaded victim (according to 4,000 Pascuan Indians)
    Whenever Chile raises its flag, it is soon shot down by either bullets or flaming arrows. Pascuans will risk their lives ensuring that flag will...'Never foul Pascuan air!'
    There is a two-hour time difference from Chile, so when my flight lands I have a longer day. It is a tiny airport for it is the most isolated populated island in the world and has all too few comforts for educated people.
    What it does have is a yet undiscovered beginning.
    In what way?
    Being so isolated we expect its first humans must have journeyed from its nearest populated island. Certainly, many background habits of the population indicate a Polynesian influence yet how could Polynesians have got so far before boats

of any description had sails? And to row would take longer than any foodstuff not be rotten.

Whoever, they deliberately set about deforesting the entire island. Even today it has few trees. It was visited by many European nations during the 18th and 19th centuries yet none found enough interest worth developing. Peru illustrated some interest and it wasn't until 1884 that it was annexed by Chile. Its natives are called Pascuan. Pascua is the Spanish word for Easter, so maybe it was Spaniards who first settled the 'modern' era islands. It also is the name of a species of fish in the South Pacific, so which came first? No one there knows nor cares.

Its population at the turn of the 19th century into the 20th is recorded at near 9,000.

It is best known for the strangeness of the Moai, the monolithic manlike monuments thought to be of ancestors. Many are singles and many up to fifteen statues lined up side by side. With one exception all statues have their backs to the ocean. Most are erected close to the shoreline. They have been assessed to have been erected 'between years 1250 and 1500.' Most are huge in size, up to 10m high and weighing 90 tons. Only in the centre of the island are there rocks of that size, the inner walls of one of the three dead volcanos. It is believed that all idols were carved inside a volcano mouth then moved up and over the wall and down to the site where erected...some 900 of them. How they were moved without the wheel remains a mystery.

The first Europeans ventured onto the island in 1722 to find many statues had been deliberately toppled...how, when and by whom remains unknown. Some say by earthquake, others during internecine tribal wars.

An information board at the airport lists only two hotels, with prices and a map illustrating locations. Hotel Orongo has 5 guestrooms, is central and medium priced. The other is large, more modern and more expensive.

I'm trying to restore an overspent budget.

Taxis? The island has few cars but many pick-ups. One of the latter is as much a taxi as anything and it brings me to Hotel Orongo in the tiny town. Nothing on the island is 'far' and everyone knows everyone else.

Orongo's Raoul is taxi-driver, reception manager, room serviceman, chef, cleaner and handyman, in his thirties, eldest of his parents' ten children and huge! He looks down on my 830cm (6ft) and makes it very clear that he is a 'screaming queen' who: quote: "doesn't like girls at all." He has brought three of us from the airport placing the Viennese Maria in front of the pick-up with him while her English husband Fred, of the British Embassy in Brazil, and I are in back with all the luggage and filth. In the house, however, rooms are large and clean with double beds and everywhere and everything spotlessly clean. There are bed-sheets but no blankets.

"Do you want anything for lunch Mr. Ric?"

"Yes please, Raoul. Do you have fresh or canned fruit? And tea? Or beer?"

"We have fresh red and green apples and passion fruit. Tea, yes, but beer no. There is a bar/come/café just down the road."

Everything I've seen so far is 'just down the road' and there is nowhere else!

"Thank you, that will be fine. What time?"

"Oh, any time."

"Thirty minutes?"

I receive a deep bow and he leaves. I hear him telling Maria and Fred, "Will you come with me now? Your room should be ready."

A little later he knocks on my door…"Lunch is in the dining room, Mr Ric."

"Thank you," I call as I put away the last of my clothes in the small wardrobe.

Maria and Fred are already there and we chat over lunch for quite a time. They then return to their room to finish unpacking and I go off to reconnoitre the town layout.

We are on the main street, meaning the one with intersections. The other three streets cross it. The name of the town is Hanga

Roa. In one of the cross streets, I see the other hotel, the only two storied building on the island. But yes, there are many cottages in sight in the distance.

When no further from my hotel than 100metres, I am addressed by a little lady in a Peruvian type cap.

"Hello sir, I am Marsella. Where are you from?"

"I am from Australia, Marsella. Are you a native of Rapa Nui?"

Rather than a hesitant sort of response, she bursts with a voice like a machine-gun with, "I've been to Australia, my daughter is a nurse at Wollongong hospital and I know everyone on this island, so anything you want you just ask me and I live in that blue house just there," she says in one breath, pointing across the street. "Anything you want, rent-car, horse, motorbike, souvenir, travel guide, I can point your way or I can be your guide, my rate is cheapest on the island. Did I tell you I know everybody here so I can be a great help..."

I put a finger to her lips and felt like putting my other hand around her throat.

"Is there a public toilet in the city, madame? I suddenly need one."

She looks astounded and points behind me.

"You can go right back there. I saw you come from Hotel Orongo."

And I'm bloody sure she knows what colour my jocks are!

I leave her pointing her finger back at Orongo, cross the dirt road, 'dirt' because there are nowt else. I can hear the surf not too far away so I make for it.

In short time I am there and up comes a young fellow in his late teens...

In impeccable English he asks, "Hello, you must have come on today's plane. My name is Kris. Are you looking for a seafront Maoi?"

"Are there any this close"

I'll use him, just in case Marsella comes after me. I'm beginning to realise that here, everyone recognizes a tourist. It seems all try to make a buck or two.

During the next half hour before I head for home, he's taken me to see the nearest Moai and tells me its known history. Also about himself, that he is 26, born on the island, son of a Polynesian father and Russian/French mother, educated in Tahiti where he now works with a team of archaeologists. He travelled ahead of them to book accommodation and is staying with his mother.

Is everyone I meet going to give me their life history?

"I must leave you, Mr. Ric. Can you find your way back?"

"Thank you, Kris yes, but can I offer something for helping me find my first Maoi?"

I reach for my wallet.

He holds up his hand. "No, but thank you, that was just my boy-scout act for today. You will see me around. Ask if you need help."

And away he goes.

Hey, that's how I like them.

Dinner at Orongo is plain but good, a huge tuna steak, coleslaw, avocado, tomato, cucumber and yam with fresh grapes for dessert.

I like that too. Raoul says there is a little bar down the road, only one on the island and calls it 'the only place to go' It is but 100 metres so I'll have a look.

When halfway there it begins to rain.

Tevake is more than a bar, it is a café come restaurant with four tables for four and many chairs, a club of some sort where regulars can watch Screen News broadcasts from Santiago on plane-arrival days, Tuesday and Saturday.

And I bet this little guy who runs it, Sixto by name, is part of Raoul's gay life. He wears his hair in a snood thick with sequins. He says he is Polynesian although looks no more Polynesian than me.

Also, my attention is turned to a lone guy named Luis, thoroughly pissed! And who should arrive to sit with him? The talkative Marsella. About a dozen arrive to see or hear the news that is piped out through the island from a transmitter. Most seem to have brought their own food. It seems Sixto doesn't consider them customers, rather neighbours or friends. Then Kris arrives.

I order a pisco-sour which is as common in South America as is beer anywhere else. A large proportion of people on the island too, it seems, like it. I reckon very few have money. There is no industry and no stores other than verandas on some houses and a souvenir shop selling knitted handicraft. Everything for sale or barter or swap is available twice a week at a street market. If someone wants bread, they go to the baker's house, if for a lettuce to whoever grows them, if butter or milk surely one of the hotels is likely to have some to spare in exchange for something or other. If there are no regular jobs, one can spend a day repairing the provider's fence or cleaning windows or mending a portable gramophone or some such service in lieu of money.

Yes, another sensible idea. So far, with maybe Luis the exception, all seem satisfied with life.

The rain stops about 11:00pm and a score more arrive. Kris's aunt Laveda lives in a shanty next door that turns out to be Romo's house or shack or whatever one likes to call the two-roomed shed made of corrugated iron and cardboard. Romo is her boyfriend and I assume father of her 3-month-old baby. In the moment, Tevake is also home to a horde of invading cockroaches which come in from the wet. We drink pisco and lemonade made by a neighbour. They chat in Polynesian for an hour, Kris and Marsella translating for me. It is an easy mood and no person seems to care about anything. I'm the only one to cringe when cockroaches chase each other over my feet, legs and the baby.

The disco seems the only place where bored people gather. I enquire where I can rent a car. The only things parked outside are two horses tethered to a tree. Kris says he can talk to me about that 'later,' so I say no more. I am introduced to so many strange people during the night that I lose the memory of who is who. The dancing is all communal rather than individual couples and dancing is in groups of three or four to records played at a deafening pitch from a boxed gramophone like I recall in our house when four or five years old. I sit with Kris and his friends until half past midnight.

I am stopped at the door by Maria and Fred, my Orongo housemates who have come to see what all the jocular noise is about. With them in tow, I return to the bar to buy them a drink. They are highly amused at the scene. A half-hour later, when the record playing is so dreadfully scratched with age and dancers are swapping partners and sometimes as a stunning girl gets a knuckle playfully into her waist, it's a man's voice that responds. I can generally tell from legs whether he/she is a him/he but when dressed in jeans one is never sure. One poorly made up guy spends most of his time nursing a baby yet try as I may I cannot work out who among the others is his partner. Singing, he imitates Frank Sinatra pretty well.

I feel now is the time to go and Maria and Fred come with me. Kris says he will 'contact' me tomorrow about the car.

Outside there are now six horses tethered and a few rusted old small cars. The three of us giggle as we walk through puddles of wet to the hotel, talking about the strange society. Drinks are sold only by the bottle so I had bought a pisco and another of something in a Coca-Cola bottle coloured a soft green, to chat over once home.

We remark on the fact that despite the island has a school, very few people either cannot or simply refuse to speak Spanish, but that it is clearly a community of people who do not care a damn about order.

It rains nearly all night and the wind blows an absolute gale and at breakfast we learn that the plane from Tahiti last night, one of the two each week, got to within an hour of the island; i.e: 5 hours out from its start, found the storm so torrential it turned and sped home. It will come later today.

"It happens often," Raoul told us. Maria, Fred and I only smile widely at each other as I reach for another tiny ball of garlic bread.

Kris phoned to say he can hire a car for me at a reasonable price and seeing the party on last night's plane now will not arrive until late, he can accompany me.

I jump at such a chance…a tourist guide that will not cost a fortune.

He tells me on arrival that with rent cars costing $40 to $50 per day, he has this car for $60 for all today, overnight and all tomorrow. The only cars on the island are little 4WD Suzukis (bone-shakers!) and no insurance is available 'because nobody trusts insurance companies.' I have never driven a 4WD but he will teach me, for once that plane arrives he must join their 'huddle' as he calls it. They are movie people to film the new discovery. He first takes me to visit archaeologist Edmundo Edwards who has excellent English and his Polynesian wife Mada, who has none. They make a point of calling the next-door neighbour to come and meet me.

"Something live, yet of whom we are as proud, for you to meet."

I tuck into my mind some old man of note on the island but almost explode when confronted with the most beautiful young woman I think I have ever seen, her name Titiana who greets me with a happy smile and traditional kiss to both cheeks. Just two years ago, she was crowned Miss Chile. I make considerable fuss of photographing her in various poses and everyone is thrilled. I pay her $5 and she is thrilled.

"This is not the only reason I brought you," Kris explains, "for Edmundo is the island's chief investigator into Moai history and our people."

And he certainly is a most interesting fellow and excited about me coming just to learn what I can of Rapa Nui.

I simply cannot but feel lucky to chance on such a knowledgeable source!

Over coffee, he gives me just over an hour of his busy time to talk about the monuments I'm about to witness.

Kris first leads me to Ahu Akivi, 7 statues in the very middle of the island and gives me what is known of their purpose. He does the same with several others during the day until I feel quite exhausted. He is my dinner guest at the Urana, which is considered the best restaurant in town as well as the only one...Wow, flashes through my mind, it has tablecloths! Most faces are of passengers on my flight from Santiago. It is a delightful dinner, an excellent steak imported from New Zealand and they serve a pleasant Chilean wine, a home-made dessert of which they don't know the English name, but delightfully tasty. All that plus coffee is 5,500 pesos ($16) each. I really am beginning to doubt my guidebook that claims Easter Island is expensive. And young Kris continues being a most fortunate discovery.

"For safety, Mr. Ric, I shall take the car home tonight and return to Orongo after breakfast," he announces.

"Come for breakfast," I invite him, but he declines.

At breakfast, however, Raoul advises that the island is out of bread…there has been an influx of archaeological personnel and the baker last night got so pissed he hadn't yet baked more.

"More disastrous though," Raoul tells us, "is that the island is nearly out of beer."

Maria and Fred are booked for what seems a regular trio of organised tours, one full day at $25 per head, and two half day tours at $15.

Kris's mother brings the car as I finish breakfast saying Kris is ill and she wants to keep him in bed for the day. I manage to drive her the few minutes home and yes, Kris does look ill. The doctor is to come later in the morning. He assures me it is not a stomach ache after last night's dinner but a muscular pain in his back. He gives me brochures and a map and points out the few roads the island has, and which route he would have taken me.

Disappointed, I can but wish him well. He tells me when I've finished with the car, to phone the owner to come pick it up at Orongo and be paid not a penny more than $US60 in American money.

After just a few minutes, I feel confident with the car that bumps along what they call roads when the rain starts pelting down. I bounce along the 'south' road until reaching the extinct volcano of Rano Raraku where the Maois are carved. The rain stops and I cross my fingers and leave the vehicle to start the long climb. The grass is long, wet and clinging and the going is slippery. Whilst my rain-cape keeps the top half of me dry when the rain returns, my jeans and feet are quickly sopping. It is quite a climb but I keep going, getting photographs of unfinished Maoi, recumbent. For reasons unknown, work on the carving of Maoi ceased sometime in the 3rd or 4th century AD and some 200 partly carved Maoi remain. How men transported such monoliths to their sites many kilometres away over steep slopes such as this remains a mystery…especially as the island never had beasts of burden. I don't get inside the crater because the steep slopes are too slippery. I try barefooted but still slip, so don't even want to risk getting to the top and sliding inside!

When the rain clears, I drive to the north beaches, stopping on occasions to inspect sites of restored Maoi, most still lying where they were toppled.

An interesting feature on flat land is the foundation of boat-shaped reed houses, typical of all what they called 'houses.'

All day when in the car I listen to a tape Kris loaned me, of a guide's instruction.

Edmund had told me yesterday that the Ahu (the formed base on which the Maoi stands) are today's veritable time capsules. They contain personal possessions of buried dignitaries. The actual grave is behind the Ahu.

On the north coast is the island's only sandy beach, Anakena. All my clothing is drenched so I strip naked and throw myself into the sea, just so I will forever have the unique knowledge of having braved the surf of Easter Island.

Driving back through the middle of the island I discover the 7 statues of yesterday so spend more time crawling about them. In the south-west corner of the island are ruins of the ancient city of Orongo alongside the Rano Kau crater. From the road climbing up are fabulous views of the entire island. This area is a national park and to enter is an expensive $12 atop what Maria and Fred had already paid but fortunately, with no organised tour booked to enter today, the ranger's hut is closed and I walk in for free.

The ruins of Orongo are incredible, the people having lived on the cliff-top like gannets in a rookery. Houses are excavations in the sides of a hill, roofed with slabs of cantilevered rock then covered with earth in which is growing thick grass. Entrances are tight tunnels through which everyone has to crawl. No house is deep enough for anyone to stand, only to sleep…an incredible village indeed, and quite extensive. Natural rock in the area is carved with the legends of birdmen, part of religious beliefs. A visit to Orongo is a must for visitors; it brings home the hardship of life in those days. The Orongo 'town' is indeed the cream on the Rapa Nui cake.

After a second day of exciting discoveries, I arrive home about 5:00pm to note that this tiny island is absolutely unique in the world, just as is Machu Pichu in Peru…a small community hidden from the rest of the world to develop its own culture.

Another insular experience!

I have been driving all day, covering every road the island has, yet on arriving at my hotel I espy the first other vehicle I've seen all day!

I've time to kill before the owner comes to the hotel to pick up my car 'about' 6pm, so with nothing to eat since breakfast, I call at Tavake for an empalada (a Chilean meat-pie) and coffee. Two young Polynesians sit at a table and one welcomes me in English, "Hello my friend, a stranger from where?"

"Australia."

"Ah, the most western island of Polynesia eh?"…and he bursts out laughing.

Bloody hell. Another educated Rapa Nui local? That makes it four!

"You could call it that."

"My name is Hugo and my friend here is Rano, who has no English."

"But you have obviously lived some time in an English-speaking country?"

"I had five years of archaeological study at UCLA. Come and join us?"

He beckons me to their table to learn they were part of those having to return to Tahiti in the previous night's great storms. They are on pisco-coke so I order a round and join them. He tells me a new Moai has just been discovered on Maunga Terevaka, the highest point in the island. I did not let on that I had already heard that.

Nor did I enquire if they might be of the party Kris expected.

"It is unique in that it was not entirely made in the Rano Raraky quarry but was discovered almost completed on the rim of the extinct volcano Rano A-Roi. Archaeologists have raised it only during the last few days."

"That sounds exciting. No wonder you are celebrating."

"Would you like to see it?"

My mind boggles. Here have I just completed an inspection of all the known Maoi on the island, in fact in all the world, and not only am I Johnny-on-the-spot when a new one is discovered, having lain hidden since the 3rd or 4th century, but am invited to see it?

I jump at the chance.

"No problem, my friend. Buy a pisco-coke to drink on our way, and we'll take you."

We call at Hotel Orongo that I can pick up another film and I am not surprised when Hugo tells me his parents own the hotel. He is one of Raoul's brothers. I am anxious to get there before it is too dark for photographs and I am also due to have the car at the hotel 'about 6pm.' We are pretty pissed by this stage but scrounge an empty coke bottle from Raoul and the boys mix it in the back seat as I drive.

Rano might speak nowt but Polynesian but he mixes a great pisco-sour.

We bounce and jolt over unmade terrain climbing the side of the mountain. We leave the 'road' several hundred metres across country and it is so steep in the long, wet grass that I stall the strange car. Hugo leans forward from the back seat and engages the 4WD. We make it and there is yet enough light for photographs.

The French have been there filming the raising. Despite it being small, the finding of a new Moai is world newsworthy. Lying down, its spine is yet attached to the bedrock when discovered, but unlike most statues it's been protected from the centuries of ocean winds and sea-spray. Its eyebrows, nose, chin etcetera remain unweathered. A crew of workmen still surround it and we present them with what is left from our bottles so they agree not to notice me photograph, even pose for me in the photographs I take.

Having taken five photographs and they have emptied the bottles and hold up a hand…enough is enough, so I tuck my camera under my shirt.

"Fotografia prohibido!" he then exclaims.

Hugo whispers that the French have filming and photographic rights and are due to start filming tomorrow.

I'm concerned about getting the car back on time, so Hugo drives. When near town, they put the hard word on me for another bottle of pisco. I agree on condition I get at least one drink from it and they readily accept. Back at the hotel by 6:15, Raoul phones the car-yard to tell them they can pick up the car at any time.

When the owner arrives on his horse, I pay his $60 and he touches his hat…he has no English. I ask for a receipt which throws him into a fit…Paperwork on Isla de Pascua?

I laugh and wave him off, his obedient horse trotting along behind.

My last day is a lazy day. I pack, read, phone Kris to ask after his health and thank him for his help, that Raoul would return the paperwork he loaned me, sit by the surf while recording notes not yet made, then lunch at Tavake.

An ever-so-typical event happens over my lunch, but it takes Sixto more than an hour to make me an omelette. His recipe calls for two eggs and he has but one in stock. He takes off at a saunter, stopping on meeting this or that friend and eventually arrives back with not a dozen or half dozen, but one egg!

Raoul presents me with a lei made of seashells and drives me to the airport where they add another lei of white and pink frangipani. Someone is on duty to collect my $5 Departure Tax yet no one to change my 33 Spanish pesos ($us128).

My Life, My Travels

Eighteen months later I find a friend off to Santiago on business who will change my $128 worth of dollars. They are by then worth $77.

Report on Rapa Nui...

Good news: Wonderful, wonderful, wonderful. Its people are great hosts.

Bad news: It rains heavily and walking can be slippery.

~ * ~

Tahiti...

After a six-hour flight with Lan Chile in a Boeing707 I arrive in Tahiti at midnight.

I've used it on three occasions and award them 5 Stars on each. A great airline!

At the airport in Polynysie Francais (Tahiti), the cambio at the airport is Westpac. I present my Westpac Australia Diners Club card along with the $us notes I'd so far been left with, to be exchanged to Tahiti's currency and also offered my Chilean notes.

To the latter, he laughed. "Keep them, sir. They make attractive wallpaper."

I take a taxi to the Maeva Beach Hotel for I feel I would like a day's surfing to round up my long 'holiday.' It is not so far and he asks $us27. I jump up and down and ask the hotel's doorman his opinion. He agrees that at this time of early morning, it is reasonable. I've no option but to pay it.

At the desk I get my next shock. Cheapest rooms are $us175 and rooms facing the ocean beach $us205. Petit dejeuner (small breakfast) is an additional $13.

At this hour I need to sleep, so I take it, have the small breakfast when I wake, then check out. There are shops along the street although not open now, but surely one will have something attractive to tourists.

In my quite glorious room, what do I find when undressing for bed?

In the carpet I yelp when treading on a pile of either finger nail chips or toenail chips or both. I phone the desk and complain. They give me another room. In the morning I find the 'small breakfast' adequate as a meal.

But I shall not stay here!

I go shopping and find a booklet on backpacker lodging. Some look adequate enough so I walk to Rue du Frere Alain and look at a couple of rooms. Both are spotlessly clean and I choose Un Coucou (The Cuckoo Clock) run by Chinese Polynesians, a BYO food with my own refrigerator-shelf in the hall and the kitchen is a DYO system. Rooms are generously large with a shower and toilet behind a curtain, for singles or doubles for pf4,500 ($us42) per night. I take one and have to pay daily. Next door is a restaurant near packed with backpackers, so good enough for me. I find that if ordered and paid for in advance, a good dinner is cheap by Tahiti standards at $5.00.

I have a vin ordinaire at a cost of $us20. I am out of cash so go to Westpac to get an advance on good old Diners Club but they have to fax Oz for approval and because of the time difference there will be 'several' hours delay. I simply go walkabout. The clerk has no English and when my cash eventually arrives, it is cleared.

"Maintenant je mange," (Now I can eat) I tell her.

"Bon apetite," she replies with a laugh.

I badly need a haircut so find a barber shop.

Everywhere I turn in Tahiti costs big money. A vin ordinaire costs $us20.

Papeete is a typical South Seas town, a mix of new and old, nothing sophisticated and generally untidy and the locals are litterbugs. I am out of film and no one stocks Kodachrome, only Fujichrome at pf1,575 ($us15).

"What?" All through South America I had been paying for the more expensive Kodachrome, $6 and $8.

I refuse and buy print film. A glass of beer in a kerbside café is pf350 ($us3.25). In Paraguay's 5 Star hotel I had bought such for $us2.15.

At a supermarket I buy yoghurt, bread and cheese, a 6-pack of beer and half-litre of orange juice and charge them to my Diners Club card.

I am happy at quitting Spanish in favour of French and spend the rest of the day sleeping and reading and dine in the Cuckoo Clock. Over it I chat with two girls from Nebraska and they tell me they surf at the Beachcomber Hotel.

"The natural beaches near the town are not so nice but the big hotels, just a bus-ride away, let anyone use their beaches because they tend to lunch at their restaurant or buy beer at their bar. We take our own food and nobody minds. Beachcomber even imports their white sand from Moorea."

There is also a jazz club close by Cuckoo Clock and the three of us go there. It is indeed fun. I'm sure they enjoy my company rather than walking the night streets alone.

Tomorrow is my last day before flying home so, as the girls are leaving this afternoon, I thank them for their company and take a bus to Beachcomber Hotel. Indeed, it is delightful and I have a great day and again dine at Cuckoo Clock.

At one stage I had tossed around going to Moorea whilst this close. Maggie had told me she went there on a group tour and found it delightful, but I am anxious for home.

In the morning there is hot water in the showers if up early enough, but I am indeed up too early for even that. My Qantas flight for Sydney, en-route from Hawaii, flies out at 3:50am. I settle up my rental and have a cold shower before bed with my timer set for 2:30. A wonderful idea is an all-night bus to the airport that runs every twenty minutes from just down the hill. It costs only pf50, a big improvement on my taxi at pf2,500.

At the airport cambio, I again try to cash my Chilean pesos, but no luck. They are happy, however, to swap all my Polynesian francs for $au.

Tahiti summary...

Good: Once finding your way around, enjoyable. Having a little French helps.

Bad: Expensive. There are ways to economise so do homework before setting out.

~ * ~

Qantas brings me home on my thirteenth flight on seven different airlines.

It is a practically empty jumbo with only 83 passengers in steerage class so there is ample room to stretch out and sleep for the 8 hours to Sydney. We arrive at 8:00am.

Let me add something I have mentioned in various novels: that every time one flies into Sydney of a morning, into the sun, one's foreground is a spectacular sight. You lose height as you are over the harbour, your foreground the longest bridge span in the world and all up Sydney's spectacular harbour, the city's skyline on its southern shore and the increasingly growing skyscrapers on the North Sydney shore and the expanding harbour stretching to its high rocky heads. Their background is the glistening Pacific Ocean stretching to the horizon. Left and right margins of your picture are tree-lined sandy beaches, ocean waves breaking with white crests...a glorious spectacle to brush your mind clean of any glum problem during your flight.

I never tire of that scene.

I have thoroughly enjoyed my project and The Australian is highly satisfied with my submission. There had been but the odd 'i' to dot and they had readily lodged in my account a tad more than to cover the excess in my budget.

I finish that objective a very contented journalist.

Sixteen

Christmas 1990...
 The four Frenchies fly across the Atlantic to spend several days in Disneyland and from LAX to Brisbane where I meet them. We fly straight to their first chosen target, Cairns in the Great Barrier Reef. I rent a car and apart from diving in the magnificent reef, tour the jungle lowlands and go see Aborigines perform 'Black Magic.'

We fly back to Brisbane where my car awaits and I drive them the hundred kilometres to my beach home at Broadbeach on the Gold Coast.

My Christmas present is a two-hour limousine tour of Gold Coast sights, during which we manage to consume three bottles of Champagne.

During their 8 days with me, they see many sights in Australia's greatest holiday city.

When asking the most memorable 'sight,' each answers the *Feeding of Wild Parrots!*

The millions of rainbow-coloured wild parrots in the area know that 4:00pm daily is the National Wildlife Park feeding time for them. They wait, tightly packed and noisily squabbling on every branch of every tree in the park, waiting for their moment.

The noise is then near to deafening. Every visitor is forewarned in advertisements to wear 'hardy clothing' and on arrival is given a plate of bird-food. As plates are uncovered, screaming parrots descend in their multi-thousands, scrambling to be first on every head, shoulder and arm of the public to *'get at that plate!'* It is truly bedlam with visitors screaming as loudly as each anxious parrot. It is normal for everyone to have as many as twenty or more of them struggling somewhere on you, to get at that plate.

Each of Christophe, Dom1, Dom2, Pascal, me and every other visitor, scream as loudly as each bird.

On Christmas Day, rounding up several writing-club members (of which I am president, so attract many) and families, we treat the four of them to a typical Australian Christmas dinner on Kurrewa Beach, less than a hundred paces from my house.

Every day I take them visiting somewhere, including the nearby mountain range where we barbecue lunch, for them a first time treat. We visit the Aussie Animal Park in which they run wild with kangaroos, koalas, wallabies, wombats and platypus and in its bird section ogle kookaburras, magpies, emus and colourful parrots, and from a distance, feed crocodiles. The two who could swim join me in the surf, the other two on shore edge dig up crabs and cockleshells that we take home and cook.

It is a Christmas they will ever remember.

EUROPE

July – September 1993

Germany
Denmark
Switzerland
France
Holland
England

~ * ~

SUDAN
...the country closed to visitors

September – November 1994

Wadi Halfa
Khartoum
El Fasher

Seventeen

Come, fill the Cup, and in the Fire of Spring
The Winter Garment of Repentance fling:
The Bird of Time has but a little way
To fly – and lo! The Bird is on the Wing.
—*Rubáiyát of Omar Khayyám #VII*

On my next overseas jaunt, I have specific targets:
*One Asian site to compare the basic differences in lifestyle to my western one.
*A look at Germany after a few more years.
*A closer look at a Switzerland, to compare with its neighbours.
*A quick visit with my Frenchies, visiting *Mont-St-Michelle*.
*Several English counties on my family history searches.

Asia...
A huge continent with two massive countries, a disturbed area over centuries in what we call the middle-east, in its south-east...the

uneasy trio dumped by France into independence when none had diplomatic training, the mess of islands as far north as Japan in snow country and as far south as tropical Indonesia...some 40 in total depending on which year since World War 2 that we count.

All is a mix of different lifestyles from those of Europe, Africa, Australia or the Americas.

I shall take another look at Thailand, an interesting sort of place for those seeking not only holidays, but somewhere to retire either part-time or permanently, something many do. Life in China and India both seem cluttered, and to a great extent in their outlying areas, subsistence living. Also in Asia, manufacturing industries based only in large cities is a bad habit for any country.

Since WW2 the trend has been to expand both industry and educational centres. Thailand is unique in being the only nation with a long history to have never suffered submission to a foreign power, and still retains something in the area of 80% to 90% of mechanical industry in its capital city or immediate surroundings. Finding futures for the younger generation in outer areas is difficult, so many youngsters seeking employment in Bangkok are easy bait for sad futures. It is a common fault.

Chiang Mai in its far north is unique in qualifying as the country's education centre. When I arrived to call it home in 1996 it had two universities. Twenty-four years later, it has nine, some albeit small, yet accommodating such an increase in temporary population still calls for large city conveniences which it still lacks.

During my 24 years in the country, Bangkok city has had to build two more airports, triple the services and tracks of its city train stations, even the few underground and build three more bridges over its broad river because of influx in population.

I find Thai Air so good an airline and prices so reasonable that I now use them as much as possible. I need to do more family studies in England and whilst so close to Europe, hop over there for specific interests.

~ * ~

Bangkok...

You are happily recommended to Narai Hotel, a 4 Star mid-city hotel with a popular dining room and close to a night bazaar has become a welcome home when I visit. Two nearby side-streets are simply denied vehicles every night and portable market stalls line footpaths as well as a portable mid-road 'island' on both streets. Clothing, jewellery and nick-nacks of all descriptions are available. The Narai Hotel roof has the country's only rotating dining room and it also requests diners to switch off telephones while in their dining rooms, to concentrate on food.

I lunch at the Narai's *Pizza Granchi* where a crab and clam pizza with lots of mushrooms, onion and garlic make the mouth drool. It's the only time I eat pizza. And *Singer* is an excellent beer, all at reasonable prices.

The most efficient way to travel in Thai cities is by *tuk-tuk*, pronounced 'took-took,' a 3-wheeled motor-bike taxi to comfortably hold two passengers. If not wanting to be robbed, fare must be agreed before boarding. Good advice is check what it should be with locals or at hotel desks. On one occasion when the driver 'forgot' to turn on his meter, he still refused to tell me what my fare would be... when he next stopped at a red light I hopped out and took off at a trot.

River ferries are popular and economical for long stretches of riverside targets. Bangkok is a 6 million resident city and ferries are always frequent and busy.

Museums are excellent, particularly *Wat Pho* and *Wat Phra Chetuphon* ('*Wat*' is Thai for 'Temple' of which BKK has 400.) The world's biggest Golden Buddah (reputedly 700 to 800 years old) is in *Wat Traimit*. If you've time to visit only one temple, I recommend *Wat Pho.*

An afternoon in the Thonburi Crocodile and Snake farm is good value. I see there a hilarious incident...while deadly snakes are handled live, we are told how the safest thing if caught eye to eye with a snake, is to remain still. It is quick movement that incites a snake to strike. After a demonstration of that particular snake being milked to provide safeguard injections if bitten, one of the assistants holding the next snake in the queue, stumbles and the snake flies off into the crowd. Screams rend the air and pandemonium reigns. The clamour is unbelievable. The loudspeaker bursts the turmoil into silence…"Didn't we just advise you that if fronting a snake you must 'NOT MOVE'?"

Around the city are many small tributaries to the great river and along the steep banks of close tributaries, poor families live in old houses open to view because rising water levels have over time caused foundations to crumble. Whole sides of houses have fallen. Old blankets hide some rooms but where families cook, sit, eat and watch TV, it's 'open to view.' Some use riverside itself to wash clothing as well as bodies.

"Like a Venice of the East really," I quip to fellow tourists.

Driving in Thailand? One needs care. Only God and Buddha know what the car in front is about to do and the yellow light at intersections is the signal to speed up in order to beat the red. Three or four cars will then speed through the red. I have now lived in Thailand 24 years driving both motor bike and car, (although at age 90 I've given up the bike), I have never yet seen a policeman pull up a motorcar for breaking road rules. Quite often however, after blind bends as bikies turn, those without helmets are flagged down and the rider fined on the spot. It you want a receipt the fine is 500 baht. If you do not, the fine is 200.

Wine is the only expensive food in Thailand. Thais love their beer but have never drunk wine as we know it. All wines are imported with a 100% tax to wholesalers who then add their profit to retailers. They get away with it because they know 'all Farang (white-skinned foreigners) are millionaires.'

(Another 2020 note: In my local RimPing supermarket, Aussie's Penfolds 389 which I have favoured during several of my life spans, is priced at 4,000 baht ($us127.84) per bottle! I make do with a reasonable South African 3 litre cask I buy every ten days or so @1,000 baht ($us31.96).

Notes on Bangkok:
Interesting for a quick visit.
Up-country however, Thailand is a wonderful place to live.

~ * ~

Frankfurt, Germany...

I spend most of my 12-hour flight from Bangkok reading up on *Learn to Speak German in Ten Days*. I have the guts of tourist language but need to freshen up. It is mid-morning and I have the address of my hotel booking so take a U-Bahn (underground metro) from the airport so don't get to even see anything of Frankfurt until alighting at the station near my hotel. Nor is there a bookshop that I can buy a map of Frankfurt.

Ric's luck helps when along pedals a postman on a pushbike. I flag him down... "*Verzaihen Sie bitte, wo can ich dei Rosenburger-Strasse finden?*"

I am pleasantly surprised that he doesn't question either my *Deutsch* or accent.

"*RosenburgerStrasse dort rechts,*" and he points along the very street opposite.

Oh what a break that it's so close. "*Vielen Dank.*"

It's a small backpacker hotel and I'm getting used to finding single rooms in attics are cheap. In many cases, however, one finds more interesting views from attic windows. This one is four floors up with a bathroom across the hall that I share with the other attic bedroom. I recall that my previous visit illustrated that Germans keep everything clean and everything about my small room is neat, tidy, clean and cheap at 80 *Deutschmarks* per night, including breakfast.

I unpack, and despite heavy dark clouds, I go walkabout, with camera in hand. First, being the marketplace I see from my window. It is Saturday and many people are out. Nearby is an outstanding ancient tower, obviously part of what must have been an ancient fortification tower in the old city. Frankfurt had been a major target of the Allies in World War 2 and all about me save this tower needed rebuilding. *Eschenheimer Turm* is a giant of centuries past, happily saved from Allied bombs. It is but another reminder of the futility of war. I note that the inside must also have been saved or restored, for its ground floor is now a bar and restaurant.

The Saturday market on *Der Zeil* between *Konrad Adenauer-Strasse* and *Die Schafergasse* is a lot of fun and well worth a visit. I join locals under a tree to lunch on *Sayerkraut und Bier*. When a thunderstorm arrives and I run home, I go to bed and wake at 8:10pm to find it still raining heavily. In the lounge I watch a WW2 movie with English subtitles, a movie told through German eyes. Two teenage American backpacker lads are thinking it great, but insist, "It must be from a humorist's point of view."

They are in Frankfurt not only because they had been school buddies all their lives in North Carolina, but their fathers had been mates in the USA post war occupation zone based here in Frankfurt.

When I tell them I was their age during those very years, one quickly responded... "Gees, you don't look that old," to get elbowed by his mate..."I mean, gees..."

I wave a hand at him. "Can I join you? I too am interested in seeing see how Germans cope with losing the war."

It is quite near the end so seems most of the movie is based on the camaraderie of the soldiers. The lads then tell me that as soon as the rain stops, they will run to the tunnel under the train station. "In that next street is a 'beaut' restaurant, very cheap."

"Come and eat with us and tell us how Australians saw the end of the war."

We each pay for our dinners but I buy a round of half-litre beers (0.88 pints) which keeps us there quite a while.

It rains all day Sunday so the lads join me in visiting museums.

I phone my friends in Gottingen. "It is not raining here, Ric. Come tomorrow afternoon's train so you arrive after we are home from the hospital. We will arrange an absence for Tuesday and take you to see some old German towns and villages. Bring plenty of film for your camera."

Well, what wonderful friends. I'd met them at a restaurant in Turkey and visited them since. Their son makes jewellery in Berlin and he served me well there.

I farewell wet Frankfurt and train the 200km north. One thing about Europe, wherever you are, trains are close by and it doesn't rain in trains. The cloud bank above is gradually moving south and west, which is promising. Rain ceases but thirty minutes north-east and I can hardly see another cloud. I arrive in the exact minute on the timetable and taxi to Jurgen and Emmi's house.

Oh how comforting it is (and cheaper) when taking a cab, to know where you are going and can even struggle in their language.

~ * ~

Gottingen...

"We eat in and leave early on the morrow for *Hannoversch Münden*, Ric. You will see magnificent countryside all the way. Overnight we stay in a hotel from the 17th century. Again you will see much of *Olde Germany* bypassed during every war in Europe. Next day we go on to *Kassel* which has an incredibly long history, including one major folly that still has never been explained. You will love it."

We 'turn in' early in order to leave early. Emille drives with me aside her and Jurgen sits in back with the snack basket of goodies and the map she obviously doesn't need. It is certainly delightful countryside, undulating yet no mountains but twisting rivers between deep grassy valleys. We pass Germany's equivalent of France's AVG, the very fast trains called here, the ICE.

Yes, I will use that from Gottingen to Berlin or Hamburg. I will be going to both but which in turn I haven't yet decided.

~ * ~

Hannoversch-Münden...

It is indeed a maze of crooked half-timbered houses, so crooked that I wonder why they don't collapse with even a gentle breeze. Such homes have been denying the weather since the 16th and 17th centuries...many more than Maggie was able to show me in England. The ones around me now seem centuries older...and beautifully coloured.

Or could it be that England being such a small country, had a greater proportion of country towns destroyed from the bombings? I recall that before the Americans came into the war, the Luftwaffe outnumbered British fighter planes and proved most destructive.

Here in Lower Saxony, half-timbered houses and administrative buildings make for magnificent viewing. I am somewhat disappointed that we brought a 'take-out' type lunch, deliberately chosen by Emi to give us more time seeing the views and walking around the welcoming history that the outdoors tell. I'd just loved to eat in some cafeteria or *Konditories* with stacks of inviting cream puffs and chocolate layer cakes.

Dinner makes up for it, for Emi had ensured my bedroom was in the 17th century part of the Hotel EsiSenbart (5 individual mansions of different periods joined together).

I am really in my coddled element.

~ * ~

Kasell...

Driving on to Kasell and its wonderful folly is through spectacular gorges and miniature waterfalls, yet it's the *KasellSchlosse* that 'takes the cake.' The *HesseKaiser* of the day was so smitten by waterfalls that an entire steep hillside of almost mountain proportions was excavated and contoured into a vast cascade, the architecture such that water tumbled down from the heights in symmetrical patterns. The *Schloss* (castle) is built not at the top as are castles everywhere else in the world, but right at the bottom so he could gaze up at this incredibly patterned flow of water at any time, for it is a perpetual waterfall.

~ * ~

Hamburg...

My interest in seeing Hamburg, Germany's second city and major port, is that in WW2 it was 99% destroyed by allied bombers. Bridges and wharfs all were shattered. I am disappointed to find that so much had been built in the modern style and so few areas rebuilt in their pre-war splendour, when Maintz and Cologne had gone to great pains in restoring their antiquity.

It starts to rain heavily and I have a brainwave!

Copenhagen, Denmark…

The 12-day Eurail pass I bought includes an extra free day anywhere in Europe and here I am in the very north of Germany. Why not visit Copenhagen?

I check by phone and I do not need a visa, simply jump on a train. It's an early start and for a lark I press the starter on my wristwatch as we pull out of Hamburg and the timetable says it is a 44-minute ride to Lubek. As we approach, I keep my eye on my watch and the train jerks gracefully to a halt in Lubek, right on the 43.9th minute!

How do European trains do this so persistently? Are drivers timed to the second in a competition?

I've had no breakfast, so on the 45-minute ferry crossing this far western end of the Baltic Sea, every need is available. I eat, change some cash at an exchange bureau, buy a duty-free bottle of wine to have when thirsty, as walking quickly causes me. *Kobenhaven* (as spelled in their language) is a 45-minute crossing. In comfortable lounges, I relax, read or chat, also spend time on the port-side railing seeing tiny villages on tiny islands and fishing vessels galore. Weather is overcast and breezy but remains dry until on the ferry coming home. From wharf-side I train to the city, arriving at 10:00am. From the station exit door, the city view is picturesque. The Danish flag on the post office welcomes me. Right opposite on the busy river, *Hovedbanegard* and Tivoli Gardens beckon. Wherever walking around the city, one feels himself in Hans Christian Andersen's presence, sitting in his window, quill in hand, his mind wondering which building will fill the gap in his mind. The entire atmosphere has one in a fairyland. Despite heavy clouds, the weather remains kind.

I wander down a narrow-cobbled mall packed with people and buy postcards, then alongside the little mermaid on her rock at riverside, write them. I watch glass-roofed tourist ferries drifting by, photograph the *Christiansborg Slot* (Royal Palace) and Opera House and sit among scores of people in a big city square eating a late bought sandwich lunch, drinking my wine from the bottle as were several others.

With yet 2 hours before my train leaves, I find a need to simply sit and watch those passing by, crying children running after parents, others being cuddled by fathers while mother carries shopping yet still smiling...all like an informal passing parade.

The entire city remains a busy turmoil of people and has very few motor cars.

My last free hour I spend in a museum. I had several more days but my Eurail pass already has my time filled for Berlin, Lausanne and south-east France.

As rain begins falling, I don't mind. My next few hours are spent travelling. Once on the train station I check my watch...in five and a half minutes, my train leaves.

~ * ~

A different Hamburg...

On my last day, I walk a different direction from the hotel and quickly realise this end of *ReeperbahnStrasse* is the gay district and like I'd discovered in Holland, ladies in shop windows beckon to single guys. And there is a major funny sight...Sex facilities are brazen in their promotion and one in particular grabs my attention...it is up an alleyway some 20m from the street and looking up as you pass, you see a door in an otherwise blank wall...the door itself is a black curtain. Either side of it, some 10 metres tall, a woman's naked legs are painted on the concrete wall, the width and height of the 3-story building, legs spread wide apart. So it's a giggle to see men pulling aside the curtain, walking into this great big black gap atop the parted legs.

All along the street every 'he' or 'she' is propositioned time out of number and it is yet but 10:00am.

My train is for 1:12pm and this one has no dining car. I lug luggage up to a seat on the platform where sits a youngish woman minding two large ports and a couple of long- handle bags. I guess the other in the twosome is buying lunch. I approach her.

"*Ich wil im der café essen, konnen Sie mein Gepack aufpassen bitte?*"

"I'm sorry, but I don't speak German," is the slow apologetic sort of answer in the broadest of American accents. We giggle over it. They have just arrived from Oslo in transit to Berlin and her husband is buying sandwiches. She minds my pack as requested.

They are Linda and Ed and when our train arrives, we share a compartment. They are from Baltimore. It is their first time in Europe and decided on a few days in Berlin before being picked up by a tour guide. I congratulate them on having a day or three on their own, getting the feel of a place, especially in a big country.

"You speak German then?" Linda asks.

"Yes, Linda, but what you just heard, all but exhausts my repertoire. I can find a bed, something to eat and count my change. Do you go to Italy?"

"Yes."

"Learn your exchange rate and always count your change."

Ed gives me a thumbs up for that warning.

"Do you go to the Balkans? Egypt? Turkey?"

"No. Do you speak other languages?"

"I get by in French in the north, but am told I could have trouble in the south. I go there after four or five days in Berlin. I can also find bed and food in Greece."

It is about then that the rain begins pelting down and it is a pretty rough track, one Germany has obviously not yet bothered about, preferring to build their new ICE fast track. So we have a somewhat bumpy ride in the old train.

I recommend that in Berlin they test ride the U-Bahn in what had been both East and West Berlin. "West Germans under Britain in the north and your country in the south during the entire cold war, had a much happier recovery than East Germany under the Russians. East of that border there was no recovery. The flattened cities were left in their ugliness. Given the chance, you will see the marked difference. Also there were no schools for children, so many east Germans now live with that gap in their lives."

Berlin again...

It is raining and the ICE is truly a wonderfully fast train...not as fast as the French, but claiming more comfort.

I am again 'boarding' with Emmille and Jurgen's son, Gunter, and much more of East Berlin is now under reconstruction, *km* after *km* of streets dug up in every direction. I'm atop a bus, front seat and all is laid out ahead as we wind through the city and suburbs. New sewers are being laid, and traffic lights installed as are telephone cables in street after street after street. The Russian East Berlin is being renewed in every respect.

Berlin Hauptbahnhof is interesting. It is well in the *old east*, Station Zoo having for 50 years been the main station for West Berlin and its surrounds exemplify the features ignored by Russia. The northern side is yet to be restored, but it is obvious that renewal is imminent. Everywhere in the areas that Russia ignored are being totally floored and some underground car-parks and new highways being introduced.

Oh, how much of the old Berlin I have trudged!

Sunday, I head for the *Tiergarten* Victory Monument (yes, for once-upon-a-time Germany had a war victory) but in the British/American area of Berlin, it has been saved. From the U-Bahn at *FranzosischeStrasse* I head up the *Unter Den Linden*, walk, walk, walking all the way through the *Tiergarten* Zoo and taking scores of photographs.

On my last night in Berlin, I eat a take-out steak and watch a night of Mozart's music. I am to bed immediately it finishes, for my feet are tired and tomorrow night I am on an 11:23pm train en-route for Switzerland.

For my entire last day, I again walk to my old love of *Kurfurstendamm*'s 'old church' and treat myself to an expensive lunch again in *Leyssifeus,* watching those wanting to be seen still using it as their 'show' room. I take some of its delightful confections home for Jurgen. I buy tinea powder from an alchemist store, for my toes have the dreaded traveller's disease. To ensure my Jurgen does not use my bed-sheets after I leave, I have all my bed linen laundered during the day I leave and take him to dinner from where he drives me to the *Intercity Hauptbahnhof.*

I've certainly taken a liking to the modern Germany, aided, I guess, by having befriended that Gottingen family. It is now a country with just so much to offer travellers. Its western people somehow illustrate thanks to the countries that defeated them in war. Or could it be having saved them from stronger Nazism? With many, certainly.

~ * ~

Switzerland's Lausanne on Lac Geneva...

The train change-over is made on the Swiss side of the border at Basel (pronounced Bahl). It takes an hour to sort luggage marked for 'West' (Lausanne and Geneva) and that for 'East' (Zürich).

I'm for south and west along the north coast of *Lac Geneva* as the Swiss call it, while on the southern shore, *Lac Léman* as the French call it, a matter on which I am to become confused. (Come Tuesday you can have a giggle on my poor planning).

The serious matter of vetting and stamping passports ensues during the wait and as the rain stops, we head south, mountains getting so steep that we begin switch-backing, then the *Grenchen-Nord* tunnel is the longest I ever experience. We emerge to find more mountain tops covered in snow and blossoming villages appear like those I ogled in the Bavarian Alps.

We hug mountainsides on my right while on my left is the entrancing overview of the lake. As the sunshine brightens, *Lac Geneva* glistens...totally captivating!

On the close shores, Swiss flags fly from every cottage and village square. Short tunnel after short tunnel tells how close the mountains are to the lake. Villages are on a spit of land between one and the other. As one part of my brain thinks on that, another part thinks how travel has its annoying sides. Here am I with innards agog after another delightful German meal but my brain agog that I have to forget everything German. Once I alight from the train, the language is French. Switzerland has three languages and Lausanne is in the French sector.

My Life, My Travels

Swiss ladies in the travel agency at Lausanne train station seem to know exactly how I feel...What hotel price range do I seek? Will I be afoot much? Do I realise Lausanne sits on a tiny shelf of a steep mountain dropping to lake's edge?

She recommends Hotel Alpha..."Take the metro underground to Ouchy terminus and you have a two to three minute walk through a pedestrian tunnel to this hotel. It is in the Old Town quarter and meets all the requirements you request."

I like her style and take the underground exit from the metro via the long tunnel and on emerging, right across the street is Hotel Alpha, five stories high.

What I cannot see is that it sits on a rock shelf. My room is on the top floor. Whilst double and twin bed rooms face the lake, my single room window, on the top floor, looks away from the lake but right on the very roadway from which cars enter the hotel. Yes, the back of the hotel clings to the rock wall of a mountain, its next 'shelf' of a street having not only the car entrance, but the hotel dining room, part of it open air and the front overlooking the lake.

Oh, what a steep climb this hotel is built on!

The hotel front door is on *Avenue de Montbenon,* a wide 'shelf,' for it includes the metro underground. The hotel entrance contains a waiting room with lounges, the visitor desk, a small staff office and the lift and that is all. The dining room is on the fourth floor. If diners arrive by train, they take the lift to the fourth floor. If they drive in for dinner, they approach by the *Avenue Jules Gonin,* the major highway, and turn into the hotel car-park at that level. From my room I walk down one flight of stairs to eat, but take the lift 4 floors to gain the front entrance.

It is a very steep mountainside that my hotel clings to.

Right opposite is not only the metro underground, but alongside it is a cable-car on wheel tracks set into the rock wall. A mountainside 'sit-down' cable-car on tracks descends down to the lake in four stages. At three narrow street levels, small houses cling to the rock face along each street. The fourth stage of descent is ground level and lake surface. From there, large ferries cross to the far shore.

Tomorrow, if it is not raining, I shall take that southern shore trip. For what is left of today I will exchange some money and stroll about this 'old town' area.

All I have ever seen of Switzerland had been the few hours in Zürich during the Singapore Air debacle and when visiting Liechtenstein from Austria's Bregenz.

Oh, I do look forward to that cable track down to the lake. Finding a city that is literally built into the side of a mountain is indeed a thrill!

It is clear that the hotel's street *Avenue de Montbenon* was once a Millionaire's Row, grand mansions with magnificent views over the lake, but in 1993, most are converted to doctor surgeries and clinics...and my hotel.

Tonight, I sleep around the clock. I guess last night's 'first in Switzerland' one of its national dishes *Rosti Valaisanne*, thinly grated potato pan-fried to crisp and golden, topped with salty bacon, fried egg and melted goat's cheese, served with gherkins and pickled onions...absolutely delightful.

And what a day to wake up! Nary a cloud, just blue-sky and the TV forecast is 26c.

With camera in hand, I am into the metro tunnel and on to this gliding cable car down the mountainside, every minute ensuring I'm bum-back in my seat, taking in the lake view. Shoppers with bags of goodies alight at each stop, for each is a cross-road. One steps out from the angled car on to horizontal steps in the street. After three such stops, I have the different angle to handle, yet there are plenty of handles to help. One steps out into delightful gardens with restaurants, clothes stores and sunshades.

All along lakeside are elegant hotels and restaurants with sun-umbrellas...a blaze of florid colours. To the east, mountain peaks, the beginnings of Tyrol country with white-capped peaks, and to the west, the same.

Flying the Swiss flag, the huge ferry comes in. I make for upstairs and am thoroughly enjoying the scenery when a ticket inspector informs me that my ticket doesn't qualify for upstairs. I can retire below or pay the additional fee.

It is one of those occasions when faced with a quickly spoken foreign language that one finds difficult. Downstairs I make new friends and approaching the southern shore I get quite a surprise. This your giggle bit.

French flags are aflutter everywhere. I simply hadn't considered that Switzerland shares this lake with France and my passport is in the hotel safe in Lausanne!

My wallet has various cards with my identity...*But will they send me back?*

Changing habit to meet such an occasion, I accept that ignorance can be bliss. Hadn't I learned how to become someone else when on stage with Maggie? To forget I'm me when on stage? And ain't I about to land on a stage of sorts here?

When realising no one ahead of me is stopping at the Visa window, my ill-at ease fear abates.

Are all Europeans void of needing visa into France?

I pull myself out of the throng to stand aside while concentrating on French words for 'already' for my passport has me on a current visa allowance...*And can reel off in French without too much foreign accent.*

Customs people wave everybody through en-masse and oh, what a wonderful day it is to see another side of France in *Evian les Bains*, home of pure drinking water. It is a spa resort, its waterfront furnished with firstly parks and gardens in full bloom on one side, and across the street, grand hotel resorts ranged side by side. I can well imagine seeing *Hercule Poirot* emerge from any of the brass-railed entrances, white suit, panama and spats, leaning on his walking cane.

I don't take to the waters except imbibe. I climb the town and find a natural spring in a rock face, its fountain installed in 1789, year of the revolution. It is indeed a delightful taste. Bottled Evian water becomes my stock-in-trade for the next several weeks as I tour my 'different' corner of France.

With Swiss coinage I buy postcards and get change in French francs, sufficient to buy coffee and an *eclaire*. Street artists attract large crowds and musicians stroll *Le Petit Chene* singling out the prettiest *m'moiselles* to serenade. After a couple of hours, it is back to the ferry, crush rather than queue to get aboard.

Back in Switzerland where Aussies need no visas, Murphy welcomes me. Everyone's passport must be presented. I explain I am a simple Australian who left his passport in his hotel room safe. I show my Australian driving licence, which draws a condescending shrug of shoulders.

Bloody hell, customs procedures between countries of the EC is ludicrous these days.

From the top of the rail-rack, I stroll *Ave Jules Conin* to *Ave de Tivoli* enjoying the evening shadows in the parks, then the colours of the lake as the sun dips from sight.

The twilight is delightful and the air is so mild I eat 'al-fresco' on the rooftop of the Restaurant Paradiso on Rue du Petit-Chene, a few doors up the mountain from my hotel. I find other patrons walking directly on to the roof from the street behind. An expensive meal at $56 but I eat like a king, stuffing myself with a *pate canard* lamb noisettes washed down with a *vin-rouge* followed by *profiteroles* and a *cognac*.

I've one more day of walking the city I find so pleasurable, and after breakfast the sun continues shining. My plan is to wander streets in a different direction and take more photographs of tilted streets.

Photographing a next street which is 'down over this railing' causes strange feeling in one. I am in *Rue St.Francois* one minute, and after a street crossing it has a different name that changes again at the next crossing, so *Rue FauxNez* quickly becomes *Rue de Bourg*.

Another gloriously strange sight is looking down *La Petite Denoise* to *Rue Cheneau deBourg*. *La Place de Cathedral*, high on a hill, the staircase going down is '*Scalier du Marche.*' Then there is the little market street *Rue Madelaine* at the corner of *Place de la Palud* that has street music all the time and *Palais de Justice* is in the manicured *Montbenon Park* behind my hotel, plenty of people relaxing and simply enjoying such an outdoor environment.

I could easily fall in love with Lausanne, but as easily change my mind come winter.

~ * ~

Having breakfasted, checked out and towed my luggage through the tunnel to *Ouchy* and transferred to the train platform for Geneva, I purchase my ticket and watch them setting up chairs and tables with chequered tablecloths and napkins ready to serve breakfast to business commuters, right there on the platform.

We hug the shoreline to Genove where I change trains to French, and we quickly cross the border.

This time I do have to show my passport and all is in order.

Eighteen

France...

An hour out of Geneva we are well into France hugging *Lac du Bourget* to starboard and pass though *Aix-les-Bains*. We stop at *Chambery*.

I am ensconced with five Americans, young Megan, her mother, an aunt and grandma. They too are on Eurail-pass tickets, yet ignore their benefits. Instead of watching captivating scenery, they are on the floor playing rummy. They don't even stir when a train guard halts at our door to point out *Mont Blanc*. I jump to photograph it but none of them even looks up.

Yep, everyone is surely different from the next.

As we approach Grenoble, that year's Winter Olympic site, they show a little more interest. Looking down from our high perch, I too find it fascinating, a small town unable to grow because it is squeezed by a ring of steep mountains.

To me it is 'shades of La Pas in Bolivia,' absolutely spectacular.

The line south is under repair so we backtrack through glorious hills and valleys to meet the River Rhone at Valence. From here it is "Just follow the river to Avignon."

~ * ~

Avignon...

Tucked into the province of *Provence* in the southeast corner of France, Avignon in the 14th century purchased the home of popes from Rome for cash and remained the papal city for seven successive popes. At the end of the 18th century, the French Revolution caused its return to Rome. I'm no upholder of religion, yet Christianity certainly establishes itself a business strength, especially Roman Catholics, in Europe. *Roma* made itself wealthy when selling itself to Avignon that even then had but half a bridge. Only in the 12th century did it decide for the umpteenth time, not to bother rebuilding it when it broke away under the Rhone River's pressure. The intriguing unique thing about Avignon is that the modern city is built beyond the walls of the 'old city' at this point of the 'broken bridge.' The historical wonderland remains today.

The 'old city' historical centre east of the river retains the partly ruined *Palais des Popes Cathedral* and what is left of the *Pont d'Avignon*. This ruined bridge is to become in 1995, a UNESCO World Heritage Site. To me in 1993, any bridge that just comes to a dead-end mid-river, only four of its original twenty-two arches intact yet still holds the annual *Festival d'Avignon*, is surely worth a visit.

The dramatic entrance into this 'old town' from the train station through the mediaeval walls immediately captures me to it.

I just want to be part of all that I see ahead of me down this very street!

I am immediately hooked. I must walk the same cobbles people of old centuries walked.

At my left elbow I discover the most teasing of entrances to *La Cloitre St.Louis*.

This 15th century monastery-come-hotel will cost heaps, but I want to be part of it!

I sign for 450Ff ($125) *avec petit dejeuner* (with small breakfast). Strolling its extensive cloisters, I am in my element. This historical monument has retained every indoor facet. Hallways, walls, floors and ceilings retain every timely element while still adding needs of toiletry in every room. So as not to change anything to modernity, elevators are built on the external sides of outer walls with windows into elegant gardens.

Modern extensions like swimming pool and library are built on the roof of the ancient chapel across the courtyard of plane-trees, so the centuries old indoors of the ancient chapel maintain their valid age.

At 9:30pm I am in the outdoor dining room, part of the ancient cloister. It is yet twilight and the magnificent plane-trees establish a romantic atmosphere of candles rather than electric lights. Dinner costs an arm and a leg, but is magnificent from start to finish and the service impeccable.

It is great to occasionally have such a splurge.

After dinner I walk up *Cours Jacque Jaures* that becomes *Rue de la Republique,* to arrive in the old Centro. Despite past 11:00pm, people in throngs still dine. The square *Place de l'Horloge* is chock-a-block with outdoor restaurants, canopies and umbrellas abounding, weaving waiters with trays held high, sidewalk performers, street artists, souvenir stalls...everywhere it seems, people eating as they perambulate or walk the dog...(in France, everyone takes the dog on holidays for all are welcome in hotels, buses, trains and restaurants as if they were children). By midnight, the crowded streets begin thinning, yet many are still dining.

All is a glory of which Avignon can boast!

After breakfast in the courtyard, I take to the streets and on *Rue deLimas* pass the town's celebrated garden cafe *leJardin de l'Europe.* It is packed.

From a street artist on Rue Vilar by the *Palais des Papas,* having watched him sign his postcard size painting of the 'broken bridge' as I call it in my mind, with the cathedral ruins in the background, I buy it for Ff100. He dries it with a battery charged hot-air blow-torch. In 2020, it too has its place on my living-room wall.

Have I fallen in love with yet another city?

The Old Town has only the cathedral-come-castle taller than two or three floors, all mediaeval, all adorned with clematis and bougainvillea. Modern Avignon is carefully beyond the walls to the east, invisible from inside the old walls...a million miles away across the Rhone and 'there ain't no bridge-no-more'!

Another world?

Another life?

Tonight, I dine in *Le Petit Bedon*. It had taken my eye in my early morning stroll, yes another beef-steak still red-raw and edible with just two forks. Yet again it is like so many places in France; if you don't speak a little French, or able to read, you can only point fingers at menus or maps when trying to explain how much you enjoy your food.

I post home a pair of films for $1.60. From Hamburg it had been $8.50!

Tomorrow I take a very early train. I want the long hop to Bordeux all in daylight.

~ * ~

Bordeaux...

Armed with bread rolls, fruit and cheese, I have a window seat and until Narbonne, it is flat terrain yet with constant reminders of farmers' pride in properties. We farewell the Mediterranean to turn northwest, and the only interests for me are the Rugby teams from Carcassonne and Toulouse. Once leaving them, the countryside is undulating and the villages become prettier. At one stage, I wend my way to the bar-car to buy Evian water and a sandwich and in second class, the people are herded like cattle, many sitting on the floor or on luggage in corridors.

Toulouse to Bordeaux is pretty countryside with considerable vineyards. *Chateaux* galore dot the track now in hilly terrain and along rivers, obviously a prosperous area. On the southern skyline south and west are the Pyrenees, atop which is the Spanish border.

All the way, it is no problem with animals, of which my car has some dozen or more. There are no fights, no barking of dogs or scratching by cats. All are taken on leash to toilets as if leading children by hand.

~ * ~

Bordeaux...

The Information Office is short on help. With minimal outline and no map until requested, I am given a list of hotels and told to make a choice of three. I am way behind budget and need to economise, so queue up with three of the hotels on the list…it's like a 'lucky dip.' When I ask if all are on tram or bus routes, she sighs as if annoyed, but the answer is positive. I choose Victoria Garden because it is closest to downtown.

"How do I get there?" She sighs again and gives me the bus numbers that pass the hotel on *Cours de la Somme*.

"*Merci de votre aide, madam.*" And that wasn't what I'd really like to say.

I go to a different counter, buy a city map that affirms that the city is surrounded by wineries. I find my way to the hotel, certainly not in an area I'll walk alone at night, yet it seems welcoming enough. A bus stops at the door every 30 minutes and my room is clean and comfortable. The hotel has no dining room but serves breakfast to rooms.

I decide to live cheaply in Bordeaux during my three days and because of the location, shopping is cheap. I find a Mum & Dad store and stock up with *Cinzano*, bread, cheese, paté, fruit-juice, yoghurt and fruit. I wash clothes in the hand basin and drape things over the backs of chairs and doors of cupboards, scrub my teeth, shower and dry off, then sit to dine on my lap, watching TV news.

As in Avignon, there is what boils down to "No Comment News"…simply news without comment, silent movies, film clips from around the world with no explanation, just the name of the country or city in the top left corner.

What makes it so telling, so memorable, is the impact of silence! The dramatic film clips tell in the extreme that in Brazil's Sarajevo, the heartbreak of parents at the street carnage by constabulary shooting even children in the streets. It leaves one to compose your own horror when this side of the imagined barbed wire fence.

One is simply so helpless. *A striking way to bring the news home to you.*

'*No Comment News*' indeed!

Shivering, I change to another channel and watch *Neighbours* with French sub-titles. I must be the only Australian who after all these years never bothered to watch an episode bearing the name of *Les Voisins*.

Come morning I take an early bus to town, stroll the streets, intrude behind those attending Sunday Mass in the cathedral to watch from 'just inside.' An imposing monument in the cathedral forecourt is important to all. Mass is so impressive over the sign designating *Le Memoir de les Gironins* I join those photographing it then sneak through the archway into a narrow street named *Le Porte du Jeaux*.

The weather becomes cloudy as I breakfast at a sidewalk café and rain-spots follow. It is suddenly cold, so I hie home for both anorak and umbrella.

I spend the afternoon visiting wineries in the *Gironde* district. The Office of Tourism promotes the half-day visit to two showrooms where wine can be tasted and to one in particular, *Le Chateau La Blancherie-Peyret* at Labrède…not only a majestic home but an extensive winery yielding 60,000 bottles of white wine and 40,000 bottles of reds from her (the owner) 11 hectares per-annum. I come away with three of her recommended reds, one to drink and two to take to my friends in Bretagne.

Our second winery is *Chateau de la Malle*, a 16th century National Trust classified homestead, then on to further tasting at *Chateau Myrat* (early 18th century) in the village of *Barsac*. Wine is of prize-winning quality valued at 100Ff($28) per bottle which I thoroughly enjoy tasting yet decline buying.

Back at the pub I shower and with rain drizzling, I eat in my lap then go to bed.

Monday dawns bright and sunny and I add two museums to my

notes...*Musèe d'Aquitaine,* 'regional art and artefacts' and *Musèe de Fine Arts.* Both are this side of the city and are my choice from the city's seven museums, one before lunch and the other after. I am on my feet all day, so will have my 'lash-out' dinner.

Tomorrow I head for Paris in the TGV.

Both museums are well worth the modest price for entry, and I recommend both. They open at 10:00am and I give each three very worthwhile hours.

It's a glorious day so I stroll to the river and see what they mean by 'Frances's major Atlantic Port'...scores of large ships, lots of activity surrounded by parklands.

~ * ~

To Paris...

With three bottles of wine to juggle, I take a cab to the train.

Wow, a very active station for I count 32 platforms. It's a long way with beautiful scenery everywhere, especially around Angouleme. We stop at only Tours and Orleans. I have a 3 day booking at Hotel Louxor in Republique, recommended from Lonely Planet and have a struggle with my backpack and 3 bottles. The cab costs Ff6.50 and the hotel Ff220($61) per night with personal shower and toilet and breakfast is reasonable. It's not the most salubrious area (right by the *Place Republique* where it all began for the Revolution). Host Claude tells me he is happy that my French is better than his English.

I buy a three-day travel pass beginning tomorrow, covering every type of transit anywhere in Paris. The Metro can put anyone down close to whatever goal! Several city areas are simply closed to motor traffic.

After my big day, I settle in front of the TV with a bread and cheese dinner and am again reminded how the number of ads interrupting programmes in both France and Germany are fewer by half than those back home.

In my most comfortable shoes come Tuesday, I am off to the *Champs Elysees* and *Arc de Triomphe.* Never in Paris does one have to worry about public transport getting you close to everywhere. And it is always quick.

I take a Seine River one-hour cruise for 40Ff($2.22) with commentary in French, English and Italian. Oldest bridge is the *Isle de Cite*, built 1605, taking two years. The cruise is a worthwhile investment, for it points my plan to where I will wander afoot during my three days. We pass the *Eiffel Tower*, the *Conciergerie* where King Louis and Marie Antoinette awaited the guillotine. *Hotel de Ville* (Paris Government House) is also an enormous riverside palace-style establishment.

To use the Paris Metro there are three essential requirements...

Have a Metro map. Write in French spelling the name of your destination. The French word for *exit* is *sortie*...in the maze of underground passages to change lines to that of your target, you can face three or four different passageways. Another handy hint to note is how to ask for help. Start with *Parlez vous anglais?* (Do you speak English?). I doubt you will ever find a sign of any kind printed in English, any more than at home you don't have signs in other languages.

Two more: Be ready for people begging. If you oblige, scores will rush you. At the Eiffel Tower (this is 1993 and things could have improved by now...), the queue to buy my ticket to 'go up' has me waiting on my feet 45 minutes. To avoid having to queue again at each level, buy a 'Top' straight off. I pay Ff52 ($14.45). You cannot imagine the crowds that push and shove. There really is no need to 'stop off' at levels 1 and 2. Just remember that at every level, up or down, there is a long queue to move anywhere else. But wow, that top level is something you will never forget. My guide book suggests that for the best position of the sun, late afternoon is best time, but I find near everybody else has also read that! If you do not make this visit you will ever regret it. Just remember that everyone going up there becomes Greek or Italian in pushing and shoving! You need sharp elbows.

Atop, you are indeed glad you came. In my day, it was the tallest public building in the world. I am atop more than an hour, utterly mesmerised for every minute. It is an experience of a lifetime.

Once down, I needed to visit so much of what had seen from up there that I had been granted renewed energy to walk, walk, walk all over Paris.

Has anyone else ever walked around so much of Paris?

On that day, KVR walks well into the dead of night. In the Opera district, I find a spare seat on a footpath table to again flop and drink bottomless coffee, still watching the milling crowd that in Paris never reduces. People keep coming from every direction to where I sit, as if part of the atmosphere. It is indeed a vibrant city.

In the Louvre's main forecourt, the dreadful pyramid is being constructed...a foreign building spoiling the Louvre (biggest museum in the world), one of the most wonderful forecourts of any huge historical area, brings tears to my eyes. Yet when I ask to see what will be the finish of the 'refurbishment,' they take pity on me and sit me down while spreading out what the end will look like... major new roads, no rather let's call them boulevards, for all are massively wide, will sweep from the forecourt right through to the *Tuilleries* to the *Place de la Concorde*, so when completed there will be uninterrupted views right through the *Concorde* and *Champs Elysees* to the *Arc de Triomphe*....an incredible addition to the very city centre! Meanwhile, it is noise and dust with front-end-loaders ripping great swathes out of the present *Tuilleries Gardens*, the whole presently a veritable bomb site.

And *Versailles* will be much the same as the Eiffel Tower, I'm told by other visitors who had been watching me "taking them to task for so spoiling the Louvre forecourt."

"We have just been standing in *Versailles* queues two and a half hours just to get through the forecourt...thousands of us. It must be bedlam once inside, so we simply gave up."

I say again, Paris is indeed a vibrant city. I must add though, that they are going through great pains to improve these problem spots. And yes, looking at today's Google map of Paris, those areas are a vast improvement on what I suffered.

Up in *Montmartre,* the shuttle runs from *Pigalle* and I recommend you use it rather than walk...very tiring and very steep, but the most wonderful sights await you! The shuttle drops me right outside *Sacre Coeur* on the crest, from where are magnificent views. All streets here are cobble and always there are women unprepared enough to be wearing stilt heels. Foolish!

It's great fun in the *Rue Novins*, a street of restaurants and little bars where one can eat and drink to their heart's content at reasonable prices and its marketplace is well worth visiting, even just to watch. It is where the would-be Toulouse Lautrecs and Salvador Dalis by the dozen will paint you exactly as you want to be painted and the result is well worth the money...with everyone around you in the holiday mood, it's lots of fun. The scenery itself and the happy-go-lucky atmosphere is indeed refreshing. Rather than the shuttle back, it's an easy downhill walk and just sighting the housing of people there in the holiday mood is displayed all the way down to the *Pigalle Theatre* itself...where so much musical and fun history occurred, more of which is still being made.

Rue Coulaincourt in particular for me, brings back such happy memories of when Maggie and I, with our fun crew in *Rhombus*, played *Irma la Douce* on stage in Melbourne, the musical version... it all happened on this very street.

My day is really made, however (with me being the joke!) when taking the metro shopping at *Les Halles* in downtown Paris. I leave the Metro at the *Les Halles* platform and find myself already in the 'shop of everything.' I don't buy much but love the fun atmosphere until trying to get out. I upped and downed escalators in all directions for maybe a half-hour before realising that the *sortie* of this mammoth store is by train!

I let it take me all the way to the *Palais de Luxembourg* where in its gardens literally hundreds are naked to the loins, enjoying the sunshine and swimming pool...absolutely magnificent gardens. And what a way to use it for everyone's fun!

Leaving, however, I make a discovery. I am on the *Rue Monmartre* (district I'd visited earlier in the day), is not where the metro station named *Rue Monmartre*, where I have to pick up my luggage, is situated. Yes, just more help in getting you lost in Paris!

Before picking up my luggage, however, to rest my poor feet, I sit over coffee on a street-front café where their cute idea is letting you mix your own the way you like it.

Another never-forget point for Paris is that the metro closes for cleaning at midnight. They run buses that don't necessarily set you down where you want to go. They vary according to different times. Walking alone at night anywhere in Europe is foolish. Remember my 'all vehicle transport ticket within Paris'? $26 for 3 days, a ticket for any transport anywhere? It would have cost double paying each fare each time.

On my last day I am again 'downtown' in *Place Vendome* with its big forecourt, but be prepared to pay big money. It's where moneyed people buy the best of anything but is well worth watching. The forecourt parking lot that day just while I was there included four Rolls Royces, three Bentleys, four Daimler plus magnificent European 'smart-cars' I cannot name.

I am now off to Nantes for my weekend with the 'Frenchies,' so having had my 'period ticket' stamped for TVG terminal, look forward to the 4 guys, having finished work for the week, greeting me at the Nantes terminal.

~ * ~

A weekend for Mont-St-Michel...

The fast train is again a wonderful experience. No matter how often I use it, I find it 'yet another new experience,' but the lads are not nearly as punctual as the train. They are not waiting at north terminal, so I trundle my big bag and bottles to the south terminal but nor are they there.

Again, I wonder: *Why can't some clever bastard invent a portable telephone?*

I lug it all back to the north terminal where there is a luggage locker.

I sit and rack my brain, trying to recall the name Christophe, now living with Edit and their tot, gave me as their new abode...I do recall him saying it is where her family lives.

But I do recall the name of Dominique Gueron's village...Les Touches.

I go back to the south terminal for that is where I had previously caught a bus. Only one bus waits there now but the driver doesn't know *Les Touches.*

Sheesh. I am an Australian and know I've caught a bus here for Les Touches, yet he doesn't know it? I tell him it is some 30km east but he still doesn't know it.

He tells me to ask at the bus depot so back I trek to the north terminal but the desk is closed. I ask around to several people and no one knows *Les Touches.*

On the wall is a large map. I cannot see it either, yet right on the edge of the map I do see the name *Thouare...That's it! The village where Christophe and Edit have their cottage!*

I ask a fellow behind the desk which of the several tram stations I go to for *Thouare.*

He explains that and adds, "Along that track, you change to a bus."

I drag my luggage and bloody bottles from storage and struggle on to a tram. I ask the lass straphanging beside me...

"Pardon M'mselle, est ce que vous ou je corresponde a le bus a Thouare?"

"Oui M'sr. But I the English speak if it is for you, more help."

The gods at last, are smiling? She actually lives in Thouare!

"Do you by any chance know Christophe Durand and his partner Edit?"

She does not. But yes, we shortly leave the tram and a bus waits.

After some fifteen minutes, she tells me she gets off at the next stop but two further stops is the end of the route and the post office may still be open.

It isn't, but there is a small hotel with an appropriate name... The Last Hotel.

I will stay the night and enquire at the post office in the morning.

Once in my room, I again look at the phone number Christophe had given me...*I shall give it one more futile try and see if he is yet home...*

Edit answers.

"This is Ric and I guess you are Edit? Christophe tells me you speak English?"

"Yes, and he is worried over you. He and the boys were held up at work and by the time they got to the Nantes Station, you had given up and left. He expects you will phone here. Where are you?"

"At The last Hotel. I..."

"I shall come and get you. I know the lady there. She will understand the problem."

So it turns out that they have the entire weekend organised for me, including tonight's dinner. Edit is indeed a sweetie and Christophe is at home at their cottage. The lady friend who owns the hotel refuses to take a franc from me.

"Edit is almost a daughter to me," she explains.

So I am taken to Edit's cottage and welcomed by a relieved Christophe, who hugs me like a father.

I am installed in the little attic bedroom of their tiny farm cottage.

I love it! It is quite ancient.

I look forward to sleeping in it for three nights.

The rest of the cottage is as cosy. Edit doesn't know how old it is..."But at least five generations of our family before me. All the cluster of houses around us is my family. Maybe 200 years old?"

The other three lads are called and asked to meet at the restaurant, so the entire tribe dines at *La Caleche,* undoubtedly *Thouare's* premier restaurant...a country-side style, great food and fun. We get delightfully merry, all but Edit, who does not drink spirits.

I have my morning shower kneeling in the bath, for the French still haven't learned to stand up to shower. We breakfast on fruit-juice, bread, egg and cheese and drive off to meet the other lads in Domonique 1's car. They are on time and we head north for more than 2 hours. Because of the huge tides on the north coast, we have a long walk to *Mont-St-Michel*...a most spectacular sight in the distance. (Since then, I've learned, a shuttle has been built to carry travellers to the *Mont* from the car-park, but we had to walk the 2 km, time lost for viewing the countless sites once there).

Over the centuries, the tiny island had been turned into a protective castle to ward off the regularly attacking English. As a sight-seeing element, I am in ecstasies, a most wonderful day and to save several pages of notes here, I advise my readers to go look it up on the Internet. Make sure you read up on every one of the hundreds of sites of interest on such a tiny island. They serve great luncheon and my camera clicked all of every minute we could before running to beat the incoming tide. Today of course, the shuttle overcomes that problem and effort, but it all remains an exhibition I've never been able to forget!

It certainly earns its World Heritage stamp.

Another wonderful dinner is at Dom Gueron's (Dom1) house. He has tried to make it tidier than usual for my benefit but dinner is a matter of calling at the Nort-Erdre supermarket, buying bread, cheese, frozen pizza slices for microwaving and pork sausages for frying. I contribute wine and liqueur chocolates with ice-cream. Dominique Manard (Dom2) and Pascal do most of the cooking while we others look over their shoulders with helpful hints. At dinner's end, I make several toasts calling for several more glasses of wine.

Dom 2 and Pascal are to sleep there for the little we have left of the night. Edit drives us home to *Thouare*, just an hour away. Sunday is an early start and the two carloads meet up again, this time they use Pascal's car and we follow the *Loire* (France's longest river) as far as *Saumur*. There and on the way to it and on the way back, we call at several old castles. There has been severe drought and the river is low, but we cross at Saumur's picturesque *Chalonnes-Sur-Loire*. All along the roads are spectacularly beautiful centuries-old villages with as spectacular gardens. We lunch at the *Tavern Maupassant* and I hog myself on the magnificent Hock, the supreme version of which is not only finger-lickin-good in the moment, but good to remember for years.

At the Ackermann Winery are the incredible natural caves inside which the chill is unnerving, ideal however, for the thousands of bottles of Champagne that mature there over the years. I buy a bottle ($12) that we consume on their terrace for afternoon tea. On our drive home, the rain begins in absolute torrents. After a prolonged drought, all in our car are happy. Edit handles the persistent storm well, especially when the car ahead goes into a helpless spin. Edit doesn't want to stop but keeps driving and Pascal behind, stays with us.

As we get close to *Les Touches,* the rain eases off and it is so tiny a village that I realise why so many I asked about it had never heard of it.

"So many small villages around here fall under the heading of 'Nort-Erdre,'" I am told. "But of course, you were not to know that."

We call into Pascal's family home for *aperitifs*, chickens and geese scattering as both cars drive in.

Again, I am aware of the 'quaintness' of the small farm houses, and again appreciate how all in the family cater for the lone son's guests. It's their way of life.

Monday morning, by the time I wake, Edit has left for work so Christophe and I breakfast. He helps me pack, then drives me to see Edit at her workshop, her own little business making cloth badges. After fond farewells, he takes me to the post office where I mail films home to Kodak, then drives me to Nantes to catch the train.

Nantes to Paris via TVG at its average of 260kph takes 2 hours and I go straight to another platform for Amsterdam. Today is the final day of my Eurailpass, so I might as well use it.

Like France, I enjoy Amsterdam immensely. So close to finishing my three-monthly journey in England, and with train or car tunnelling from France to England still on the planning map, I must cross the channel either by ferry or flight. From Amsterdam I will fly to London. After so much sightseeing and laughter with company to more than satisfy me, I am now ready to again enjoy being alone.

Ain't it a natural part of my sixth life?

The train journey Paris to Belgium then on to Amsterdam unfortunately bypasses several towns and villages with partly German history, places like Colmar and Strasbourg that must await a later visit. Over the border into Belgium is more an industrial area so lacks the complacency and beauty of the south, especially the area between England and Germany. Not until approaching Amsterdam do I open my camera pouch and what do I find? Tucked carefully around the camera are 400 French francs with a short note from Christophe...

From the five of us, thanking you for sharing our friendship. You will ever remain our dear friend.

All five signed it, drawing hearts and kisses.

~ * ~

Amsterdam...

I've never forgotten flying out of Amsterdam for the first time back in 1974, sitting in KLM's First Class being treated like a king, yet weeping tears of frustration at having been so close to seeing so much wonderful history.

Now here I am in a train heading for it... for what, a fourth or fifth time since?

Touring is tiring and expensive, yet I get so much from it! Not to even mention the most wonderful friends I've made to make me so much the richer. Let's face it, if Europe did not have such cold winters, I could and would, live happily in the south of either Germany or France for the rest of my life, travelling at will.

It is 9:00pm when we arrive and I change money and take a cab to The Waterfront Hotel on Singel, one of those traditional little narrow canal houses, this one all of 5 metres wide, expensive but only because single accommodation has become more than I'd previously paid. A single room with shower and toilet is now $145 per night yet it is right on the *Konigsplein* within easy walk of everywhere, and includes a full English breakfast. They give me a map of the city so

I've four days left of my holiday before flying to England to begin solid work as well as touring, on family research.

Upstairs and unpacking, what should fall out of my camera pouch but another Ff100.

Bloody hell, a round hundred francs each? That's really good friendship.

Having unpacked and it now 11:00pm, it's still right on dinner time for many. I recall the Argentinean steakhouse in *Reguliersgracht* so make for it...one of the best steaks I've had. And how pleasant it is to come onto the streets at this hour and find it busy, people and lights making it safe to walk about solo! Yes, it is still open and the only seats available are to mix in with those with yet spare chairs to their table. It is one of five French-speaking Swiss, so I feel almost comfortable chatting with them as I had felt for the last several days. We talk mostly football!

Tuesday I awake to drizzling rain and at the desk after breakfast I search the phone book for Thai Air, to affirm my on-flight to London come Friday. Then I wander my favourite streets to see what is new and in a little square off the *Kalverstraat* a crowd has gathered. I go to see what they are watching. It soon has me engrossed... mesmerised. A fully clad statue of a man with hand held to the front of him and shoulders somewhat rounded, stands with noisy pigeons settled on his shoulders and arms...

Ah, did one of those hands slightly move?

A murmur goes softly through the crowd. Both arms begin to move so slowly that it even takes time for the pigeons to realise it. They fly off. The statue freezes again. An entire minute later it moves ever so slowly to a quite different stance.

People behind me are growing in number, all seeming as spellbound as me. A huge crowd gathers and the 'statue' slowly raises a hand to remove its hat, to lay it upside down at his feet, all of which takes some fifteen minutes. Only slightly faster does he retain the posture he had held when I arrived and continued with what I had been too late to see at the start. Now however, the crowd begins pushing and shoving, every one tossing coins and notes into the hat, so many that it overflows. People then retire backwards, handclapping the entire performance.

Bloody amazing!

I walk the length of *Leidsestraat* and along the *Stadhouderskade* to the *Rijks* Museum. Three years ago, when I was last here, it was being repaired and the gallery closed but the entire series is now on display and crowded. I spend several hours taking in all the wonderful displays they now have. A wondrous several hours of wondrous art.

In the street, rain is again dribbling and it is cold. I don a windcheater over my skivvy and an anorak over all and arm myself with a brolly. Down on the street the rain pelts down. I brave it and run.

Across the street is *Charasco,* pleasant enough fine South American style food.

For the next two days rain persists, so restricts wandering; so I take trams to museums but means afoot again for hours on hours. The city has plenty of wet-weather interests available, and Thursday morning I brave the climb in the *Westerkerk* tower, highest point in Amsterdam. It is interesting that church towers here do not belong to the churches but to the city, used as watchtowers against an outbreak of fire in timber houses built before all had to be built in brick...causing the entire city to slowly begin sinking!

During the war, the Nazis took 17,000 Dutch church bells to melt for armaments, yet allowed Amsterdam to retain theirs. The major bell in *Westerkerk* weighs over 2000kg and the smaller bells each side, each 1-1/2 tonnes. An interesting fact is that there is no problem ringing the *Corrillions,* but making them stop is difficult!

I leaisurely wander along the *Prinzengracht* and *Keizersgracht* with their quaint houses and antique shops, but soon find myself on the more touristy *Brouwersgracht.* There houses have crazy tilts, held up by timber props. The sad truth is that all are beginning to sink.

Tomorrow's start is indeed early. My commuter train to *Schipol* leaves at 4:30am.

After wording up the concierge to have coffee ready at 4:00am, I am early into bed.

"Bye-bye Europe, I've thoroughly enjoyed you again."

And what a grand display they present for me as my plane rises...towards every horizon are patch after organised patch of flowering tulips in every seven colours of the rainbow...a dramatic farewell.

Nineteen

Kent, England, September 1993...
  Whilst my purpose in visiting England is to discover the history of both parents' families, Travel is a big part of it and it's those parts I use here.
  Flying from Amsterdam, Thai Air again performs well on the one hour hop to Heathrow, arriving at the same time I left. Yes, time differences can do that. The sun shines brightly on England and my rental car, a Ford Escort Manual with electric windows.
  What will they think of next?
  I need to recount here the most amazing co-incidence of all time...a couple of months ago at my regular local barbers, Chris is on the sick list and the relieving lady named Joan and I are quickly into the fact that tomorrow I leave for England. She is English... "What part, Ric?"
  "Kent."
  "What part?"
  "Edenbridge by the Surry border I..."

In the mirror, she stares at me...

"I was born in Edenbridge. My mother still lives there. Why there?"

"Starborough Castle?"

She doesn't know it.

"Will your mother help me?"

"Of course. When will you be in Edenbridge?"

"Three days from now!"

"I will telephone tomorrow."

Three days later, in her Edenbridge home, Joan's mother tells me there used to be a Starborough Castle, but Oliver Cromwell demanded it be torn down. It is at the top of the hill just a few hundred yards from her home. She gives me the name of the 'gentleman' who lives on the site now and points out his house on a pencil drawing.

Twenty minutes later, I park at the end of the long drive of this grand manor. On its gate is the name *'Moat House,' George Hammond, Esquire.*

I toll the doorbell and the door is opened by a portly gentleman with a waif of a little lad clutching his father's trousers, a finger to mouth.

When I explain the purpose of my visit, Mr. Hammond announces, "Yes, I can show you Starborough Castle from my study window. Follow me."

He picks up the lad and carries him.

"I won't introduce you to my son. He is home from school with chicken pox. Even my housekeepers are staying away."

He points to an extremely large lake beyond a tennis court, beyond which again is a forest. "That forest is all that is left of Starborough Castle. My lake was its moat. The forest you see is an island. That vague timber construction you see is the 'folly castle' built by my wife as a jest. We call it Starborough Castle."

He gives me considerable time over tea telling me the little he knows of its history.

"I know not the name Richardson, yet believe a *de Bourg* owned the castle."

"My Richardson of the time married a *de Bourg* daughter. All I know of him is that he had a seat in Parliament."

He gives me leave to wander the grounds taking photographs.

At least that answers the wonder about Aunt Estelle's scribbles, that one of our Richardsons 'owned Starborough Castle in Edenbridge Kent.'

I photograph the folly castle and the forest behind it.

I take off for Brighton where I plan to overnight, concerned that this being the Friday of a Bank Holiday weekend I could find accommodation difficult. I top up petrol at 55.9pence, exactly double the Australian price...pretty countryside and villages but the car radio reports people 'streaming out of London for the south.'

It is yet only 3:00pm and Cornwall is a long way off, so I decide against Brighton and head for Salisbury overnight. I miss the by-pass at Lewes and find myself bogged in Brighton traffic. During the next half-hour, I stop to study my map but map and roadside signs differ. I am lost somewhere south of Salisbury. All is colourful countryside. *New Sarum* is a name in my Wm. Woolley history (a convict given 7-years for trying to steal a purse in a Salisbury pub) and I feel nerve ripples as I see a signpost to *Old Sarum*...not on my map! I drive into Old Sarum and enquire, to be told New Sarum no longer exists. It is now all privately owned land. I seek digs nearby but get caught up in traffic queues. 30 frustrating minutes later I discover The Inn at High Post, a modern motel but no one can tell me where New Sarum used to be. I dine at the St. Emillion at a cost three times that of Paris.

Come morning I visit *Old Sarum Castle*, now nowt more than mounds of earth and some stone retaining walls. A sign tells me William the Conqueror was crowned there in 1083. I meander by A and B roads west to Cornwall and am caught up in miles of traffic.

On the A30 through Bodmin Moor, I'd been stalled, not even making a centimetre in the queue. As far as the hill ahead, no west bound car was moving. I lock the car and walk past the score of cars on the crest of a hill, to see what is beyond it. The queue reaches as far as the eye can see to the next hill. There is no exit road, only private homes and fences.

1 hour 26 minutes later, the queue ahead is moving and when I get atop the further hill I had seen on my inspection, is a left hand road with cars moving around it. When I reach it, it is to St. Austel. In it are two pubs and a B&B with signs up saying, 'No Vacancies.' Eventually I find myself back on the road I had left and just out of Redruth near the north coast of Cornwall is 'businessman's pub,' The Inn for All Seasons.

No sign up so I drive in and yes, they have a bed for me.

I'd been given that my mother's grandparents married in Redruth, so very late in that Saturday I'm directed to the two Anglican churches in the town. On the first is a plaque dating its founding in 1883, far too late for my great-grandparents. The other church, St Euny, is locked and the next service is listed for 11:00am tomorrow.

After a restless night, I am awake early and drive into the hillside town with narrow winding streets. A high railway viaduct soars overhead. St. Euny keeps no documents, all are held in the Cornwall Records Office in Truro. It won't be open on a holiday weekend, so I sightsee along the tops of the cliffs that arise from sea-level between Portreath and Hell's Mouth. The wind blows an absolute gale, yet people are out in shirtsleeves, shorts, some stripped to the waist, hiking. The temperature is but 14 and I am rugged up in skivvy, shirt and anorak zippered to the neck, even with a cap to keep my head warm.

Oh, but what a coastline this *Jamaica Inn* type territory has... smuggler coves, caves and all that one can imagine, when from these very cliff-tops over several generations, lanterns deliberately guided ships on to rocks that their cargos could be plundered. My pub is on such a road and at the holiday Monday breakfast I'm told this is normal Cornwall weather, cold wind and sleeting rain, but I could nowt more than sightsee.

By lunchtime, however, I'd had enough of the chilly wind and spent the afternoon playing chess and poker.

Cornwall Records Office is a let-down. Records here are different from those in Australian libraries, but there should not be too many 'Mitchell-Mitchel' marriages, even allowing spelling differences.

So were my mother's grandparents only imagined?

I slap my wrist.

In Truru, where her grandfather was born and lived until despatched to Australia delivering the latest in tin-mine machinery, the sun is shining and I bury myself into finding what records are available...not easy when BDMs are not indexed and there are 219 parishes in Cornwall, each to be searched according to dates. Only guide I have is family records in Tasmania claiming her grandparents sailed four months after their marriage. But this does not agree with any M-M records here in Cornwall. The 1851 census? These figures are not held at this centre but at the Municipal Library where to visit, one must make a bloody appointment two to three weeks in advance.

Shit, eh?

~ * ~

Northampton...

On driving to Northampton, one inn in the Cotswolds that I pass looks so tempting I pull to a halt, make a U-turn and drive back to it.

Fossbridge Inn on the Cirencester-Northleach road I later learn, is highly praised.

"This is it! This is it," It is a building that just 'gleams' history!

I don't even think about cost...the gulp will come when checking out!

I just want to eat and sleep in this rickety old pub!

By the time I reach the desk my wallet is out, Diners Card ready.

The 'old' part of the hotel, stone and half-timbered, dates back to the 1400s, floors creak, doors no longer fit frames, stairs are irregular in both width and tread heights, the roofing is crooked and the chimneys are twisted.

Whilst I love the history and geography of England, I become more convinced its people can be downright rude. Hotel staff is always great, professional about hospitality, but other guests not so. With an exception or two, Europeans at least smile at strangers and make one feel welcome, but here, one feels an intruder. I love their country but find their attitude to strangers abrupt. Even Maggie admits to that.

I spend the rest of the day wandering the gardens...ducks and chickens getting under my feet, piglets, sheep and lambs reminding me of home, fishing rods and bait are free for guests to catch your own dinner in the lake. A veranda bar tempts one from strolling as do squeaks as you mount stairs and I hear quiet music reaching from somewhere.

Fossbridge Inn dinner attracts many locals. I follow Pink Breast of Chicken with a Supreme of Scottish Salmon in a most delicious sauce and top it off with Stilton and Cognac with coffee. Short menus and a long wine list invariably promise a great meal. With a most satisfied belly, the teen-age son of the family at the next table makes a liar of my criticism when he asks if I might join him at the chess table. His parents, obviously locals, are already at a game of their own.

With considerable patience he spends much of the game-time showing me how I might have better handled this or that move, each of which I appreciate.

I awake after a long sleep to the crowing of successful cocks, cackling geese and grunting pigs and am not shocked at the cost of my overnight, just thoroughly satisfied.

Northleach is not a beautiful name for such a pretty town but I stop to walk about its little square. I then drive through Oxon to Northampton.

~ * ~

Brixworth...

When the Vikings came to Britain, *All Saints* Brixworth was already old. Built in 680AD and still standing majestically on its hilltop after 1,300 years, it is the largest Anglo Saxon building still active as a place of worship. It also claims to be the best preserved 7th century building north of the Alps.

Much of the blood in the veins of 'the Notable Mr. Richardson,' as my reviewer and publisher chose to call this work, is of that era, my inheritance proven. Please go see the covers of *Faith and Frenzy*. With the help of Dr. David Parsons FSA, Emeritus Reader in Church Archaeology, University of Leicester, I once back in Australia make an in-depth study of Brixworth's *All Saints*. Many of my ancestors were baptised, wedded and interred there, even active officers in the parish.

~ * ~

Long Buckby...

Eight miles west of Brixworth is home of a Third Great-Grandfather, Adam Newitt, the 'devil,' and last of my eight convict ancestors, he who could not even write his name or have anything but pride of nineteen years of convict history during which he kept absconding. He 'defeated' his twentieth year only because in 1868, Australia closed its convict prisons. He proved himself a good father yet hardly a good husband to his two wives in turn. The felony that cost him his transportation was for the second time, stealing shoe leather in order to fulfil his cobbling profession.

I park in Long Buckby's village square. There were two churches in Adam's day and I crawl through both graveyards. In St. Lawrence CofE I find a few Newitt graves, yet the tangle of blackberries and brambles are too impenetrable to read most stones. I have more luck, though, in seeking a pub, for there is but one, The King's Head. I pay him the honour of a toast at its bar, that I am sure he must have often attended.

I also photograph the old Coach-house from which his Ann and all the children will have departed when sailing from London aboard *Hydery* in 1832, when allowed to join her husband 'so the children can be fed,' she dictates to the clerk when boarding.

~ * ~

St. Sepulchre CofE, Northampton City...

Charles Richardson married Martha Billing of Brixworth in the city rather than in Brixworth, where most of the Richardson and Billing families abided. Charles' father had made Northampton City his home and had been buried at St. Sepulchre and the rest of the family remained in the city. His mother, however, to see son

Charles wed, was too ailing to face the dangerous ten-mile journey to Brixworth, so he married in the city.

St. Sepulchre is unique in that it is a replica of the circular Jerusalem church of that name. It was begun in Northampton in 1100 and added to little by little, century by century, and when I visited, it was locked most of each day. I give another full day to the Northampton Records Office where nothing is indexed. You choose what lists you need but must know beforehand, the parish name.

Bloody Hell! I've come half way around the world to be given this much help?

When you guess the name of the parish, you wait an hour and they bring you the very massive tome in which records are written in a hand you can hardly read, centuries ago.

Bloody hell yes, this is how the Northampton Records Office maintains its records!

The Long Buckby Parish record could not be found...

"Maybe a church borrowed it and hasn't yet returned it!"

In Northampton there is a total gap in Brixworth records from 1812 through 1821.

However, there are some notes recorded to make one smile. Like these...

Date 1546: John the Husband of the said Mary Dyer went as a Soldier into Flanders above a year before the said Daughter was born and did not return since. This daughter therefore is violently suspected to have been begotten in Adultry.

Sixtenthe Aug 1598: Joshua Salmon, a bastard Childe without a Doubt...

From the 'burials' ledger:
11th Mar – Mr. Allyn, a poor traveller, also the infant sonne of Alis Cowper, Spinster which must have been begotten unlawfully.

My Life, My Travels

I had to come away seething in annoyance at gaining nothing about several branches of my Richardson family, nor my convict Adam Newitt. All the Richardsons were literate, Adam Newitt not so.

~ * ~

Bedfordshire...
An hour down the road is Bedfordshire's Records Office.

Lo and behold, here is every soul born, married or died in the county over centuries, listed in alphabetical order and one is allowed to photograph any document. Also in Bedfordshire, I gleaned the entire early life of my convict, larrikin son of an educated family who arrived in Van Diemen's Land (old name for Tasmania) with a 'life' sentence. 'Larrikin' life? He married his pregnant girlfriend Bess in Bedfordshire's Millbrook in 1816, stole and skinned a sheep and tried selling it to his policeman 'friend,' was shipped in chains to Van Diemen's Land in 1817, married Sarah (a daughter of my two First Fleeters) in 1818 and fathered 8 children to her. At age 80 he died on Christmas Day 1868, a wealthy sheep grazier.

Bedfordshire has the best library of family records that I visit. Everything is well organised. I followed this convict's life back several more generations. But then, this is the only one of my 8 convicts with educated parents (except Cornwall with no recorded order). In my father's family, however, in what had been Westmorland (since become Cumbria) I am given current local families to approach! In many cases of the 35 churches where I 'crawl' through churchyards, I am given personal good help, including names and phone numbers for particular family branches.

Getting out in the field, however, often provides more help than wasting hours in record offices.

~ * ~

London...
Having every time in London sworn I would never be so wild as to try driving a car, I find myself driving down Earl's Court Rd but a half kilometre of Buckingham Palace where I'd been recommended to a hotel where visiting Aussies are welcome. I've to either pay another month on my rental-car or surrender it, and I have to return

it at a nearby office, so had to drive it here. Thai Air Flies London-Sydney twice a week, most of it during the night, which suits me fine and I intend finishing my studies in a week or ten days. I've many a church and graveyard to find, yet fear most is in London's 'old' half, which suffered the nightly bombings of the 1940s, many now having been replaced by modern high-rise apartments, as London then became.

The pub I seek is Philbeach Hotel on Philbeach Rd. I book for a week and am close to the underground rail services. Having unladen the car, I study the Shoreditch-Spitalfields area and find I can buy a four-day free travel pass effective all over London.

My belly is hungry and I espy an Italian bistro on Earl's Court Rd with a mouth-watering blackboard menu, Osso Bucco, a glass of red, profiteroles and coffee for £18.

At breakfast I give top marks to the hotel waiter, who calls after a departing house-guest, "Bye-bye, look after yourself," then in an undertone to only those left, "better than you have been bloody doing!"

That day I search great-grandparent's various homes. Two of the streets on which they lived don't even exist anymore and the one that does no longer has the church where they married, but only the small ruin of one on the centrepieces of four-way intersection. I have better luck during the afternoon, finding the ruin of another church of the same family branch in Bloomsbury, near the British Museum which occupies an entire city block which takes me two entire days to inspect and photograph. On my second night, I treat myself to the St. Martin's in the Field Theatre by Trafalgar Square to see *The Mousetrap!* A neighbour is St Martin's Church where my *Gerard Rawes* married.

During this London visit, I will fill fifty-three 'quarto' pages of typed notes once home, plus many page-fulls of photographs, including the Brick & Brown's Lane corner Bethnal Green bookshop and premises of George Wagstaff and family, all three floors of it.

From Piccadilly circus I wander through Burlington Arcade where royalty has shopped since the 1700s. I don't buy there, but on the way home grab a French loaf, some paté and cheese and a *Jacobs Creek* Shiraz Caberbet 1991 at £3.95, cheaper than I can buy in Australia! I eat imagining all is bought at *Fortnum and Mason* while watching TV, which interrupts programmes only half as much as in Australia.

The rail tube at Earl's Court takes me with only one change to Heathrow terminal.

Thai Air again gives me every reason for keeping them on top of my list for travel. After Amsterdam, we fly over the Baltic Sea, Latvia, Moscow (all covered in cloud). As we sweep south over Pakistan and India into Bangkok, I sleep. After an hour we are off for 8 hours to Sydney, then another hour to Brisbane, from where I catch a door to door bus service to Broadbeach, Gold Coast, only twenty metres from home. Great travel service! My head hits the pillow at 1:30am and I recall nowt more than just 36 hours since getting out of bed in Earl's Court after Bangkok, Frankfurt, Gottingen, Hamburg, Kobenhaven, Berlin, Lausanne, Avignon, Bordeaux, Paris, Loire Valley, Amsterdam, England from Kent to Cornwall, Cumbria, Northampton, Bedfordshire and London.

Twenty

With Australia seeming intent on making itself an expensive country for living in retirement, and becoming so over-ruled as to feel I'm losing all sense of freedom, I begin looking at places visited that might be suitable in which to retire.

Germany's Mittenwald in summers and France's Avignon in winter really draw me, yet one of my major reasons for parting from Maggie was to quit winters in Melbourne. Also, in the last ten years, prices in Europe have soared. Friends of friends have retired in Thailand. I certainly don't want Bangkok and its millions of people in a hurry. But Chiang Mai in the north seems popular. The big negative of leaving Australia is losing free hospital treatment. After a two-year trial, I check the cost of joining Thailand's health insurance scheme, but at my age it is extremely costly. To all Thais, all Aussies are millionaires and private hospitals are outrageously expensive.

Other than my cancer attack which has never reappeared, I've never been seriously sick, so decide to take a trip to look at the country's two best surfing beaches and are given references to retirees in Chiang Mai.

An hour proves enough on treading the beaches around Pattaya...litter is abounding, beach-side rats are mostly brown in colour and I hate brown and there is nothing that I'd call surf, just oil trailing motor launches sharing swim areas with people.

Phuket island is delightful. A reasonable surf and a choice of beaches that are clean and no rats. It is a most attractive sub-tropical island with ample holiday-maker services.

Chiang Mai is a small city invaded by motorbikes, yet with no thick motor traffic. It is the area's winter, yet morning shivers are not too cold and are short-lived...by 8:00am it is bright sunshine and one can dispense with sleeves.

I go home and sell up.

~ * ~

Chiang Mai, Thailand...

Thais have never learned how to cook beef which they import. It is years before I find the few restaurants that employ imported chefs.

Time has changed so much...the first underpass built for motor traffic took six years to build. In my 24 years here, to date the population has doubled, traffic tripled, has countless underpasses and overpasses, universities increased from 2 to 9 and lost all the delights I enjoyed on arrival, but it is still 'home.'

Too old to enjoy travel as a rewarding pastime, what do I do now?

Those first few books have become twenty-seven and this makes twenty-eight. I decided to take the advice of Agent Selwa Anthony and take that two year leave of absence. That's how I discovered Chiang Mai. My first book *Gurrewa* is now in its third edition. Every one of my books has been awarded by American and Australian reviewers either 5 Stars, 5+ Stars, 5++ Stars. Two received from Conger Book Reviews its only ever 10 Stars.

~ * ~

The Sudan… The three week visit to Sudan that takes three months…

I wangle my way into a country that doesn't allow foreigners, but then they won't let me out!

Sudanese people are banned into near every country in the world, certainly 100% of English-speaking countries. Sudan has had unstable governments ever since the UK forced independence onto it after WW2.

Being such an inquisitive and determined bastard, I aim to break that embargo.

Remember *Amr Ali el-Haq Daoud,* the Egyptian born lad forced to live a life of idleness, not allowed to ever work in Egypt because he was son of a foreigner? In his case, a Sudanese? On my return to Australia, I manoeuvre against Sudanese, Australian and English laws, three visas…one for me into Sudan, one for Amr-el-Haq, a Sudanese into Australia and from the British Embassy in Canberra, one for him into England!

Travel? Yes, It has taken me a year of insisting help from Australian politicians in both Queensland and Canberra, and even a special visit to London to be interviewed by officers there, but I am at last getting my pleas on having visas issued for Amr (travels essential for selling Britain's obligations to stupid laws in the countries they 'abandoned,') heard. But I had to be careful to hide my feelings to it in that manner.

I won! But only on the basis that I first travel to Sudan to gain documents ensuring Amr is of that particular family. And it meant I had to travel to his family home in El Fasher of Sudan on its western border with Chad. I was given promise of this access to the politicians involved in this venture, in Canberra.

The three weeks I had allowed myself to complete that interview and get the required documents, turned out to take three months! Yes, I was given a written visa by Amr's father, who assured me it would assist me gain a visa in Australia…yes another visit to Egypt and Canberra, but I did get that visa…first one to admit any Australian but the few specific politicians visiting once or twice a year. There was no embassy there.

Oh, what an adventure I was in for!

And yes, I got that exclusive visa for Amr to travel alone to Sydney airport and I was responsible for him for its thirty-day licence.

I travel into a country with closed borders!

I am limited in the work you now read as to the length of this novel so I refer interested readers on my visit in detail in my award winning *A Soul Forsaken*. It tells all, even some of the political intriguing I had to create!

I must admit that a few things in the book, published as a fiction, have some spurious areas designed to aid the pressure on governments. Elfleda is a spurious character. The attack on me by camera robbers is fiction (that attack occurred, in truth, in Bogota in 1992). Also spurious are the English reporters I meet on the train...they are included to help illustrate how difficult is that journey, the most uncomfortable train journey in my life. My entrapment when trying to fly out indeed took three months. Only then could I get back home to take up the 'getting Amr here' that is also spelled out there.

At 90, I really do find it difficult to believe that particular travel journey to El Fasher really happened. Never had I been more frightened. But it was indeed all real.

~ * ~

'Tis all a Chequer-board of Nights and Days
Where Destiny with Men for Pieces plays:
Hither and thither moves, and mates and slays,
And one by one back in the Closet lays.
　　　　　　　　　—*Rubáiyát of Omar Khayyám #XLIX*

Meet Kev Richardson

Once retired from management of a major printing works in Australia's Melbourne, Kev happily happened on an opportunity to tour the world for a period each of most years inspecting areas popular with tourists, to write articles for airline magazines. Alongside his twenty-seven novels to date, including several award winners, many wayside and city sites are outlined here.

Other Works From The Pen Of

Kev Richardson

Letitia Munro Series

Letitia Munro - Australia's white settlement. In witless ignorance, convicts transform the world's biggest prison into a land of free enterprise and pride.

To Plough Van Diemen's Land – Australian children of founding convicts spawn a new ethos. They establish their own taboos and their nation's spawning culture.

The Terrible Truths - As society values change, grandchildren must hide their convict heritage. A beehive of mining begins showering riches on the land.

The Brogan Series

Brogan – Born in the sands of Australia's far outback, Brogan typifies the blood-and-guts characteristics by which Aussies still remain recognised.

Brogan's Bust - Flying an Amazonian jungle courier service, Brogan twists planned rackets into tangles that slide into snowballs that turn into avalanches.

Brogan's Bella – Highjack victims find their holiday an ongoing terror. Even discovering its cause has them fearing for their very lives.

Misadventure - On a spine-tingling adventure in South America, Brogan faces FARC, military coups and drug-smuggling... a tale to keep you turning pages.

Brogan Abroad – In three simultaneous adventures Brogan is trapped. "What can a man do, when to accomplish one, I must fail at another?"

A Family Series

Faith and Frenzy – In England's Civil Wars, each religion is ripped into shreds. Faith in God is itself torn asunder.

Gerard Rawes – A man's life transforms from rags to riches. In England's industrial revolution he finds himself catapulted from serfdom into London's elite.

An Epic Life – A true tale of two couples risking similar safeguards, together create on the far side of the world, a dynasty.

A Welcome War (An Award Winner!) – In WW2 a young lad is influenced more by wartime's bathos than by parents. "In learning life, it beats schoolwork, hands down!"

Beresford Branson... World War 2 Series

Pacific Paradox - A British son is banished to the South Pacific to discover responsibility. When Japan invades Guadalcanal, he discovers it all.

My Red Cross (First ever 10 Star Award from Conger Book Reviews !) –In war-torn France, Red Cross agents face fear, love, hate and pleas for help. He can but offer tenuous hope.

A German Stirring (Second 10 Star Award!) - Deprivation in occupied Germany after WW2 seems greater than during wartime. Are Allied victors guilty as charged, of major malpractices?

Beresford at Bay – The Allied Control Council is formed to rebuild Germany. But how can democrats and communists ever see eye to eye?

Romance

A Home for Old Ladies - The love of a couple renewing life for a derelict hospice, demands every instinct demanded by a true labour of love.

Summy Lu - A gripping tale of the ingenuity of a woman's love in a time when war's influence was tearing families apart.

Turtle Island - The movie *Blue Lagoon*'s exotic location proffers a pampered holiday for those who can afford it...in the Top Ten of the world!

Adventure

What If? Had Hitler maintained Russia as friend rather than foe, WW II would have been his. With Britain so weak at the time, a second front was foolish.

A Soul Forsaken (Award Winner) - Abandoned by his own country, a victim of an antiquated law finds a 'Boy Scout' to relieve his dilemma.

Connor's Cabal – A journalist's young Thai tour-guide is kidnapped. When even the police refuse action, what can the poor fellow do?

Shadows - A tremendously exciting French Resistance tale in World War II. It strikes fear, love, hate, terror and glee into all.

Soul of Australia Series

Gurrewa – *(Award winners in both Britain and USA)* Australia's white settlement empties the vacuum cleaner with which Australians are at last cleaning under the carpet where for generations, the dust of truth was swept.

Son of Gurrewa – A true tale of Australia's advancement into the democratic world. Lady Luck lends a hand and the odds for Adam fall a little each way.

Dreamtime Drift - Australian Aborigines find their very ethnicity torn asunder as the city of Brisbane is founded as a Convict Prison for Second Offenders.

Memoir

Positive Paradox – Into his 90s, Kev Richardson divides his exciting lifetime into 'series', in childhood, both marriages, business successes and a retirement of world travelling.

Letter to Our Readers

Enjoy this book?

You can make a difference

As an independent publisher, Wings ePress, Inc. does not have the financial clout of the large New York Publishers. We can't afford large magazine spreads or subway posters to tell people about our quality books.

But we do have something much more effective and powerful than ads. We have a large base of loyal readers.

Honest Reviews help bring the attention of new readers to our books.

If you enjoyed this book, we would appreciate it if you would spend a few minutes posting a review on the site where you purchased this book or on the Wings ePress, Inc. webpages at: https://wingsepress.com/

Visit Our Website

*Quality trade paperbacks and downloads
in multiple formats,
in genres ranging from light romantic comedy to general fiction and horror.
Wings has something for every reader's taste.
Visit the website, then bookmark it.*
We add new titles each month!

Wings ePress Inc.
3000 N. Rock Road
Newton, KS   67114